INSISTENCE OF THE MATERIAL

Insistence of the Material

. . . .

Literature in the Age of Biopolitics

Christopher Breu

University of Minnesota Press
Minneapolis
London

The University of Minnesota Press gratefully acknowledges financial assistance provided for the publication of this book from the Department of English and the College of Arts and Sciences at Illinois State University.

Portions of the Introduction were previously published as *The Insistence of the Material: Theorizing Materiality and Biopolitics in the Age of Globalization*, Institute on Globalization and the Human Condition Working Papers Series 12.2 (August 2012): 1–20; reprinted with permission. An earlier version of chapter 1 was published as "The Novel Enfleshed: *Naked Lunch* and the Literature of Materiality," *Twentieth-Century Literature* 57, no. 2 (2011): 199–23. An earlier version of chapter 4 was published as "Disinterring the Real: Dodie Bellamy's *The Letters of Mina Harker* and the Late-Capitalist Literature of Materiality," *Textual Practice* 26, no. 3 (2012): 263–91; reprinted with permission of Taylor and Francis.

Published by the University of Minnesota Press
111 Third Avenue South, Suite 290
Minneapolis, MN 55401–2520
http://www.upress.umn.edu

Library of Congress Cataloging-in-Publication Data
Breu, Christopher.
Insistence of the material : literature in the age of biopolitics / Christopher Breu.
Includes bibliographical references and index.
ISBN 978-0-8166-8891-3 (hc : alk. paper)
ISBN 978-0-8166-8946-0 (pb : alk. paper)
1. American fiction—20th century—History and criticism. 2. English fiction—20th century—History and criticism. 3. Materialism in literature. 4. Biopolitics. I. Title.
PS374.M395B84 2014
813'.5409—dc23   2014001436

Printed in the United States of America on acid-free paper

The University of Minnesota is an equal-opportunity educator and employer.

20 19 18 17 16 15 14   10 9 8 7 6 5 4 3 2 1

Contents

Origin Story

The body as a material fact is given, but sex is not.

—Katrina Karkazis, *Fixing Sex*

This book had its initial genesis in an open-ended sequence of hospital beds or, more precisely, in the catheter-punctuated body that occupied those beds. The disjunction between the ideal male body posited by my surgeons and the recalcitrant flesh of the body they attempted to correct provided the context in which I began to think about the disjunction between language and other forms of materiality. It is this disjunction that lies at the heart of the countertradition of late twentieth-century writing that this project engages. And while in the pages that follow I will address this disjunction in a wide array of texts and global phenomena that seem (and often are) far removed from this initial context, the three- through thirty-eight-year-old body that found itself returning to the seemingly same operating room and allowing itself to be perforated by many of the same instruments is never far away, at least on an affective level. As far as I can reconstruct it, there were fifteen surgeries in all, a number in that first year, and they were all a product of "complications" from the first unnecessary surgery.

As psychoanalysis reminds us, all stories are, in part, about the body. The story told by *Insistence of the Material*, while conceptualized within the language of critical theory and literary criticism, is no different. In many ways unremarkable, my body is relatively distinct in its genital configuration. I have a relatively pronounced version of a condition called *hypospadias*, a "disorder of sex development" that is often categorized as a form of intersex.[1] According to the United States National Institute of Health, hypospadias occurs in four out of every thousand births and is characterized by the opening of the urethra on the underside rather than the end of the penis.[2] The standard medical practice (still in use today, despite the best work of intersex activists) regarding hypospadias is to rebuild the urethra, restoring the penis to ostensible normality. Unfortunately, this unnecessary surgery regularly produces complications due to urinary tract strictures, which, as in my case, manufactures the need for multiple necessary surgeries. Indeed, it is only since I have returned my body to something approximating its original state with my last two surgeries (actually, the urethra had to be taken down further because of the scar tissue, which may have been produced by the catheters or other instrumentation from my many surgeries) that I have achieved some relief from the seemingly eternal return of the hospital bed.

While there is no evidence available for the frequency of hypospadias in earlier eras (the condition as a "birth defect," rather than a specific configuration of the body, being something of a discursive invention), its medical "treatment" does have a history that is relatively traceable and rather recent. As Elizabeth Reis tells it, there is documentation of the medical treatment of hypospadias and intersex in the nineteenth century.[3] Indeed the presence of the surgical "repair" of hypospadias in the nineteenth century has recently been turned into relatively common knowledge by mystery writer Patricia Cornwell, who speculates (probably erroneously) that Jack the Ripper's misogynist violence was the by-product of the trauma experienced by her candidate for the famously elusive London serial killer, painter Walter Sickert. Sickert underwent extremely painful surgeries (without anesthetic) for hypospadias.[4] Thankfully, given the violence of this Grand Guignol scene of medical horror, surgical procedures for hypospadias have largely occurred during the era of anesthesia. Indeed, as Kartina Karkazis has noted, they only became routinized in the United States (and then only for those subjects who came under and could afford medical scrutiny) in the middle decades of the twentieth century.[5] Outside this relatively limited temporal and geopolitical context, hypospadias has gone "untreated." This routinization can be seen as an early version of the forms of overmedicalization that Adele Clarke et al. argue characterizes the regime of "biomedicalization" in the contemporary United States—one that exists in dialectical tension with the lack of access to basic medical care throughout much of the world and in the United States itself.[6]

As my description of it as a form of overmedicalization begins to suggest, the treatment of hypospadias is unnecessary, as is its categorization as a medical disorder. Instead, the treatment of the hypospadias body reveals more about our fantasies of the way in which the male body should appear and the way it should be biomorphically distinguishable from the female body.[7] As I have already noted, because it challenges gender biomorphism, hypospadias is often, although not always, categorized as a form of intersex.[8] While I have written about it in the past as a form of intersex, the inclusion or exclusion of the "condition" or, better, "embodiment" as a form of intersex seems less important to me than attending to the material differences presented by all bodies that challenge our binary understandings of sex (and the often still binary conceptions of gender attached to them).[9]

This insistence on and of the material is the central focus of this book. I not only work to theorize the material but also work to theorize the material's insistence and its refusal to regularly conform to our cultural, linguistic, and indeed theoretical scripts. Instead, I posit the material as it refuses full symbolic recuperation—in its contingency, obduracy, and recalcitrance yet also its vulnerability and fragility. The forms of materiality theorized in *Insistence of the Material* range from the vulnerable yet sometimes resilient materiality of bodies, to the often obdurate yet deteriorating materialities of our late-capitalist built environments, to the endangered yet dynamic materialities of various ecosystems, to the changing yet recalcitrantly material dimensions of political-economic production.

In tracing this insistence of the material, then, I am working outward from my body and its own refusal to follow the cultural scripts assigned to it. The best writing always works in two directions at once—both outward toward the contradictions and inequalities that shape the world and inward toward the complexities and knots of contradiction that shape our subjectivities and embodiments. In my first book, *Hard-Boiled Masculinities*, I both worked outward toward a larger cultural fantasy about masculinity in the interwar years and also worked through (although I did not reveal this at the time) my own investments in fantasies of a hard-boiled masculinity. Thus if the inner life of my first book, *Hard-Boiled Masculinities*, was about the violent fantasies produced by my medical experiences (perhaps Cornwell's account of Sickert holds a kind of psychoanalytic truth), in the inner life of this book, I am trying to stop clinging to that prophylactic tough guy and exist within and work outward from my vulnerable, aging, and much worked-over, yet resistant and willful, body.

In *Insistence of the Material*, then, I attempt to work from my body outward to the forms of materiality and material contradictions that characterize life (primarily but not exclusively in the global North and the

United States) in the second half of the twentieth century and in the early years of the twenty-first. In working outward, I have taken care to not simply project my own experience onto what I am analyzing, yet I have also attempted to stay true to the basic insight afforded to me by my body's refusal to fully adhere to larger medical, cultural, linguistic, and even personal scripts. This insight has enabled me to see and thus theorize the way in which the recalcitrantly material is a relatively untheorized yet crucial dimension of everyday life, as well as a crucial preoccupation of literature in the last fifty years.

Attending to this basic insight has thus allowed me to theorize the representation of materiality in a range of late twentieth-century literary texts. It has also given me a different perspective on the emergence of biopolitics and biopolitical production (political and economic practices that directly shape and manage life itself) in the same period. The way in which my own body resisted the biomedical discourse in which it was shaped enabled me to think about the way in which materiality can form one site of resistance to and divergence from the dominance of biopolitical forms of governance and economic organization in twentieth- and twenty-first-century life. It is to the theorization of the relationships among literature, biopolitics, and materiality that I will turn next, but throughout *Insistence of the Material*, if you read closely and psychoanalytically, you can still see those ghostly hospital beds, which formed the initial, inchoate site of this book's material genesis.

Theorizing Materiality in the Age of Biopolitics

In terms of theory itself, finally, we are summoning a new materialism in response to a sense that the radicalism of the dominant discourses which have flourished under the cultural turn is now more or less exhausted. We share the feeling current among many researchers that the dominant constructivist orientation to social analysis is inadequate for thinking about matter, materiality, and politics in ways that do justice to the contemporary context of biopolitics and global political economy.

—Diana Coole and Samantha Frost, *New Materialisms*

Thinking Materiality: A Necessary Contradiction

This book takes materiality as its object. In doing so, it is, by necessity, inadequate to this object. One of the central arguments of *Insistence of the Material* is that the various forms of materiality in contemporary social existence—the materiality of the body, the object world of late-capitalist life, the material elements of political-economic production, the various forms of materiality we group under the signifier "nature"—cannot be adequately or completely accounted for by language. *Insistence of the Material* takes this contradiction between language and nonlinguistic forms of materiality as its fundamental preoccupation. It attempts to attend to what Diana Coole and Samantha Frost describe as matter's "restlessness and intransigence" and what Richard Terdiman posits as "the brute and often brutal difficulty of materiality," even as it recognizes the inability of language, representation, or theory to fully do so.[1]

However, *Insistence of the Material* does not take the inability of language to fully account for its object as a reason to turn away from the attempt at such an account. Instead, in an era in which economic and cultural production have become increasingly fascinated with the virtual, the immaterial, and the textual, it becomes crucial to theorize the material. It is also crucial to theorize the material in an age in which political and economic organization have taken on a decidedly biopolitical and thana-topolitical character.

To broadly summarize, for the moment, what are actually very distinct deployments of these concepts by a range of theorists, biopolitics and its deathly double, thanatopolitics, describe the direct management of life and death by political and economic power.[2] My characterization of this era as simultaneously an era preoccupied with immateriality and one defined by biopolitics is not coincidental. Both the privileging of the so-called immaterial or virtual and the idea of complete biopolitical control imagine a material world that is a passive site of inscription and unprob-lematic manipulation. My theorization of materiality in this book, then, tries to posit it as a limit to biopolitics, even as it also charts the way in which material life is shaped in ever more intimate ways by biopolitics, thanatopolitics, and biopolitical production. Materiality, in this formu-lation, can be likened to biopolitics' and virtuality's unconscious flip side—one that resists integration with the world of biopolitical control. For reasons bound up with the very dynamics I am describing, then, it is crucial to both theorize the material and keep in mind the way in which such theorizations are always inadequate to their objects. *Insistence of the Material* is thus organized around two imperatives: (1) theorize and attend to the material in the era of biopolitics, and (2) recognize language's limits in doing so.

As the epigraph from Coole and Frost indicates, I am not alone in wishing to tarry with the material. There has been widespread frustration at the limits of what has alternately been called cultural or linguistic turn in much recent theoretical writing. To briefly summarize, the linguistic and cultural turns elevated language and culture as placeholders for social life itself. Indeed, in the moment of their greatest ascendency, the 1980s and 1990s, it was common to hear each of these concepts evoked in ways that refused the ability to posit their limits or theorize that which resided outside of or in tension with them. While it is important to recognize the cultural and linguistic turns as having distinct genealogies, the linguistic turn in the reception of poststructuralism in the United States and the cul-tural turn with the ascendency of cultural studies and culturalist forms of Marxism in the nineteen eighties and nineties, they overlapped and gener-ally functioned as mutually reinforcing concepts, finding common ground in that other fetishized signifier of the era: postmodernism.[3] The two turns shared philosophical underpinnings as well. Both were grounded in what

Quentin Meillassoux describes as the post-Kantian philosophical doctrine of correlationism, which he defines in the following way: "the idea according to which we only ever have access to the correlation between thinking and being, and never to either term considered apart from each other."[4]

Recently, however, there has been a growing frustration with the limits of the cultural and linguistic turns, as well as with the logic of correlationism that underpins them. This frustration has led a number of scholars to theorize and tarry with forms of materiality that exist partially outside of and in tension with the cultural and the linguistic. As Stacy Alaimo puts it, "What has been notably excluded from the 'primacy of the cultural' and the turn toward the linguistic and the discursive is the 'stuff' of matter."[5] In contrast to the linguistic and cultural turns, Alaimo and Hekman propose what they term the "material turn."[6] I too work to theorize the stuff of matter and thus ally my argument with the material turn and what Frost and Coole term the "new materialisms."[7] In doing so, however, I don't so much want to abandon the important work done by the linguistic and cultural turns as theorize the limits of this work and begin to account for (while recognizing the impossibility of fully doing so) that which they are not able to discuss: the forms of materiality that resist, exceed, and exist in tension with the cultural and linguistic. One of the dangers of a wholesale rejection of cultural and linguistic turns is that we merely invert their logic, rewriting the same set of theoretical moves onto materiality that characterize the cultural and linguistic turns. If we really want to be attentive to the challenges that the heterogeneity of materiality presents to critical theory, to the study of literature, and to everyday life, we need to think about how various forms of materiality differ from, intermix with, and place limits on the cultural and linguistic, rather than merely supersede or replace them.

My approach also echoes Sarah Ahmed and Sonia Kruks in suggesting that new theoretical work of the material turn needs to be brought into dialogue with older forms of materialist scholarship.[8] Thus, while it draws upon much of the new materialist work in areas as diverse as feminist theory, critical science studies, object-oriented ontology (or OOO, for short), biopolitics, and political ecology, *Insistence of the Material* puts this new work in dialogue with the older materialist traditions' associated psychoanalytic and Marxist theories in order to theorize the relationship of materiality to subjectivity and subjective embodiment, on the one hand, and to political economy and globalization, on the other.

In what follows, then, this introduction will first provide an account of what I am retaining from the cultural turn. It will then map out some of the trajectories of the recent material turn, putting them in dialogue with older materialist approaches. It will conclude by suggesting the way in which this theoretical approach can illuminate a countertradition of literature—what I am calling the late-capitalist literature of materiality.

Beyond the Cultural and Linguistic Turns

Culture and *language* are the totemic words around which literary and cultural studies have circled for much of the last thirty years. Even as the critique of the linguistic and cultural turns has become more force-ful in recent years, it is still not uncommon in contemporary scholarship and pedagogy to find each of these terms elevated to the position of a placeholder for social life itself.[9] Indeed, in the moment of their greatest ascendency, the 1980s and 1990s, it was common to hear each of these concepts evoked in ways that refused the ability to posit their limits or theorize that which resided outside of or in tension with them. Instead, each term became part of a self-contained language game (to use the Wittgenstein-derived rhetoric of the time) that allowed, for all the atten-tion to otherness, no space for the radically heterodox to be understood or even posited.

This is far from what was intended by these epistemological "turns" and by the forms of social constructionism associated with them. Each of these turns emerged around the same time for reasons both political and epistemological. They emerged as a way of challenging ideological habits of thought associated with earlier moments of cultural or political *doxa*. The cultural turn, for example, emerged out of the impasses produced by vulgar Marxism, with its reductive account of culture as merely a reflection of the economic infrastructure or base. Similarly, the linguistic turn represented a new and necessary awareness of the ways in which language and repre-sentation worked to constitute the very objects they ostensibly described.

The power of the constructivist interventions is nowhere more pal-pable than in the theoretical impetus they have provided in the last thirty years for the theoretical critique of racism, sexism, homophobia, and class habitus. Many of these interventions have turned around the critique of the ideological production of cultural difference as natural difference and the ways in which a reified or essentialized conception of nature was used to justify various forms of social inequality. This critique of various processes of "naturalization" remains an invaluable and very necessary contribution made by social construction to theoretical critique. And, indeed, social construction continues to remind us, as do theorists of discursive productivity such as Michel Foucault and Judith Butler, that we should posit that which is outside of culture and language with the utmost care, lest we reproduce the forms of essentialism that the critique of the process of naturalization was designed to undo.

One of the most powerful innovations of the linguistic and cultural turns was the way in which they enabled a political conception of subjectivity. Subjectivity in this formulation is not presocial or predicated on an invariant and authentic core. It is instead shaped and reshaped by political and cultural forces. Within such a conception of subjectivity, race, gender, sexuality, and class habitus are not natural properties of certain bodies, nor are they merely external forces that place limits on the self-same bodies. Instead, they are forms of discourse that intersect with and shape subjectivity and embodiment, which itself is often conceptualized, in Butler's often-misunderstood term, as performative.[10] Perhaps the most powerful conceptions of subjectivity proffered by the cultural and linguistic turns manifested in post-Lacanian psychoanalytic accounts of subjectivity in feminist, gender, and queer theory. In the work of theorists such as Teresa de Lauretis, Elizabeth Grosz, Bruce Fink, and Lee Edelman, subjectivity becomes more than just an effect of discursive inscription.[11] Instead, discourses and ideologies are understood to intermix with structures of fantasmatic identification and disidentification, bodily inscriptions, the workings of drives and desire, and an unconscious in which social meanings mix with affect and dream work. Such an approach underscores the complex causality of psychoanalysis, with its displacements and condensations, projections and disavowals, repetitions and reversals, and incorporations and excorporations.

This psychoanalytic conception of subjectivity already begins to push beyond the cultural/linguistic turn by attending to aspects of subjectivity that exceed and complicate discursive and cultural coding. As de Lauretis puts it, "Freud's own terms—the drive, the unconscious, the ego, and other terms of his metapsychology—are conceptual figures or tropes which inhabit the space between mind and matter, a space not traversable by referential language."[12] The account of the material turn to follow retains this psychoanalytic conception of subjectivity, even as it pushes it in a more materialist direction, attending not only to the way in which discourses like race, gender, sexuality, and class get subjectified, lived, and to use Frantz Fanon's phrase, produced as part of an "epidermal schema," but also to the way in which subjectivity and various social discourses and cultural practices intersect with the irreducible materiality of the body.[13] It is important to retain this psychoanalytic understanding of subjectivity for two reasons. First, it still provides, to my mind, the most sophisticated and least deterministic account of subjectivity, more so than the recent turn in some humanities scholarship to cognitive science, yet it also opens out onto a complex account of the materiality of the body and of psychophysical processes. Second, positing such a subjectivity, however materially shaped, seems crucial for attending to the difference and challenge presented by objects and other forms of materiality to the linguistically situated subject. One of the dangers of the material turn is that, in our drive to correct the excesses of the cultural and linguistic turns, we merely invert them, writing everything under the sign of the material; in doing so, we would not posit the difference and challenge that forms of materiality make to theorizing culture and subjectivity. Preserving the psychoanalytic subject, even as we work to make it more materialist, forestalls such a danger.

Like all orthodoxies, the cultural and linguistic turns have, over time, become as constraining as they were once liberating. What began by returning a politically powerful understanding language, subjectivity, and culture to the center of academic inquiry in the humanities and social sciences has itself become naturalized into a new kind of essentialism: one that presents culture, language, or rhetoric (or some combination thereof) as autonomous and, as Louis Althusser put it in a different context, "in the last instance" determining the privileged medium by which we can comprehend the social.[14] One of the ways to know that a concept has become part of a problematic orthodoxy is when it can no longer theorize its limits. This is precisely what has happened to the terms *culture* and *language* as they are typically invoked and metaphorized in literary and cultural studies.

It is the aim of *Insistence of the Material* to contribute to the material turn in contemporary scholarship and pursue its implications for literary study by engaging the conceptions of materiality put forward by a diverse range of writers in the second half of the twentieth century: William Burroughs, Thomas Pynchon, J. G. Ballard, Leslie Marmon Silko, and Dodie Bellamy. It is my contention that these writers made the material turn long before contemporary scholarship and that we can learn a great deal about thinking through the coordinates of our early twenty-first-century world by attending to the way in which they posit the material dimensions of life in the second half of the twentieth century. Before turning fully to literary critical matters, however, it is important to map out the coordinates of the material turn and indicate the ways I will be drawing from and reworking aspects of it in *Insistence of the Material*.

The Material Turn

The recent material turn in scholarship holds a great deal of promise. As a corrective to the cultural and linguistic turns that preceded it, the recent turn to theorizing various forms of materiality has been salutary, working to demonstrate the limits of both textual and social constructivism as dominant paradigms for work in the humanities. This materialist turn has taken many forms: the OOO of Graham Harman, Levi Bryant, and Ian Bogost; the material culture of objects charted by Bill Brown through the engagement with the agency of things in the ecotheoretical work of Bruno Latour and Jane Bennett; the emphasis on biological life in much recent work in biopolitics, feminist theory, and animal studies; and the emphasis on geopolitics and political economy in globalization theory and Marxist accounts of neoliberalism.

The Material and Biological Body

It is in the context of the cultural and linguistic turns that preceded it that the materialist turn has made its important interventions. Thus social constructivist accounts of the body have been complicated by the emphasis on the biological and material body in the writings of Rosi Braidotti, Elizabeth Grosz, and Anne Fausto-Sterling, and in the work collected in *Material Feminisms*.[15] Elizabeth Grosz initiates this line of inquiry with her groundbreaking text of 1994, *Volatile Bodies*, with its emphasis on producing a theory that can account for "some sort of articulation, or even disarticulation, between the biological and the psychological."[16] Working in a similar vein as Grosz, Braidotti has produced a vitalist theory of feminist embodiment—one that draws on the work of Luce Irigaray and Gilles Deleuze, in order to emphasize the intertwining of the biological and the subjective as they are bound up in a process of becoming. Perhaps most compellingly for the work I am undertaking in this book, Anne Fausto-Sterling presents an account of intersex that demonstrates the way in which the material and biological body of the intersex individual disrupts the sexed meanings projected and often violently inscribed on this body by the medical establishment. Similarly, a number of the essays collected in *Material Feminisms* work in different ways to theorize the materiality of the body and of biological processes, often in relationship to other forms of materiality.

All these theorists push our understanding of embodiment beyond the parameters of cultural and discursive construction. Indeed, each of them asks us to reckon with the materiality of a body that resists as well as conforms to cultural scripts. Moreover, what is particularly notable about the work of Fausto-Sterling and other theorists of intersex and transsex, such as Alice Dreger and C. Jacob Hale, is that they produce an account of the materiality of the biological body that does not reproduce the binary of sex.[17] Thus their work maintains the necessary critique of sexual binarism that is central to Butler's work while also insisting on the materiality of the body as that which can and often does resist or exceed discursive construction. My own more psychoanalytic account of the body in what follows is deeply indebted to the materialist line of inquiry opened up by Grosz, Braidotti, Fausto-Sterling, Hale, and the essayists in *Material Feminisms*.

Many of these theorists emphasize the way in which the oppositions between language and material body can be deconstructed or seen as part of a material continuum. Such an emphasis is important, demonstrating the ways in which the linguistic and other forms of materiality, subjects and objects, interpenetrate. What Grosz describes, drawing on Lacan's category of the imaginary as a reworking of Freud's body ego, as an "imaginary anatomy" represents one particularly fruitful account. As she articulates it, this imaginary anatomy is a crucial locus where the biological and the subjective intersect.[18] It is in the imaginary where the biological body becomes encoded with subjective meanings, even as it is necessary to recognize the often radical discontinuity between the imaginary body or body ego as a map of the body and the material body itself. The body ego's image of the body is shaped and refigured by desire and by the erotogenic mapping of the body; thus certain organs and surfaces are emphasized, while others are deemphasized, if not altogether occluded.

This disjunction between the imaginary and material body suggests the importance of not just theorizing their overlap or interpenetration but also theorizing the ways in which signification and the more obdurate materialities of the body are importantly distinct and sometimes form in opposition to each other. While much materialist work on embodiment emphasizes the way in which the opposition between language and the material body can be undone, I want to shift this focus for our purposes: in order for us to fully attend to the materialities of our bodies, we need to insist on the ways in which the materiality of language (as well as the forms of subjectivity shaped by language) and the materiality of the body not only interpenetrate and merge but also remain importantly distinct and sometimes form in contradiction to each other.

In order to theorize the material body that is in tension with, even as it is also bound up with, the body ego, I employ a version of Lacan's concept of the real. In contradistinction to the imaginary and symbolic, the real is one of the most elusive and controversial concepts in Lacan as well as one of the categories that underwent the most revision during the course of his teaching. It is elusive, in part, because that is its nature. It is easier to define it negatively, in terms of what it is not rather than in terms of what it is: the real is everything that remains outside of the symbolic and the imaginary, even as it haunts and disrupts the logics of both. Thus the real can be used to talk about trauma, death, the fetishistic status of what Lacan calls the *objet petit a* (or little bit of the other) and about uncoded materiality itself. While recent texts by Slavoj Žižek and Alain Badiou have emphasized the *real's* nonmaterial nature as a gap, hole, or excess around which the symbolic is organized, I will primarily be using a materialist understanding of the term.[19] At different points in my argument, I make reference to a number of the different valences of the real; yet it is the definition of the real as uncoded materiality that I will use most frequently, as befits a book on materiality.[20]

This latter understanding of the real comes out of developmentalist accounts of Lacan. Thus the child begins as a "fragmented body" in the locus of the real—a realm of uncoded materiality in which the line between inside and outside, self and other is not yet formed.[21] Bruce Fink designates this first version of the real as uncoded materiality *Real 1*, or *R 1*, and contrasts it with the functioning of the real with the advent of the symbolic (that he terms *Real 2*, or *R 2*), in which its status becomes closer to what Žižek describes as the gap or what Lacan describes as the *objet a*, or the little piece of the real that functions as a fetish.[22] Yet there is always a relationship between R 2 and R 1—the various avatars of R 2, such as the *objet a*, but also trauma and the gap in the symbolic, point to those forms of materiality that have not been fully coded by the symbolic and thus recall the undifferentiated state that preceded symbolization.

I use this notion of the real as uncoded materiality in order to talk about the aspects of the body that exceed or refuse our symbolic and imaginary constructions of it. Theorizing this real body (which should be understood as distinct from any naïve empirical understanding of the "reality" of the body, since "the real" is always a relational phrase) enables a discussion of the resistance that the body has to, for example, gendered, sexual, and cultural scripts, as well as contemporary scientific, philosophical, and theoretical accounts and mappings of the body. This concept of the real body, then, allows an attention to what Anne Fausto-Sterling has theorized as the resistance of bodies—particularly intersex bodies—to the sexual scripts placed on them by culture, by the medical establishment, and even sometimes by the subject herself.[23] In emphasizing this real body, I am not trying to maintain a Cartesian mind/body split. Our thinking selves and our speaking selves are always embodied, and this embodiment shapes the knowledge and speech we produce. Yet I think it is dangerous (and still a legacy of the linguistic turn) to imagine that all forms of materiality are continuous with language and can be understood in terms of linguistic models.

Objects, OOO, and Political Ecology

Another strain of recent materialist work can be grouped under the banner of object studies. This work encompasses the material history championed by Bill Brown in his studies of the centrality of objects in American culture; the queer phenomenological work of Sarah Ahmed; the OOO of Graham Harman, Levi Bryant, and Ian Bogost; and the political ecology of Bruno Latour and Jane Bennett.[24] Each of these theorists has disrupted the cultural turn's and modern philosophy's central preoccupation with subjectivity by pointing out the material objects and entities that are obscured by this focus. If the cultural and linguistic turn decentered the subject, it is still the subject who is the focus of this decentering. These theorists have each, in different ways, pushed us to attend to the objects and forms of matter that lie outside this exclusive focus on subjectivity. These material things are central to culture yet irreducible to it.

Bill Brown's work in *The Material Unconscious* and *A Sense of Things* argues for the importance of theorizing and attending to "the poetics and politics of the object[s]" that proliferate within everyday life in the United States.[25] Central to Brown's argument is what he theorizes as a *material unconscious*, or the relegation of material objects and their heterogeneity to the unthought background in formalist and poststructuralist accounts of literature.[26] *Insistence of the Material* employs Brown's concept of the material unconscious to theorize the disavowal and fantasized transcendence of the material (what I term *avatar fetishism*, which is detailed more fully later in this introduction) that is central not only to the linguistic and cultural turns but also to the alluring promises of digital culture and so-called immaterial production in contemporary life.

Brown's work thus emphasizes the intersections between subjects and objects. Sarah Ahmed's genesis of what she terms *queer phenomenology* in her book of the same name similarly charts the relationship between subjects and objects. Returning to the work of Husserl and Merleau-Ponty, Ahmed rethinks their work within the political framework of queer theory. Central to her project, as to Brown's, is the notion of attending to objects (and objectified subjectivities) that are overlooked, relegated to the background, or naturalized. To counter this work of naturalization, Ahmed proposes developing a queer phenomenology, which would "function as a disorientation device" and "allow the oblique to open up another angle on the world."[27] In what follows, I take up Ahmed's challenge to disorient our conventional, culturally, and linguistically constructed maps of the world and instead provide alternate orientations capable of recognizing and valuing materiality in its force, intransigence, and vulnerability. Such a project does not imagine an abjuring of subjectivity so much as its reorienting. With such a reorienting, as Ahmed notes, comes an ethics and a politics of materiality—one that is ecologically and economically attentive to material limits as well as possibilities. Such an ethics and a politics begins by recognizing and valuing the being of materiality rather than just treating it as so much raw material or as the alternately ignored or exploited background within which culture takes place.

The emphasis on the being of objects is central to the work of the object-oriented ontologists, who propose, perhaps, the most radical challenge to the cultural and linguistic turns. The work of Graham Harman, Levi Bryant, and Ian Bogost all challenge the bracketing of the object world and the emphasis only on what can be subjectively apprehended (as is central to Western philosophy since Kant)—what they term, after Quentin Meillassoux, correlationism. In contrast to correlationist *doxa*, OOO theorists posit the being of objects that necessarily exceed our linguistic, subjective, or scientific access to them. As Levi Bryant, who is to my mind the most compelling (because he is the most political) of the OOO theorists, puts it in his *The Democracy of Objects*: "What an object is cannot be reduced to our access to objects . . . As such, *The Democracy of Objects* attempts to think the being objects unshackled from the gaze of human in their being-for-themselves."[28] Thus OOO theorists posit the being of objects in themselves (and, more controversially, for themselves) separate from and exceeding any human apprehension. *Insistence of the Material* shares this central emphasis on the being of objects in excess of human perception with OOO—for it enables the positing of the intransigence, resistance, and insistence of the material over and against human manipulation and control. As Bryant argues, such a position enables us to begin to attend to the "role played by non-semiotic actants such as natural resources, the presence or absence of power lines, road distributions and connections, whether or not cable internet connections are available, and, so on, in their exploration of why certain social formations take the form that they do."[29] OOO thus allows us to begin to theorize objects not only as resistant but as what Bryant theorizes as political and ecological actants in their own right.

In theorizing objects as actants, Bryant draws upon the work of Bruno Latour. In their respective work, both Latour and Jane Bennett theorize this concept of objects as actors (or what Bennett terms their "agency") as central to what they term "political ecology."[30] Both theorists posit political ecology as a way of talking about the political and economic stakes between the human and the nonhuman by conceptualizing what they both describe as "the collective" (which Latour defines as a "procedure for collecting associations of humans and nonhumans").[31] Thus, to engage in political ecology is to begin to attend to the insistence of the nonhuman, whether such nonhumans are animals, plants, minerals, or ecosystems. In contrast to Latour, however, I will use political ecology alongside the more established term, political economy, because I think it is essential to maintain the economic critique advanced by Marxist theory and because this critique much too quickly falls out of the work of both Bennett and Latour.

In theorizing materiality, I also side more with the OOO theorists than Bennett and Latour, who tend to conceptualize objects in terms of processes of becoming and in language still derived from the linguistic turn: for example, Latour invokes object's "speech" while Bennett discusses "agency."[32] In contrast, I attend to the resistance and recalcitrance of objects—to their *being* as much as their *becoming*—as well as to their heterogeneity to (as well as intersections with) human motivation and action. Thus if Bennett willfully errs on the side of anthropomorphism in her argument, I err toward the opposite—toward the radically non-human dimensions of the material, including, at points, the materialities and material prostheses of our bodies.

It is this emphasis on the nonhuman dimensions of materiality that I derive from the OOO theorists. Yet, since I am still interested in theorizing the relationship between subject and object, even as I want to place more emphasis on the object side of the pole, I also draw not only from Sarah Ahmed's queer phenomenology but also from Theodor Adorno's older account of the relationship between subject and object in *Negative Dialectics*.[33] Adorno's model provides what is perhaps the most thoroughly realized account of the relationship between subject and object that still insists on what he terms the "object's preponderance."[34]

While writing in an earlier moment of materialist critique, Adorno presents an account of the negative relationship between subject and object that is quite valuable for the work undertaken by the current material turn. For Adorno, the pressing question of the moment in which he was writing, a moment defined by what he described as the administered society and that can also be understood as a Keynesian version of biopolitics, is that of the status of the object. For Adorno, as he and Max Horkheimer articulate it in the coauthored *Dialectic of Enlightenment*, the heterogeneity of the object is threatened by instrumental rationality and the logics of identity and equivalence that it underwrites.[35] The qualitative dimensions of objects are effaced in a political-economic and scientific logic in which "equivalence itself has become a fetish."[36] Adorno also sees this same logic at work in language, especially as it is reshaped by the dictates of instrumental rationality. For him it is "the concept," as it was used by the subject to appropriate the object, that inevitably does a form of epistemological violence to this self-same object: "The prevailing trend in epistemological reflection was to reduce objectivity more and more to the subject. This very tendency needs to be reversed."[37] His positing of what he terms *negative dialectics* insists on the object's preponderance by refusing to posit its full negation via the subject in the movement of the dialectic. This is a radicalization of the Hegelian or Marxist dialectic in the sense that it theorizes aspects of the object that are not appropriable by the subject but instead remain heterodox to the workings of subjective appropriation. Thus, even as they can be dialectically transformed by their interactions with the subject, they also necessarily exceed and resist subjective and linguistic control.

Such a negative dialectics, then, allows us to attend to what Ahmed theorizes as the subject's orientation toward the object and to the way in which objects are transformed via their encounter with subjects, while still emphasizing the irreducibility and heterogeneity of objects (what Bogost terms their "alien" qualities) to human fantasies of mastery.[38] Such a negative dialectics also suggests the theoretical limitations of biopolitics in not theorizing the resistance and intransigence of objects (and of subjects, for that matter) to the direct political and economic management of life. It is the engagement with biopolitics as part of the material turn that we will turn to next.

Biopolitics and Thanatopolitics

The recent theoretical engagement with biopower and biopolitics, as well as its inversion, thanatopolitics, holds much promise for the material turn. Both biopolitics and thanatopolitics present a version of politics in which biological life itself (and its cessation in death) is directly invested and managed by political and economic forms of power. Thus it is an understanding of power that attends directly to the shaping and management of biological life and as such can be defined as part of the material turn. It also, as Adele Clarke et al., Giorgio Agamben, Roberto Esposito, and Michael Hardt and Antonio Negri differently articulate it, a growing form of power in the neoliberal and globalizing present. Yet, as Foucault and Achille Mbembe point out, biopolitics has a longer history than accounts of its growth in the second half of the twentieth century would suggest. So while this book takes its subtitle, *Literature in the Age of Biopolitics*, from the notion that biopolitics has become a more prominent and generalized form of political-economic power in the second half of the twentieth century and the first part of the twenty-first, this should not obscure its older history. It is an older history bound up with the history of Euro-American imperialism—one that is theorized at a number of moments in *Insistence of the Material*, most notably the chapters on Silko and Pynchon.

As powerful as biopolitics and thanatopolitics are as concepts, they need to be theorized more fully in relationship to both materiality and political economy. Before doing so, however, I will provide a brief over-view of the different theories of biopolitics and how they theorize the relationship between power and biological life.

As Michel Foucault posits it in *The History of Sexuality, Volume 1* and in three different volumes of his recently published lectures at the Col-lège de France, biopower is a form of power that takes biological life itself as its focus, particularly as it is regulated and ordered by the workings of governmentality in terms of technologies of population, statistics, pub-lic health, and eugenics (thus he links it to modern forms of racism). In the *History of Sexuality* and in "Society Must Be Defended," he contrasts this form of power, what he also calls bio*politics* to emphasize its political dimensions, with two other understandings of power: the power of the sovereign, which he sees biopower as replacing, and the forms of disci-plinary control of the individual body that he describes in *Discipline and Punish*.[39] So, at first glance, biopolitics seems distinct from the otherwise pervasive engagement with the body in Foucault: "Unlike discipline, which is addressed to bodies, the new nondisciplinary power is applied not to man-as-body but to the living man, to man-as-living-being; ulti-mately if you'd like, to man-as-species."[40] Yet Foucault goes on to suggest that the two forms of power are bound to each other and are interwoven in the functioning of modern governmentality. As we will see further, the relationship of the body to the forms of life regulated by biopolitics will be a recurring issue—one that runs throughout the different theories of the biopolitical and thanatopolitical.

While Foucault's accounts of biopolitics in *The History of Sexuality, Vol-ume 1*, and "Society Must Be Defended" are his most commonly cited and have exerted the most influence on scholars such as Agamben, Mbembe, and Esposito, his account in *The Birth of Biopolitics* presents a crucial development of his thesis—one that ties it directly to economics and specifically to the growth of neoliberalism in the second half of the twen-tieth century (which continues apace into the twenty-first century).[41] While Foucault never fully theorizes the connection, he suggests that a relationship between the biopolitics and neoliberalism can be adduced in relationship to the neoliberal concept of "human capital" as the means by which human life and biology are regulated under neoliberalism.[42] Human capital assumes that all aspects of human existence can be quantified and thus regulated by the market. All aspects of what formerly was understood to be civil society and aspects of the public trust (such as health care, education, child care, social well-being, etc.) under Keynesianism should be privatized in order to maximize the production of human capital. Moreover, the maximization of human capital is the responsibility of individuals; it should be a competitive system, so that there is an impetus to maximize one's share of capital. The effects of this form of privatization are manifold and, while Foucault does not theorize this, have a direct impact on embodiment and the construction of materiality. The body is shaped and reshaped via the demands of human capital, from the violence done to the working body in an economy that no longer protects workers to the uneven forms of what Adele Clarke et al. have termed *biomedicalization*.[43]

Under the regime of biomedicalization, medicine is defined as a process of the maximization and normativization of health; medical care is driven further by profit and individuals are increasingly interpellated by a moral discourse of wellness (in which the maintenance of our health becomes our own responsibility). What was once defined as a right of citizens and thus was tied to notions of national and democratic sovereignty is now defined as a product of the market or of governmentality. Circumventing earlier, if radically imperfect, forms of mediation via notions of citizenship and sovereignty, biomedicalization directly shapes and invests life itself.

It is this opposition between citizenship and biological life that is central to Giorgio Agamben's reformulation of the term. For Agamben, biopolitics is about defining which lives are included within the political community (what he terms *bios*) and which lives are seen as excluded and thus are capable of being killed with impunity (what he terms *zoē*).[44] Central to Agamben's analysis is the way in which *zoē* is defined as bare life, or life reduced to its purely biological dimensions. If the material body seems to be absent in some of Foucault's accounts of biopolitics, then it returns with a vengeance in Agamben. Agamben sees the reduction to a purely material and embodied existence, without a claim to citizenship or subjectivity, as the defining feature of those who are defined as *zoē*. While Agamben uses this concept to theorize those who by their status as infrahuman were constructed as *zoē* during the Holocaust, it also has other political-economic resonances in the neoliberal present, marking, for example, those who labor in "offshore" contexts, where both labor laws and environmental protections are often altogether absent.

Drawing on Agamben and Foucault, Achille Mbembe has theorized the application of biopolitics to the context of colonialism and neocolonialism, arguing compellingly that colonialism itself renders its subjects as *zoē*.

Mbembe articulates a position that was implicit but not fully developed in Agamben—that biopolitics in this sense is also a politics of death, what he terms *necropolitics*.[45] The colonial or neocolonial state exerts direct control over human life, "dictating who may live and who must die."[46] Thus Mbembe crucially adds the element of negativity to what Foucault theorizes in terms of positive power. Roberto Esposito develops this notion of the politics of death even further with his notion of thanatopolitics. Esposito returns to the context of the Holocaust to theorize the way in which biopolitics turns into its deathly opposite, thanatopolitics. Esposito argues that this transformation from a positive (if still violent) form of governmentality into its negative double takes place around the logic of immunity. For him, biopolitics is always split or double—privileging one community, nation, or group as immune, while marking another segment of the population as outside the *cordon sanitaire*. In the name of immunity, biopolitics turns around into thanatopolitics, justifying violence against those who are outside the sphere of protection. In the name of maximizing the health and vitality of all those who are immunized in the body politic, biopolitics becomes a ceaseless campaign of death (since health itself can never be guaranteed).[47]

Esposito's and Mbembe's different accounts of necro- or thanatopolitics add a crucial dimension of negativity to theorizing the effects of contemporary biopolitics. They also push beyond the limits of social constructivism by theorizing death—something that was never really fully possible within the sphere of the cultural and linguistic turns. (One could theorize about the representations of death or discourses around death but not the material finality of death itself for organic beings.) As we will see in the reading of Dodie Bellamy's AIDS novel, *The Letters of Mina Harker*, in chapter 5, it is no accident that death, for Lacan, is one of the dimensions of the real; it is a phenomenon that, like materiality (and the link here is not coincidental, since death is a material process for organic life), refuses full representation in the space of the symbolic.

While neither Esposito nor Mbembe really theorize this, thanatopolitics can be theorized in political-economic terms as well: the way in which maximizing profit or human capital on one location often produces death (in the form of starvation, reduced life expectancy, economic neglect) on another. Michael Hardt and Antonio Negri are the theorists who articulate most fully an economic understanding of biopolitics. They theorize what they term "biopolitical production" as the core component of economic production in the neoliberal present.[48] This restoration of the political economic to the category of biopolitics is both necessary and extremely valuable. Indeed, given the centrality of economic power in our globalizing present, the exclusive emphasis on governmentality in most accounts of biopolitics feels, at best, inadequate. For this reason, Hardt and Negri's economic reconceptualization of the term is crucial for thinking about life in a world in which the economic, the biological, and the bodily are becoming ever more complexly and intimately intertwined.

Yet, even as Hardt and Negri link biopolitics to economics with their conception of biopolitical production, they do so in the name of what they term "immaterial production" or the forms of financial, service, and affective labor that represent the leading sectors of the global economy.[49] While they are right to emphasize the importance of these sites of production, their conceptualization of such forms of production as "immaterial" becomes easily complicit with the fantasies of dematerialization that form one of the central ideologies of our digitalizing present and indeed are a key ideological formation of the last fifty years, with the emergence of image culture and what Guy Debord presciently terms *the society of the spectacle*.[50] Hardt and Negri are careful to argue that immaterial production is intimately tied to material production. It is, in their terms, only the product of the production that is immaterial—the production itself is, of course, still material (whether this materiality is the body of the affect or service laborer or the material processes that produce and power our electronic devices). Moreover, they are also clear that in describing immaterial production as the leading edge of the current economy, they are not arguing that it is the largest sector (this is still agriculture, as it was under industrial capitalism) but rather that it shapes and directs the conditions of all other forms of production—which are reworked in its logic—and is the locus of the largest profits. Yet Hardt and Negri stake their whole revolutionary vision on the forms of autonomous productivity that are central to the relatively high-end and high-pay work associated with immaterial production. Thus the material is finally muted in their account—not just the recalcitrant materiality of bodies but also the recalcitrantly material process of late-capitalist production itself.

In order for biopolitics, thanatopolitics, and biopolitical production to realize their full critical potential as analytic categories, then, they need to be rethought in relationship to the insistent and resistant materiality of bodies and of large sectors of the production process itself. This is not to situate the body or materiality as fully outside the sphere of culture;

indeed, as much biopolitical thought has demonstrated, the history of the last half century can be productively thought about in terms of the increasing ability of culture to shape and discipline the body and for it to socialize and commodify evermore fully different aspects of everyday life. Yet this is also to refuse to make the material and the cultural coincident, for even as the cultural and the discursive shape our bodies in ever more intimate and subtle ways, the materiality of our bodies resists and interacts with such dynamics in ways neither fully controllable nor predictable. Moreover, the bodily and the biological, even as they are transformed by biopolitical and economic processes, also form sites of limit and resistance to those very same processes (limits and resistances that are historically specific and changing but partially determining nonetheless). Such an emphasis resists the fantasies of bodily transcendence that are increasingly central, as N. Katherine Hayles has so cogently pointed out, to our digital age, particularly in a psycho-geographical space of the global North, which is fully immersed in the transformations produced by "immaterial production."[51] In an era in which the dominant ideology of digitalization is the virtual imagined as a process of dematerialization, it becomes especially important for reasons both political economic and ecological to attend to the material resources and still very material forms of production that underpin these fantasies of virtuality.

Political Economy and Globalization

The emergence of globalization theory and the resurgence of work in political economy can also be considered part of the material turn. While globalization theory has both a cultural and a political-economic component (not to mention ecological, political, and environmental components), in almost all its guises, it has placed an emphasis on the limits of the cultural by emphasizing it as only one dynamic in the process of globalization. Thus even a culturally oriented theorist like Arjun Appadurai presents the cultural aspects of globalization as linked to the political economic and the technological.[52] The break with the limits of the cultural turn is even more evident in much of the other work done in globalization theory, from Arif Dirlik and David Harvey's different meditations on the relationship between neoliberalism, post-Fordism, and the ideology of the cultural turn, to the large-scale political-economic interpretations of the capitalist world system in the work of world-systems analysts such as Aníbal Quijano, Immanuel Wallerstein, and Giovanni Arrighi.[53] It is also evident in the impressively integrative work of Saskia Sassen on global cities, which attends to the political economic and the cultural in equal measure.[54]

Insistence of the Material employs world-systems theory and Sassen's and Harvey's social-geographical understandings of globalization in order to provide a longer and more complex account of the spatial and temporal dynamics of globalization than is usually evident in present-oriented accounts of the phenomenon.[55] While the dynamics of globalization have accelerated greatly in the last thirty years, the process, as the world-systems theorists argue, needs to be understood as part of a much longer dynamic—one that has its roots in what imperialism, which in this account is bound up with the history of capitalism.[56] This long view of globalization enables us to theorize the dynamics of capitalist development in a more spatially and temporally complex and recursive manner. Thus, as Aníbal Quijano argues, so-called primitive accumulation (or what David Harvey nicely renames "accumulation by dispossession"), in which resources and land are appropriated wholesale by the capitalist (and often the colonialist) class, not only occurs at the beginning of capitalism but instead represents a recurring dynamic within all phases of capitalism.[57] Accumulation by dispossession underscores the forms of material appropriation (of the minerals and resources of the earth, the land, and bodies themselves, as they are defined as possessions) that subtend the exploitation of wage labor and the production of commodities within capitalist production. For Quijano, even wage labor itself is the exception rather than the rule in Latin America (and I would add Africa)—one that is tied to whiteness. While the industrial proletariat as well as the new service proletariat are exploited via wage labor, this labor is often dependent on unwaged (and thus often thanatopolitical) labor on another scene. Thus the dynamics of accumulation by dispossession, and the forms of imperialism to which they are bound, form what Slavoj Žižek terms the "obscene underside" to the dynamics of capitalist wage labor.[58]

While there is certainly nothing new about political economy, with its genesis, according to the canonical narrative, in the eighteenth-century writings of Adam Smith, there has been a notable rehabilitation of it as a discipline in the last ten to fifteen years. After the seeming dismissal of political economy during the cultural and linguistic turns, a dismissal that was also influenced by the triumphalist market rhetoric that attended the end of the Cold War, there has been a resurgence of interest in political economy, even in fields such as queer theory and cultural studies, where the critique of it was sharpest.[59]

While political economy is often considered a materialism of the Marxist kind rather than the materialism of physical matter that I have so far been addressing, there is a relationship between the two forms of materialism—one that is sometimes obscured in the present by the emergence of financialization and so-called immaterial production. Marx's notion of materialism is organized around the ability of humans to effectively use and control the forms of physical matter associated with the earth and its products. He links this notion of the physical transformation of the earth to the various modes of production and the development of the productive forces and the means of production each one enables. Where this gets complicated is when the products of the capitalist mode of production become increasingly dematerialized, as in the affective, service, electronic, and financial sectors. In the context of these newer political-economic developments, it becomes necessary to trace the material underpinnings and material forms of production upon which they rest.

One way of attending to the material underpinnings of ostensibly immaterial production is suggested by Immanuel Wallerstein in his book, *The Decline of American Power*. He presents Fordism and post-Fordism, usually periodized as radically distinct periods, as A and B phases of a single economic cycle—what he terms a *Kondratieff cycle*. In such a cycle, material production is central to the A phase and financial accumulation is central to the B phase, yet the two phases have to be understood in relationship to each other and as dominant tendencies in what is an interconnected and interlarded process.[60] Thus elements that are subordinate yet present in the A phase become dominant in the B phase and vice versa. This allows us to understand the way in which post-Fordism and the forms of immaterial production usually associated with it are dependent on the forms of material production and the built environment (what Harvey terms *fixed capital*) produced by Fordism and by forms of industrial and material production that continue into post-Fordism.[61] This theorization, then, allows us to trace the material objects and structures beneath the flickering images and seemingly insubstantial commodities of the era of immaterial production. Another way in which I attend to the relationship between Marxian materialism and physical matter is by reworking the

Marxian concept of the commodity fetish in order to critique the fantasy
that underpins the idea of immaterial production and more fully engage
the forms of materiality that it occludes.

Avatar Fetishism

The material turn is an important and necessary development in humanities scholarship, not only because it represents a corrective to the excesses
of the linguistic and cultural turns that preceded it, but also, and perhaps
more importantly, because it can serve to combat the fetishization of the
immaterial. The latter is one of the central ideologies of our time in the
spaces of the global North that have shifted toward the information, financial, affective, and service economies. This fetishization of the immaterial,
which is a dominant feature of everyday life in the global North, takes the
form of what I refer to as *avatar fetishism* (or what could be described as
commodity fetishism 2.0).

I model my conception of avatar fetishism on Marx's notion of the
commodity fetish; it is a subspecies of commodity fetishism.[62] Whereas Marx, in the era of industrial capitalism, organized his conception
of commodity fetishism around a dynamic of materialization, with the
relationships between people becoming transformed into a fetishized
relationship between things, in our era of "immaterial production," the
commodities themselves have become resolutely secondary—so much
degraded and messy materiality—to the fetishized self-image (i.e., a
virtual self or avatar, to which they provide access). What is disavowed,
then, in avatar fetishism is not only the social labor of production but the
material processes, objects, and embodiments that structure and enable
everyday life in our ostensibly postindustrial era. In psychoanalytic terms,
this process can be seen as akin to the construction of an ideal self or an
ideal ego, as in the Lacanian mirror stage. Lacan's conception, with its
emphasis on the simultaneous imaginary organization and supersession
of the material body, is especially resonant in this regard—for such a
fantasy of imaginary organization and supersession of the body is a key
component of avatar fetishism.

Central to the workings of avatar fetishism is a fantasy of the transcendence of the material: most immediately the material body but also the
mundane objects of the material world and the messy business of various
forms of material production, from industrial production, to electronic

production, to various types of so-called eco-friendly production. Avatar fetishism also produces a corollary structure of envy as its dialectical flip side: what I term *embodiment envy*, in which those who have the privilege of imagining that they can transcend embodiment become envious of those who are defined as excessively embodied through their lack of access to avatar fetishism and their relationship to the more material dimensions of the production process. Thus embodiment envy, as I explore more fully in chapter 5, functions as a late twentieth- and early twenty-first-century version of the forms of racial borrowing and primitivism that were central to the formation of white subjectivity in the early twentieth century.[63] It is against avatar fetishism and its corollary, embodiment envy, that *Insistence of the Material* is written.

Rethinking Late Twentieth-Century Literature

Materiality is not only the focus of this book but a core, if unacknowledged, preoccupation of that strain of experimental literature that we inadequately call *postmodernist*. Indeed, *Insistence of the Material* takes its argument and its theoretical cues from a practice of postwar writing that is engaged with materiality and its relationship to biopolitical forms of power. It is my contention that a certain counterpractice of writing in the postmodern era, the late-capitalist literature of materiality, presents the issue of materiality as one of the core questions of contemporary existence. The late-capitalist literature of materiality engaged questions of materiality long before the materialist turn was made in literary and cultural studies. Accordingly, we can profit greatly by looking to the texts themselves for clues as to how to think about materiality in the context of our globalizing present. This materialist vein of literature also pushes us to reconsider the categories by which we understand writing in the second half of the twentieth century.

The End of the Postmodern?

Is postmodernism still a viable analytical category? This is one of the theoretical questions shaping much scholarly debate and inquiry in our early twenty-first-century moment. Mirroring the diverse array of meanings attached to the signifier *postmodern* in its 1980s and 1990s heyday, signifying everything from a set of stylistic practices, to theoretical antifoundationalism (as such its links to the cultural and linguistic turns are obvious), to, in its most compelling formulation, the "cultural logic of late capitalism," contemporary challenges to postmodernism are extremely variable in their presuppositions and political resonances.[64]

Some theorists have rejected the category of the postmodern altogether as an analytical mistake—one that is more effectively replaced by an alternate conception of either modernism or modernity. Thus Marjorie Perloff has argued for the continued validity of modernist aesthetics with her argument for a "twenty-first-century modernism," while globally minded scholars such as Arjun Appadurai and Andreas Huyssen have proposed the differing models of "modernity at large" or "alternate modernities" for thinking about contemporary culture on a global scale.[65] Others do not so much reject the concept of postmodernism outright as define it as an era, set of aesthetic practices, or set of theoretical assumptions whose time has come and gone. Thus a number of writers and scholars have argued for the emergence of post-postmodernism, an aesthetic that reacts in turn to the dominant aesthetics of high postmodernism.[66] In a similar, if more nuanced, vein, Marianne DeKoven has defined the postmodern as emerging from 1960s and the shift from the utopian politics of the grand narrative to the more limited and (to her mind) more ethical politics of local struggle and reformist transformation.[67] In this context, the postmodern, like the 1960s, is both distant from our present yet, paradoxically, still very much with us in the way in which it haunts the cultural imagination. A similar historicizing impulse informs Rachel Adams's argument that the postmodern needs to be periodized as a cultural product of the Cold War and that the literary production of the last two decades in the United States can be better conceptualized as part of what she terms "American literary globalism."[68] Philip Wegner, in turn, suggestively argues that the period of high postmodernity died two deaths, one with the end of the Cold War and the second with the aftermath of the terrorist attacks of September 11, 2001, with a period of genuine political possibility emerging in the 1990s that has now vanished.[69]

As with the critique of the cultural and linguistic turns, these critiques of literary postmodernism are necessary. Indeed, it is through the convergence of disparate critical accounts around a singular (if sometimes vaguely defined) object that real change often happens in culture, academic or otherwise. The cultural structure of feeling about postmodernism has clearly shifted—the once fetishized becoming the rejected, old fashioned, or reviled. This critical shift may indeed enable the emergence of something new, and, as such, it is salutary. Moreover, it allows us to begin to move beyond a theoretical category that even during its heyday felt like it excluded too much, as well as left too much of the world and too many forms of literary production outside its purview.

One of the dangers of such a shift in intellectual common sense, however, is that the object being rejected becomes reduced to a flat caricature of itself—one that, in its one dimensionality, is easier to dismiss and seemingly put behind us. Postmodern aesthetic practices, for example, are reduced to pure metafictional play, as the irresponsible aesthetic of a dominant class of cultural producers in an era when political-economic solutions seemed nowhere to be found and when cultural production seemed divorced from any larger forms of political struggle. If this refrain sounds familiar, it should: it echoes, almost word for word, the charges leveled by postmodernism against the aesthetic practices of (late) modernism in the former's moment of emergence. One of the risks of the present moment, then, is to blindly repeat the ideology of the postmodern (an ideology that was always inadequate to the multiplicity of cultural practices that it claimed to encompass) in our very fantasy of overcoming it. (In this context, nothing seems more postmodern than the positing of a post-postmodern; if we really are beyond the age of the "posts," the claim certainly cannot be congruent with the cultural or material present.)

The Late-Capitalist Literature of Materiality

Perhaps another strategy, one that I pursue in *Insistence of the Material*, is to return to the reviled object that is postmodern literature in order to posit a difference or, more forcefully, a rift within the very category itself. It is only by returning to the category and seeing the complexity and heterogeneity contained therein that we may be able to generate critical categories adequate to the literary practices it describes as well as to that which it covers over or excludes. While the standard take on postmodern fiction sees it as a metafictional enterprise, this definition only describes one tendency within the literature conventionally grouped under the banner of the postmodern. Within this framework, most postmodern fiction is conceptualized as fiction about the process of fiction making itself.

In contrast to this dominant tendency within postmodern fiction, I posit the counterpractice represented by the late-capitalist literature of materiality. This alternative vein of postmodern fiction holds much richer possibilities for thinking about the relationship of literature to our globalizing present. Often grouped under the rubric of the "fiction of transgression," the writers of the late-capitalist literature of materiality use language experimentally to engage the increasingly obscured yet ever proliferating material underpinnings of everyday life in the era of late capitalism. Late capitalism, in this context, applies to the whole period that extends from the economic cycle that begins with the post–World War II Fordist boom in U.S. production and continues through the post-Fordist era that follows it. Such a definition thus incorporates the eras of both high Fordism and post-Fordism. In Wallerstein's schema, and in contrast to Jameson's and Harvey's famous formulations of the postmodern as coterminous with post-Fordism, high Fordism and post-Fordism can be theorized as interpenetrating parts of a continuous cycle—one to which the writers of the late-capitalist literature of materiality were responding.

A quick glance at the writers I have grouped under the banner of the late-capitalist literature of materiality (William Burroughs, Thomas Pynchon, Dodie Bellamy, J. G. Ballard, and Leslie Marmon Silko) reveals their largely metropolitan and first-world status. This is not accidental nor merely a product of my inevitably partial and parochial reading practices. While there are many other materialist traditions and practices of literature, the practice that I am calling the late-capitalist literature of materiality is a product of the overdeveloped core of the capitalist world system. This literature of overdevelopment is a product of the context these writers find themselves situated within or at least (in the case of Burroughs and Silko) partially situated within: a world in which the built environment, modes of representation, the figuration of the body, and the experience of everyday life are profoundly intertwined with late-capitalist production, consumption, and signification practices that both remake the material world and produce an ever-growing fantasy of its transcendence. Central to such a zone of overdevelopment is the fantasy that life itself is becoming ever more malleable, discursive, and indeed, "metafictional"—a fantasy bound up with the emergence in the postwar period of biopolitics and biopolitical production as a core organizing principle of everyday life, in which the body and subjectivity are immediate products of the process of economic production (rather than adjuncts to it) and thus are entirely socialized.[70] Yet these fantasies of dematerialization and complete socialization, like the orthodoxies of the cultural turn, work to disavow the very real ways life in late capitalism was and continues to be characterized by the opposite—by the proliferation of the intransigently material.

In short, then, the late-capitalist literature of materiality is engaged in tarrying with the material unconscious of late-capitalist existence. In contradistinction to metafictional forms of postmodernism, the literature of materiality engages with the material underpinnings of our globalizing world. The literature of materiality reveals that the roots of current processes of globalization are in the postwar era and continue throughout the two phases of late capitalism. In the first phase, the United States oversaw and benefitted from the neoimperial construction of a relationship between the first-world core as the site of production for both the United States and the war-ravaged economies of Europe and a periphery, as the locus of raw materials, which was made up of the newly postcolonial nation states of the third world. In the core state, this phase was also characterized by the growth of forms of technocratic and biopolitical governmentality, what Adorno called the administered society, that were central to the Fordist and Keynesian regime of accumulation. This postwar society, as commentators from C. Wright Mills to William Whyte noted, was characterized less by modes of democratic participation and more by a mass organization and administration of everyday life—in a word, *biopolitics*.[71] Also central to this period was the emergence of what Guy Debord described as the society of the spectacle, shaped by the appearance of televisual culture, the proliferation of communication technology, the initial moments of the cybernetic revolution, and the exponential growth of commodity culture.[72] These tendencies would become even more pronounced in the second phase of late capitalism, but it is important to remember that they have their moment of initial impact in the first phase of Fordist production. Similarly, industrial production would not disappear in the second phase of financialization but would be a continuing, if devalorized and less profitable, dimension of production—one that was increasingly outsourced to deregulated zones in the third world. Meanwhile, redefinition of their economies around the finance, electronic, and service sectors precipitated a shift from biopolitical governmentality to biopolitical production in the core countries of the world system. While these two phases are distinct and involve distinct political-economic, ideological, and affective formations, they are also overlapping and have interlarded tendencies. Indeed, both phases depend on structural relations of overaccumulation and disaccumulation, as well as shifting forms of biopolitical regulation.

It is unsurprising, then, that late-capitalist literature of materiality, with its preoccupation with the material underpinnings of everyday life in a world dedicated to the transcendence of the material, spans both eras.

Transmodernity and Postmodernism

Now, after considering both the critiques of the term as well as its persistence, we are in a better space to assess the value of the signifier *postmodern*. Given its familiarity and embeddedness within critical discourse, I will still use it, at points, as a periodizing shorthand. I find it primarily useful on a local and descriptive level as a way of talking about certain set of literary practices that broke with modernism and that responded to life in the overdeveloped first world. Such an account includes what I am terming the late-capitalist literature of materiality, yet it is also challenged by it and at points exceeded by it. Postmodernism thus should be understood as a category that has theoretical and descriptive limits. Also, my intertwining of postwar eras that are usually seen as diametrically opposed produces a different understanding of postmodernism than is conventional within Jameson and Harvey's formulations. I want to suggest, as more aesthetically minded theories of postmodernism also do, that postmodernism's genesis can be located in the 1950s and 1960s and is as much a reaction to the emergence of administered forms of life produced by Keynesian and Fordist biopolitics as it is the seeming textualization and marketization of life produced by neoliberal biopolitics.

This understanding of the aesthetic practices of postmodernism should be seen as a set of tendencies rather than absolutes—tendencies that are bound by temporal, spatial, and generic constraints. Thus the narrative about the relationship between literature and contemporary life will be a different one when considering literature produced in other cultural locations—whether those locations are geoculturally, temporally, or generically different (and the forms of modified realism that continue to be central to most forms of popular writing also complicate these distinctions). One of the problems with some of the more expansive theories of postmodernism, such as those of Jameson and Harvey, is that while they represent an important and necessary materialist corrective to purely aesthetic or theoretical conceptions of the term, they tend to generate an application that is simultaneously both too broad and too narrow—too broad in reading all textual production in terms of a cultural dominant and too narrow in being marked by the conceptual limits of an unconscious privileging of first-world experience.

It is here where I find Enrique Dussel's concept of "transmodernity" to be an important corrective to the limitations of Jameson's and Harvey's otherwise compelling theoretical models.[73] While, if anything, transmodernity is an even broader term, it is also more flexible and less prescriptive. Dussel attends to successive waves of modernization and globalization within the long frame of capitalist modernity beginning in the sixteenth century, arguing that such waves do not simply replace or eradicate the forms of culture or production they encounter. Instead, such forms of production persist and are rearticulated in relationship to their encounter with the forces of modernization. Within such a paradigm, all spaces within the globe need to be understood as composite spaces made up of different forms of cultural production and different regimes of political-economic organization—ones shaped by and subordinated to the dominant mode of production but ones that also contain other forms of production within them.

While Dussel is concerned with producing a new "interpretation of modernity in order to include moments that were never incorporated into the European vision," his paradigm also works productively to think through the complexity of cultural production in spaces that have been central to the European vision of modernity.[74] Thus what emerges from Dussel is a model in which cultural producers can draw on a range of political, economic, and cultural dynamics that are existing in differential spatial, political-economic, and temporal relationships to each other in order to produce accounts that challenge modernity and postmodernity as much as conform to them. Novelistic production emerges in this model as more flexible in aesthetic terms as well as spatiotemporal ones. Novels can embrace or challenge dominant aesthetic practices; similarly, they can cast back or point forward to social and economic developments that move in a different temporality to those that are dominant in any given moment. Thus while I will continue to use the term *postmodernism* in *Insistence of the Material*, it should be understood as operating within the larger frame provided by Dussel's transmodernity.

Dussel's transmodernity also suggests a different understanding of temporality and periodization that is common in contemporary literary studies. Since the growth of new historicism in the 1980s and 1990s, a specific, localized, and linear understanding of historicism has been instituted as proper practice in literary studies. While much else has changed in contemporary literary criticism, this new historicist framework has rarely been effectively challenged. And yet such tight and linear forms of historicism can be as distorting as they are illuminating. They can obscure as much as they reveal.

The point is not that we should stop historicizing or return to a transhistorical framework of analysis (though some objects as well as some ecological and economic systems, if we take the material turn seriously, may need much larger temporal frames to properly understand their historicity) but that we need to be alert to the longer rhythms and recursive, often spiral-like dynamics of historical change, especially as we attempt to be attentive and adequate to the spatial and temporal disjunctions produced by a more global framework. It is important in this regard to emphasize something that Jameson has always done in his historicism: all modes of production are mixed ones, in which the older modes and newer modes exist in tension with the mode that is dominant in any given moment. This composite understanding of temporality is even more complicated when one starts to think about the complexities of how spatiality and temporality are interlarded, such that what may not have occurred or is already seemingly finished in one spatial location may be the dominant formation in another.

The geographies depicted by the novels I examine present us with just such an interlarded conception of space and time. Thus Ballard's London, Bellamy's San Francisco, and Silko's San Diego have more in common with each other than, say, Silko's Sonoran Desert, which, in turn, has more in common with Pynchon's representation of German Southwest Africa. Within this remapping, a space's relationship to larger dynamics of accumulation and disaccumulation, biopolitics and thanatopolitics, and imperialism and colonialism are much more reliable guides for thinking about the relationship between spaces and times in these novels than any straightforward notion of culture as bounded by the nation state or a thoroughly linear conception of temporality. What I am arguing for then is what Victor Burgin has theorized, in a nicely materialist metaphor, as a "brecciated" conception of both time and space.[75] A brecciated rock is a rock that is a composite of different rocks and different materials, each produced within a different temporality. Within a brecciated conception of time and space, then, dynamics like accumulation by dispossession or biopolitics do not have a single history or a single temporality but are rather spatially and historically recursive and dynamic, as they are shaped by and intersect with distinct forms of materiality and material practices. This brecciated understanding of time and space, then, enables us to attend to the seemingly prescient dimensions of texts like *Naked Lunch* or *Almanac of the Dead*, which, because of their authors' specific positioning in the world system, point forward to dynamics that are barely emerging in most places at the time of the text's composition. Such an understanding of time and space also helps us attend to the long temporality of a novel like Silko's, which takes as its extended present the five hundred years of imperial conquest in the Americas. This, then, is the conception of temporality and spatiality I will work with in *Insistence of the Material*. Now that I have laid out the conception of time and space that operates in *Insistence of the Material*, I am finally in the position to summarize the argument made in the chapters that follow.

Attending to the Material

Chapter 1 advances a reading of William Burroughs's *Naked Lunch*, arguing that Burroughs's transgressive watershed articulates a prescient vision of the intersections of three forms of materiality in the emerging era of globalization and biopolitics: the linguistic, the bodily, and the political economic. *Naked Lunch* also suggests that we need to attend to the most obscene and degraded forms of material existence (those that are most directly shaped by biopolitics and thanatopolitics) if we want to think about the possibility of a more just future. As such, Burroughs's novel becomes the template for thinking about the literature of materiality in the chapters that follow.

Chapter 2 engages Thomas Pynchon's *V.*, arguing that the writer's first novel presents a prehistory of late capitalism, tracing the emergence of biopolitical forms of control in both the first-world metropole and the colonial periphery. The novel also stages a series of encounters between those who construct themselves as subjects of history and those people and things that are constructed as the objects of history, foregrounding the increasing inability of the former to control the latter in the era of decolonization.

Chapter 3 reads J. G. Ballard's *Crash* as a secretly political novel. Ballard's infamously amoral chronicle of the erotics of car crashes insists that we recognize the built environment of high Fordism that persists beneath emerging post-Fordist fantasies of flexibility and immaterial production. It asks that we tarry with the material unconscious of the post-Fordist moment: the hard city that persists beneath the "soft city" that David Harvey equates with postmodernism.[76] In its emphasis on the violence to vulnerable bodies by the technology of this hard city, the novel insists that we attend to the forms of violence that the notion of immaterial production both obscures and perpetuates.[77]

Chapter 4 reads Dodie Bellamy's *The Letters of Mina Harker* in order to theorize more fully the materiality of the body as it resists biopolitical scripts of performativity and discursive control. Bellamy's experimental chronicle of the forms of biopolitics and thanatopolitics that characterized the AIDS crisis in San Francisco represents an important feminist and queer intervention into accounts of the body as discursively constituted. Bellamy insists that a truly progressive feminist and queer politics needs to attend to the domains of the body that elude our fantasies of symbolic control—aspects of the body that are constituted as abject or real but also those aspects where biology asserts its imperatives separate from our cultural scripts. Thus she suggests the necessity of putting the category of the resistantly biological back into biopolitics in order to imagine a body politics adequate to contemporary existence.

Chapter 5 takes up the political vision articulated by Bellamy and reorients it toward a collective politics articulated from a Native, fourth-world perspective. Leslie Marmon Silko's *Almanac of the Dead* presents a vision of the world caught in a struggle between a thanatopolitical culture of overdevelopment and death and a vision of life that emphasizes the importance of attending to and respecting the material world and the forms of life bound to it. I read Silko's novel as consciously in dialogue with the largely metropolitan tradition I have thus far been tracing. The novel both employs the same forms of critique of late-capitalist life evident in Burroughs, Pynchon, Ballard, and Bellamy, and posits an antidote by imagining a conception of everyday life that incorporates pan-Native practices that value the ecological and the material grounds upon which human existence is lived.

The conclusion of *Insistence of the Material* makes some provisional assessments based on the readings that have come before. It is written in a speculative and aphoristic style, advancing a set of theoretical possibilities rather than firm conclusions. Such openness is necessary if we are going to be able to begin to adequately theorize the material. This introduction began with the recognition that we can never be adequate to our objects—to the forms of materiality that escape our linguistic categories for them. Thus it is crucial that we maintain a theoretical openness that both tries to better account for its objects while also recognizing the impossibility of fully doing so. This double imperative lies at the core of the chapters that follow.

CHAPTER 1

The Novel Enfleshed

Naked Lunch and the Literature of Materiality

The most accessible version of the "New Flesh" . . . would be that you could actually change what it means to be a human being in a physical way.

—David Cronenberg, *Cronenberg on Cronenberg*

The Prescient Mr. Burroughs

William Burroughs's fiction resists temporal categorization.[1] While often defined in the popular imagination, along with Ginsberg and Kerouac, as one of the three major beat writers (an appellation that obscures the diversity of literary production and producers associated with the beat movement as well as Burroughs's own rejection of the term), he is often presented as the odd man out in this fetishized triumvirate. Whereas Kerouac's jazz-inflected and Ginsberg's Whitmanesque writings seem comfortably of their time, Burroughs's fiction, with its resolute antihumanism, darkness, and wildly experimental prose, seems to be generated as part of an alternate temporal trajectory—one that both points backward to early twentieth-century experimentalists such as the Dadaists and surrealists and forward to our time of postmodern or "post-postmodern" experimental fiction, globalization, neoliberal biopolitics, and so-called immaterial production.[2]

Indeed, I am not the only one to notice the strangely prescient dimensions of Burroughs's fiction. That Burroughs's fiction can be read as prescient—indeed as prophetic—is the central gambit of the recent collection of essays on Burroughs and globalization, *Retaking the Universe: William S. Burroughs in the Age of Globalization*.[3] That this collection succeeds as well as it does points to the ways in which Burroughs's writings refuse to become merely the literary production of another era. Similarly, Ann Douglas, in the magisterial essay that opens *Word Virus*, notes the way in which Burroughs's fiction speaks to the concerns of the present as much as to the times of its genesis.[4]

At first glance, to describe a novel as prophetic seems to be a strange claim for a book about materiality. Surely, nothing is less materialist than the claim that a text is an index of the future. Yet I think that such a claim appears irredeemably idealist only if we employ a limitedly linear and implicitly evolutionist conception of temporality, in which economic and literary forms are both tightly bound to each other and imagined as constituting entirely discrete and consistent categories. While Fredric Jameson is often the name most immediately associated with such a critical paradigm, to read Jameson in this way is to do a disservice to the more complex and dynamic conceptions of both temporality and literary form that shapes his work at its most supple.[5] His conceptions of modes of production, for example, are always mixed, with the dominant, the emergent, and the residual mixing in ways that are both conflictual and complimentary.[6] His conception of literary and artistic form is similarly flexible, with figures like Stein and Duchamp pointing proleptically toward an emergent postmodern aesthetic in the moment of high modernism.[7] Indeed, Jameson specifically discusses the prophetic dimensions of fiction in *Marxism and Form*, in which he suggests that this ability to examine the entrails of the present for signs of what will be dominant in the future is one of the privileged tasks of literature and of cultural production, more generally.[8] When we combine this supple and complex conception of temporality with the recursive, brecciated conception of time that I describe in the introduction as characterizing world-systems economics and, more specifically, Enrique Dussel's conception of transmodernity, what emerges is an account of temporality that is as complex and mixed as the various spaces and ways of life that make up the capitalist world system.[9]

Such an approach thus allows a longer and more recursive sense of temporality than literary critical categories such as postmodernism and post-postmodernism. My reading of the temporal disruptions produced by Burroughs's prose, then, is one example of such an approach. The prophetic dimensions of Burroughs's narratives of the late fifties and sixties and *Naked Lunch* in particular are a product of space as it mixes with time: Burroughs moved geographically in the years just prior to the novel's genesis, from cities of core countries in the global North such as New York to the urban spaces of the periphery and semiperiphery, Tangier and Mexico City. This movement is repeatedly traced in the novel itself. As

Brian Edwards compellingly documents, Burroughs wrote much of the novel (and parts of the cut-up trilogy) in the international zone in Tangier, and this extranational space also contributes to its prescience: life in the international zone pointed forward to late-capitalist forms of economic and social organization that were just emerging or becoming newly dominant in the fifties and sixties.[10] The specific space and juridical status of the international zone, which, much like the contemporary free enterprise and special development zones produced by neoliberal globalization, was a deregulated, transnational space produced by the specific history of colonialism in Tangier (and Morocco, more generally). Such a space enabled Burroughs to address forms of economic organization and biopolitical as well as thanatopolitical forms of power that only became more generalized at a later moment. The colonial location of Tangier (as well as the neocolonial location of Mexico City, where he lived before he moved to Tangier) thus allowed Burroughs to construct a fictional landscape that is built around biopolitical production, including sex work, the trade in narcotics, the biomedical economy, and the traffic in life and death that would only become a more dominant part of the world system (one not primarily situated in colonial and neocolonial spaces) in our own moment.

In the reading of *Naked Lunch* that follows, I will not treat Burroughs as an author whose writings are primarily of historical interest. Instead, I will read *Naked Lunch* as a fictional text that has much to teach us about the world in which we live today. Indeed, I treat it as a work of theory as much as a work of literature—one that is crucially engaged with dynamics that continue to shape our biopolitical and neoliberal present. Central to Burroughs's engagement with late capitalism and biopolitics is his text's meditations on materiality, especially the materialities of violated and reshaped bodies, as they intersect with the forms of economic and biopolitical violence depicted by the novel. It is to this engagement with materiality that I next turn.

Materialist Burroughs

If what I am calling late-capitalist literature of materiality represents a counterpractice of writing in an era dominated by postmodern metafiction, then this practice can be said to be inaugurated with William Burroughs's publication of *Naked Lunch* in 1959. While Burroughs's text is often situated uncomfortably between modernism and postmodernism, it is best characterized as the founding text in the tradition of materialist literature that I am tracing here.[11] In this context, the question of its status as either modern or postmodern is of less importance (though my discussion of it as prescient suggests that, if pushed, I would categorize it as the latter) than its inauguration of a tradition of writing that responds to the world of overdevelopment that emerged with the advent of U.S. hegemony during the short American century. In contrast with the primarily linguistic concerns of much metafiction, Burroughs's texts are focused relentlessly on the material.[12] This engagement with materiality is nowhere more evident than in Burroughs's experimental watershed, *Naked Lunch*. Indeed William Burroughs's materialist urtext can be read as providing a theoretical account of the intersections among three different registers of materiality—linguistic, bodily, and political economic.

The form of novelistic praxis undertaken by Burroughs's novel can only be fully understood in terms of its engagement with the interrelationship among all three forms of materiality. Indeed, the text can be read as proffering a distinctive aesthetic—one predicated on the charged relationships among these differing registers of the material. Burroughs's novel is certainly engaged with the materiality of the signifier, but, unlike the largely metafictional concerns of postmodern writers like Italo Calvino or John Barth, the central obsessions of Burroughs's text cannot be limited to the linguistic domain. Instead, language, as a form of discourse, becomes as significant for what it obscures and refuses as for the ways in which it is productive. As his repeated theorizations of language as a virus suggests, Burroughs's novel (in spite of the ambiguity of the concept of virus in his hands) is written against language as much as it is written inevitably within or through it.

Burroughs and Lacan

I want to suggest that the function of language in Burroughs is best theorized in a Lacanian register. In contrast to the metaphoric privileging language and linguistic metaphors (such as discourse and textuality) in most poststructuralist theory, Lacan's conception of language, which is coincident with his category of the symbolic, is only one part of his tripartite schema of subjectivity and its relationship to the social. The other two parts are, of course, the imaginary and the real. While the imaginary largely overlaps with, even as it overdetermines, the symbolic, the real is precisely that which eludes, resists, or traumatically underpins yet is disavowed or excluded from the symbolic.[13] Lacan's tripartite formulation is particularly valuable for theorizing the status of materiality in the spaces of overdevelopment that define late capitalism; for while most postmodern theory tends to take these spaces at face value as sites in which the material has been fully socialized and the actual has been replaced by the virtual, Lacan's formulation, in contrast, emphasizes the intransigent forms of materiality and abjected aspects of everyday existence that form in tension with the material signifiers that constitute language.[14] It is Lacan's category of the real that can help us theorize that which resists full integration into the linguistic and that which the linguistic can only misname. In other words, the real can help us theorize those forms of materiality in late capitalism that exceed and resist symbolic coding in *Naked Lunch*: the domains of the body and political economy.

Burroughs's conception of language as a virus suggests the applicability of Lacan's theory for the analysis of his works,[15] for Burroughs conceives language very much along the lines of the Lacanian symbolic. Language is for Burroughs a viral yet necessary imposition on biological life and the material world that functions as a system of social control that structures our very conception of reality. Or, as Burroughs puts it in *Nova Express*, "Word begets image and image *is* virus."[16] Burroughs and Brion Gysin concisely formulate this capacity of the word and image viruses to construct reality in their jointly produced art and print collage, *The Third Mind*: "'Reality' is apparent because you live and believe it. What you call 'reality' is a complex network of necessary formulae . . . association lines of words and image presenting a prerecorded word and image track."[17] Here, as in Lacan, what we perceive as reality is largely a by-product of the forms of symbolic and imaginary language-constructed and image-based mediations that organize our everyday understanding of the world. Burroughs is instead interested in accessing the real via the symbolic. In order to do this, though, the symbolic must be used against itself in order to expose that which it attempts but fails to account for and which exists in contradiction to it: the real. As Timothy S. Murphy puts it, Burroughs is interested in using the "material of the reality film against itself."[18]

Naked Lunch is especially invested in two distinct resonances of the Lacanian real: the real as trauma and the real as materiality. Materiality and trauma are linked everywhere in Burroughs's novel. At the most general level, Burroughs presents materiality itself as the traumatic repressed in a global order increasingly organized around the dematerializing effects of media and commodity culture in the core countries of the world system and biopolitical forms of discursive control. In such a context, the forms of materiality that disrupt the subject's imaginary identifications and symbolic fictions of the world function as a traumatic return of the repressed, especially for those members of the global bourgeoisie for whom the material appears to be forever displaced on another scene. This other scene has been theorized by Giorgio Agamben as the locus of "bare life" or forms of brutely material existence that are defined in contrast to the more privileged forms of biopolitical subjectivity that correspond to those who possess the rights of citizenship and political voice.[19] Such forms of bare life, a product of biopolitics in its most violent register, form one of the key loci of the material repressed to the symbolic constructed by first-world forms of citizenship. As Roberto Esposito argues, such forms of "bare life" are linked not so much to biopolitics but its opposite: the political-economic production of death, or what Esposito defines as *thanatopolitics*.[20] Thanatopolitics, as well as the political-economic divides that underwrite it, become the repressed of the global North that Burroughs is interested in making manifest in *Naked Lunch*.

Moments of the return of the material repressed, then, become the sites where syntax breaks down and where violated, exploited, and abject forms of materiality break through the web of the symbolic and forcefully intrude into the subject's field of perception, insisting on an accounting in the field of desire. Indeed, this return of the material repressed is one of the central meanings of the novel's title: "The title means exactly what the words say: NAKED lunch—a frozen moment when everyone sees what is on the end of every fork."[21] Such a frozen moment suggests precisely an instant when the symbolic breaks down, when the familiar becomes strange, and the uncoded stuff that is the material remainder of that which we consume becomes visible on the end of our forks.

The Language of the Real

Burroughs's engagement with the real is not merely thematized in *Naked Lunch* on the level of content, but, as I have already begun to suggest, it is also stylistically enacted on the level of language. In its engagement with language, Burroughs's text is continuously pushing against the symbolic confines of representation in order to foreground the materiality of the signifiers that are the building blocks of his (and all our) narratives. While this emphasis on the materiality of the signifier seems initially to replicate metafictional postmodernism, Burroughs, in contrast to many postmodern writers and thinkers, emphasizes the connection of the materiality of the signifier to other forms of abjected materiality. This connection is made explicit in the logic of trauma that I have just outlined, in which material as well as symbolic trauma is linked to certain occulted signifiers that take on full resonance in specific material contexts. Thus, in Burroughs, the materiality of the signifier becomes a privileged link to other forms of materiality. *Naked Lunch* emphasizes this linkage by employing the materiality of the signifier in order to analogically stand in for the other forms of materiality engaged by the text.

Burroughs's use of language plays with syntax only to finally undo its logic. This move from syntax to radical parataxis—from semantic legibility, through isolated moments of signification, to the very materiality of the signifier itself—is strikingly as evident when the text appears to be mimicking the relatively realist narrative structures of earlier (at least in terms of initial composition) novels such as *Junky* or *Queer* as it is in the text's more overt flights of fantasy. Take, for example, this description from early in the novel, which begins as a relatively realist account of the federal policing of the trade in opiates, which began in earnest in the postwar moment but ends somewhere beyond representation and conventional syntax: "The Vigilante is prosecuted in Federal Court under a lynch bill and winds up in a Federal Nut House specially designed for the containment of ghosts: precise, prosaic impact of objects . . . washstands . . . door . . . toilet . . . bars . . . there they are . . . this is it . . . all lines cut . . . nothing beyond . . . Dead End . . . And the Dead End in every face" (9).

Representation breaks down into discrete signifiers here, with each cluster of signifiers separated by ellipses. It is significant, though, that this derailing of representation begins in a sentence that appears entirely "prosaic," to use the term that is deployed by the sentence itself. While the first part of the sentence relies on street slang such as "lynch bill" and "nut house" that may lend it a certain opacity, depending on the reader's familiarity with such terms (and Burroughs's attraction to such terms may be in part for the way in which their metaphoricity and subcultural specificity already works to render strange the prosaic), it reads as a relatively conventional sentence—one more associated with the compressions of pulp narrative than with the explicit experimentation conventionally associated with Burroughs. The second half of the sentence, however, more than lives up to the latter billing.

Yet if we examine the details of this refusal of narrative, it becomes clear that while Burroughs's language is at war against the prosaic, in the sense of the conventional prose narrative, it is also interested demonstrating the way in which the "impact" of the prosaic (in the sense of ordinary) "objects" of everyday life are irreducible to a prosaic form of representation. Indeed, the list of discrete objects emphasizes what Levi Bryant describes as "the being of objects unshackled from the gaze of the human in their being for-themselves."[22]

Of course, Burroughs doesn't situate the objects as not present for the human gaze, nor is this what Bryant means in describing them as "unshackled" from such a gaze. Instead Bryant and Burroughs are emphasizing "the non-semiotic or non-representational differences" manifested by "nonhuman objects" over any ability of the subject to fully represent or appropriate them.[23] Instead, the lines of communication are "cut" and language rushes forward into a "dead end" of decontextualized signifiers. Yet the death implied in this dead end seems to be that of a subjectivity securely anchored in the symbolic, because the signifiers take on a life of their own, glowing with asyntactic vitality. Thus the language of the sentence becomes a linguistic analog to the Lacanian real. The second half of the sentence emphasizes the materiality of the signifiers deployed and, in clustering these signifiers together, creates discrete subsyntactic units such as "all lines cut" or "nothing beyond" that become entities unto themselves. In other words, the text continuously shifts from the language of realism to the antirealistic language of the real (in which signifiers become a form of uncoded materiality).

This creation of a language of the real characterizes the distinctive form of linguistic experimentation associated with *Naked Lunch* and Burroughs's other experimental texts. Indeed, this technique reaches its apotheosis in the cut-up trilogy, with the cut-up process working precisely by juxtaposing different texts to produce asyntactic and non–narrative linguistic conjunctions. But it is also evident throughout much of the writing in *Naked Lunch*. The narrative passages in the novel are often derived from what Burroughs describes as his routines—"completely spontaneous" oral performances that "proceed from whatever fragmentary knowledge you have."[24] Thus even in its most conventional, Burroughs's text is derived from the embodied practice of oral improvisation. In these routines, fragmentation is valued over coherence and the rhetorical effect of obscenity and hyperbole on readers' or listeners' bodies over any commitment to representational or conceptual truth. The language of the routines thus represents one version of the novel's language of the real.

This language of the real takes two other characteristic forms in *Naked Lunch*: descriptions of random detritus that overload initially realist descriptions until they collapse under their own junk-filled weight and narrative fragments that break off after a few paragraphs only to shift radically in content and location in the next fragment.

A particularly resonant version of the first technique is evident in a passage that irrupts into the infamous "Hassan's Rumpus Room" section of the novel, with its endlessly staged sexual lynching rituals and pornographic film diegesis. This irruption reads like an inverted pastoral interlude, calling attention to the abject materials that accumulate in the waste spaces of Interzone and other global urban spaces: "He plummets from the eyeless lighthouse, kissing and jacking off in face of the black mirror, glides obliquely down with cryptic condoms and mosaic of a thousand newspapers through a drowned city of red brick to settle in black mud with tin cans and beer bottles, gangsters in concrete, pistols pounded flat and meaningless to avoid short-arm inspection of prurient ballistic experts. He waits the slow striptease of erosion with fossil loins" (64).

Form mirrors content here. These sentences maintain a tenuous relationship to syntax and can be read for narrative meaning, yet their general movement is toward dissolution (or "erosion," as the sentence puts it) into the stagnant pools of accumulated objects the sentence describes. Words are "pounded flat and meaningless," even as they are the objects of "prurient" inspection. The representation of space is presented as analogous to this collapse of language; it is unmappable and dreamlike, suggesting, as Fredric Jameson has noted, the "mutation of built space itself" that accompanies late capitalism.[25] The sentence also disrupts conventional mappings of subject and object through a process of chiasmus. Objects become the focus of sexual interest, while semen and other sexual fluids and finally the subject of the sentence himself become just waste products open to the process of slow erosion. The word and the subject thus become analogs to the various abject and excremental objects that are the waste products of the global economy that *Naked Lunch* details.

John Vernon has called attention to the emphasis on the excremental and the anal in Burroughs's writings, and such an emphasis is evident everywhere in this passage.[26] Indeed, what the passage articulates is an analogy between the abject dimensions of the subject—what Kristeva describes with a set of excremental metaphors as those aspects of the subject that are repudiated as locus of "defilement, sewage, and muck"—and the abject and excremental waste of a globalizing capitalist world system.[27] The muck in Burroughs takes on registers that are at once socioeconomic, psychoanalytic, and linguistic: it is those aspects of existence, including the bodily, deathly, excremental, and basely material, against which the ego typically defines itself. It is also the waste products and forms of degraded materiality, including the materiality of bodies defined as bare life, that form the obscene underside to the dominant symbolic produced by commodity culture and the logic of governmentality in the short American century.[28] Finally, it is the muck of language itself, shorn of narrative certainty and throbbing in its materiality with a kind of erotic intensity.

A final stylistic characteristic of Burroughs's texts is the juxtaposition of narrative fragments:

> The gangster in concrete rolls down the river channel . . . They cowboyed him in the steam room . . . Is this Cherry Ass Gio the Towel Boy or Mother Gillig, Old Auntie of Westminster Palace?? Only dead fingers talk in Braille . . .
> The Mississippi rolls in great limestone boulders down the silent alley . . .
> "Clutter the glind!" screamed the Captain of Moving Land . . .
> Distant rumble of stomachs . . . Poisoned pigeons rain from the Northern Lights . . . The reservoirs are empty . . . Brass statues crash through the hungry squares and alleys of the gaping city . . .
> (166)

Like the lists of random detritus, the juxtaposition of narrative fragments works to disrupt narrative meaning and call attention to the materiality of the signifiers themselves. However, the lists maintain the ghost of syntax even as the sentences buckle under their own weight of accumulated junk. The juxtaposed fragments work through the logic of montage. Like avant-garde film (such as *Towers Open Fire* or *The Cut-Ups*, both of which Burroughs and Gysin made in the 1960s), the passage juxtaposes isolated, disconnected images in order to challenge the prerecorded image tracks associated with the word *virus*. The cutting up and transposing of technologies of word and image construction, as well as the word and images themselves, works to create a kind of synesthesia in which language and image, vision, touch, taste, and smell become disoriented and jumbled together, thereby disrupting the smooth functioning of the reality film—or, as Burroughs puts it here, "Only dead fingers talk in Braille."

The other effects, besides those of ideological demystification produced by these moments of montage, are spatial. Not only do they contribute to the spatial dislocations that are central to the novel, but they also work to produce its globalized landscape. In the previous passage, we move swiftly from Mississippi in an alleyway, to some place where the Northern Lights are visible, to an anonymous urban space. The isolated fragments of language thus become analogous to the isolated and confused snippets of place in such passages. Similar spatial displacements run throughout the novel.

The New Flesh of Late Capitalism

The materiality that Burroughs is most interested in examining is the materiality of the body and its relationship to the economic underpinnings of late-capitalist existence. The body in Burroughs's text is one deformed and reformed by the political and sexual economies depicted by the novel. The reconstituted flesh of this body can be opposed to the idealized mappings produced by the conventional imaginings of the body ego.[29] Thus the body in Burroughs exists in opposition to the imagined coherence produced in the mirror stage; the body, instead, often appears without imaginary coherence or as, in Lacan's term for the body in the dimension of the real, the "fragmented body."[30] The mutated flesh of this fragmented body is presented as the product of the various forms of economic production and exchange depicted in *Naked Lunch*. The body in the novel is perforated and reshaped by drugs, penetrated and reconfigured sexually, and mutated by exploitation and addiction: "The physical changes were slow at first, then jumped forward in black klunks, falling through his slack tissue, washing away the human lines . . . In his place of total darkness mouth and eyes are one organ that leaps forward to snap with transparent teeth . . . but no organ is constant as regards either function or position . . . sex organs sprout anywhere . . . rectums open, defecate and close . . . the entire organism changes color and consistency in split second adjustments" (9).

The bodily transformations detailed in this passage echo similar trans-formations throughout Burroughs's narrative. These transformations are variously produced by addiction, sexual exploitation, and economic exploitation, but what is most notable about them is the ways in which the biopolitical economy presented by the text directly impacts the body, reshaping its substance and producing radically new forms of embodi-ment. These bodies elude symbolic fixity and even clear description. They are constituted instead as a real flesh of continuous transformation in which the bodily and the political economic are constant interchange.

As such, this *real* flesh can be read as the product of the forms of biopo-litical production that Michael Hardt and Antonio Negri argue are central to the emergence of the transnational political subject that they term the "multitude."[31] However, in order to fully theorize this real flesh in relation-ship to Hardt and Negri, I need to rearticulate their conception of flesh in the Lacanian register that I have elucidated. Hardt and Negri posit the new flesh as not bodily but immediately social: "Looking at our postmod-ern society, in fact, free from any nostalgia for the modern social bodies that have dissolved or the people that is missing, one can see that what we experience is a kind of social flesh, a flesh that is not a body, a flesh that is common living substance."[32] Hardt and Negri articulate a vision of late capitalism that is very close to the one imagined by Burroughs, with its emphasis on the intersections between bodies and economic systems of production, exchange, and consumption.[33] The flesh here becomes the immediate object of social and economic production and investment, in contrast to the body's status in industrial production as an object that aids in production but must be largely located in "nature."

Where Burroughs's and Hardt and Negri's visions differ is in the concep-tion of this new flesh. This difference in conception has less to do with the nearly fifty-year difference in time between the publication of *Naked Lunch* and that of *Multitude* than with a differing conception of the relationship of late-capitalist production to the fleshly. Whereas Hardt and Negri imag-ine the new flesh to be common substance beyond the bodily, produced by the forms of immanent communication and production that define the workings of capital in the era of financialization, Burroughs, writing (albeit presciently) near the end of the regime of high-Fordist production and with the post-Fordist regime that Hardt and Negri take for granted as just emerging, refuses such a sublation of the bodily and is suspicious of the kinds of abstraction from the material that is suggested in Hardt and Negri's vision of this new flesh, which seems more virtual than material.

In order to understand Burroughs's conception of the reformed flesh of the late-capitalist era, then, we need to supplement Hardt and Negri's conception with the Lacanian framework that I have elucidated previously. In this context, uncoded aspects of the body and other forms of uncoded materiality become the real upon which this symbolic and material system of biopolitical production is grounded. Burroughs is thus interested in the flesh of this excluded remainder as much as in the forms of flesh that are a valorized part of the economic and social investment that Hardt and Negri detail.[34] However, both the theorists and the writer agree in their assessment that this transformed flesh not just is the product of exploitation but has resistant possibilities as well—both see the flesh as a key site of resistance as well as exploitation in late capitalism.

Interzone: The Dreamscape of Late Capitalism

While *Naked Lunch* was written during the first part of a Kondratieff cycle that privileged production over financialization, Burroughs's economic vision is one of the most prescient dimensions of his narrative, and his text points forward toward the practices of contemporary globalization as much as it addresses the forms of global exploitation that were central to the Fordist era.[35] This prescience is aided by the geopolitical location of the composition of much of *Naked Lunch*: Tangier's international zone. As Brian Edwards argues, the geopolitical specificity of Tangier is more central to the composition of *Naked Lunch* than most critics have allowed.[36] Much like contemporary free enterprise zones, the international zone of Tangier, which morphs into the delocalized Interzone of the novel, was a deregulated extranational space.

The distinctive sociopolitical geography of the international zone thus becomes the basis for the fluid conception of space imagined by the novel. As Allan Hibbard argues, in the novel, space is conceptualized as fluid yet disjunctive: "Aspects of Mexico and Latin America blur with those of North Africa, London, Paris, Cairo, and the Midwest of the United States."[37] The experience of space in *Naked Lunch* is defined by the kinds of time-space compression that David Harvey argues underpin the spatial logic of late capitalism: "In Yemen, Paris, New Orleans, Mexico City, and Istanbul—shivering under the air hammers and the steam shovels, shrieked junky curses at one another neither of us heard, and The Man leaned out of a passing steam roller and I copped in a bucket of tar."[38] What is striking is not only the collapsing of geographically diverse locales

into one indistinguishable urban location but the emphasis on the material forms of production and consumption that underwrite the emergence
of this spatially compressed transnational urban space. The spatiotemporal compression that Harvey describes may depend, in part, on the forms
of communication technology that are integral to the exponential growth
of the service, financial, and electronic economies in late capitalism and
that are more readily associated with post-Fordism, but as Saskia Sassen
has noted, these economies in turn depend on traditional forms of material and infrastructural production that are conventionally associated with
the Fordist era.[39] The latter forms of production are indicated here by the
steam shovels and air hammers, which are crucial to the construction
of the global city's infrastructure, while the immaterial economy is metonymically suggested here by the spectral presence of heroin, or "junk,"
which, as a commodity that is more about the embodied effects it produces than the material form it takes, suggests the biopolitical goods and
services central to post-Fordism.

The disjunctive temporality of the novel parallels its disruptive representation of space.[40] Much like the temporality of global financial speculation
in the post-Fordist era, time is presented in the novel as simultaneously
recursive and disjunctive. Time can jump in the space of a sentence: "Time
jumps like a broken typewriter, the boys are old men, young hips quivering and twitching in boy-spasms go slack and flabby, draped over an
outhouse seat, a park bench, a stone wall in Spanish sunlight, a sagging fur-
nished room bed" (79). Here the span of a lifetime is annihilated in a verb,
paralleling the ways in which financial transactions of the global market
compress time or eradicate it altogether. The invocation of the typewriter
as a midcentury instrument of recording can be seen both as a mechanical writing device that is an analogue to the mechanized factory spaces of
Fordism and as prescient of the logic of post-Fordism in the sense that it
suggests that communication technologies are central to this effacement
of time. The sentence in its instantaneous shift from youth to old age and
potency to decrepitude also parallels the way in which the body becomes a
commodity in biopolitical production—one with a limited shelf life.

Thus the body not only is reshaped by processes of commodification
and various biotechnologies (such as heroin) but represents one of the
central commodities circulated in the pages of *Naked Lunch*. The novel
details a biopolitical and finally thanatopolitical culture of sexual predation in which the bodies of teenage youths have become the central

commodity exchanged in the colonial yet deterritorialized space of Inter-zone.[41] It depicts the organization of desire within an ever more pervasive global commodity culture in which the commodity itself shifts from the sublime promises of transcendence to the abject real of decay, disposabil-ity, and death (signified by the "slack and flabby" bodies and the "outhouse toilet seat," associated with both waste and abjection) once the metonymic movement of desire within the biopolitical dimensions of late capitalism has shifted elsewhere.

Interzone is the novel's most fully realized vision of this emergent economy of biopolitical and thanatopolitical production: "Panorama of the City of Interzone . . . The Composite City where all human potentials are spread out in a vast silent market" (89). Here the space–time com-pression that Interzone embodies is made explicit: it is the "composite city," a condensation of the undersides and black markets of any number of the world's cities. As this description already suggests, it is a space that is defined by its relationship to the market. Indeed the space itself is "one vast market" in which everything is for sale: "[The city is filled with] sell-ers of orgone tanks and relaxing machines, brokers of exquisite dreams and memories tested on the sensitized cells of junk sickness and bartered for raw materials of the will, doctors skilled in the treatment of the black dust of ruined cities, gathering virulence in the white blood of eyeless worms feeling slowly to the surface and the human host, maladies of the ocean floor and the stratosphere, maladies of the laboratory and the atom-ic war . . . A place where the unknown past and the emergent future meet in vibrating soundless hum" (91).

In this passage, the proleptic dimensions of Burroughs's narrative are made explicit, even as the time compression that characterizes late capi-talism is also suggested in the mixing of the emergent future with the unknown past. What is being represented here is indeed the "emergent future" of what Hardt and Negri term *biopolitical production*—in other words, forms of production in which subjectivity and the body are inte-gral parts of the product and not merely the process. The will is bartered, dreams and memories are brokered, orgones are produced, and biological and atomic maladies abound. The corporations that operate in this space also reflect the emergent economy of biopolitical production ("Amalgam-ated Images," "Islam, Incorporated," "Friendly Finance") as do the people ("Autopsy Ahmed," "Hepatitis Hal," and, in one of the novel's most darkly humorous globalized names, "Salvador Hassan O'Leary, the Afterbirth

Tycoon"; 96, 121, 102, 122). Burroughs's emphasis on the trade in human organs, fluids, and diseases insists that the reader attends to the thanatopolitical underside of this global economy of biopolitical production—the side that represents a disavowed real to the sublime promises of the symbolic created by commodity production.

The Dialectic of the Material and the Immaterial

Central to the biopolitical and thanatopolitical economies presented by *Naked Lunch* is a negative dialectical relationship (in Adorno's sense) between the material and the immaterial. This negative dialectic can be linked to the novel's complex positioning between Fordism and post-Fordism—for it refuses to fully negate the former in its prescient account of the latter. The text insists on the material underpinnings of the global economy it presents, emphasizing material production as centrally as it does various processes of dematerialization. This emphasis also serves as a corrective to the idea that post-Fordist production is primarily immaterial, underscoring the material dimensions that underpin various forms of "immaterial" production.

The dialectic between the material and the immaterial manifests itself most directly in the relationship between heroin or "junk" and the body. Junk is represented as the ultimate commodity in the era of biopolitical capitalism: a superaddictive drug that interacts directly with the substance of the body, reshaping and reorganizing it on a microcellular level. If, in the initial moment of the fix, the junk has the effect of partial dematerialization, in the moment of withdrawal, it has the effect of rematerializing the body in new and strikingly mutated forms, producing flesh that is at first "soft, tentative," and "ectoplasmic," and then "a mass of scar tissue hard and dry as wood" (60, 7). This movement toward rematerialization underscores the way in which the promise of dematerialization represented by late-capitalist commodity culture is dependent upon disavowed and abjected forms of materiality; once the fix wears off, the junky is returned to a body that is rendered all the more abject by becoming raw material upon which the fantasy of dematerialization is staged.

The dematerializing effect of junk, which the novel presents as taking place when the junky first fixes, suggests the ways in which the commodity form in post-Fordism is organized around the promise of material transcendence. While, as Marx demonstrated, the idealization of the material has always been a part of the logic of commodity fetishism, this logic takes on a new potency in the era of the society of the spectacle and immaterial production. As Marx described it, the materiality of the production process was effaced by the logic of commodity fetishism in which "the social characteristics of men's own labour [appear as] objective characteristics of the products of labor themselves."[42] If Marx's description is definitional for commodity fetishism in the era of high capitalism, what has taken place in the late-capitalist era is a further idealization, in which the fetish itself has become immaterial. The dematerialization of the fetish takes two forms. Most immediately, what has become fetishized in the era of late capitalism is not so much the commodified object but the fantasy of a sublime body that transcends temporal and material constraints. This fantasy of a sublime body is everywhere visible in our late-capitalist moment, from the promises made by the beauty industry, plastic surgery, and other forms of what Adele Clarke et al. term *biomedicalization*, to the various avatars encouraged by video games, televisual culture, pornography, and web-based technologies such as Facebook, Twitter, and so on.[43] Similarly, as the very notion of the sublime body suggests, what is most forcefully fetishized in late capitalism is the immaterial. The immaterial body (or "avatar" to use current lingo) is only the most striking feature of a general fetishization of the immaterial. In this sense, Hardt and Negri's valorization of immaterial production (even as they recognize the forms of material production that are part of immaterial production) can be seen as a symptom of this fetishization of the immaterial. Writing during the emergence of this logic of fetishism—what I call avatar fetishism, as distinct from classical commodity fetishism—Burroughs is ideally situated to critique this logic in its initial moments of genesis. From such a vantage, for all their value, theories such as Hardt and Negri's run the danger of becoming junk-fueled fantasies of transcendence.

The dialectic of de- and rematerialization is also evident in the sexual economy mapped in *Naked Lunch*. The complex intertwining of exploitation and pleasure represented by the sexual trade in bodies is another exemplary instance of the novel's prescient engagement with the biopolitical and thanatopolitical dimensions of late-capitalist existence. There is, of course, nothing inherently late capitalist about the sex trade as such. Moreover, Burroughs's depiction of the sex trade is certainly modeled on his own ethically fraught participation in the sexual economy of the not yet postcolonial space of Tangier and the neoimperial space of Mexico in the 1950s. However, like much of *Naked Lunch's* representation of the economy of Interzone, its depiction of the sex trade points toward its specific reconfiguration via communication technologies and biomedical transformations in late capitalism.

The sexual economy of the novel and its relationship to film and televisual culture are staged by Burroughs in the infamous "Hassan's Rumpus Room" and "A.J.'s Annual Party" sections of the novel. In these sections, nonconsensual and consensual sex acts are staged for the pleasure of a predatory and voyeuristic bourgeois audience: "Gilt and red plush. Rococo bar backed by pink shell. The air is cloyed with a sweet evil substance like decayed honey. Men and women in evening dress sip pousse-cafés through alabaster tubes" (62–63). The thanatopolitical snuff act that takes center stage in the rumpus room is the simultaneous hanging and rape of a "boy" by a "Mugwump," which is Burroughs's science-fiction reworking of the nineteenth-century term for an "important person, bigwig or boss."[44] Burroughs presents the Mugwump as a predatory posthuman being (representing a mixture of drug dealer, capitalist, and politician) that has been completely transformed by addiction. Mugwumps "have no liver" and are addicted to "sucking translucent, colored syrups through alabaster straws" (46). They, in turn, "secrete an addicting fluid from their erect penises which prolongs life by slowing metabolism." The fluid is fed upon by addicts who are termed "Reptiles" (46). In sum, the Mugwump, with its transformed flesh, its participation in an economy that is at once pharmacological and sexual, and its figuration of the promise of transcending death through prolonging life, represents a perfect figuration of the biopolitical economy depicted by *Naked Lunch*.

The Mugwump is presented as the ultimate sexual connoisseur and predator in the rumpus room scene:

> "Stand up and turn around," he orders in telepathic pictographs. He ties the boy's hands behind him with a red silk cord. "Tonight we make it all the way."
> "No, no!" screams the boy.
> "Yes. Yes."
> Cocks ejaculate in silent "yes." . . .
> The Mugwump dips hot perfumed water from alabaster bowl, pensively washes the boy's ass and cock, drying him with a soft blue towel. A warm wind plays over the boy's body and the hairs

float free. The Mugwump puts a hand under the boy's chest and pulls him to his feet. Holding him by both pinioned elbows, propels him up the steps and under the noose. (63)

The Mugwump's connoisseurship is indicated by the delicate and "pensive" way in which he washes the boy's body before guiding him to the gallows. A late-capitalist reworking of the Sadean figuration of the sexual libertine as apathetic in his sadism, the Mugwump is presented here as the ethically detached connoisseur of a fleshly commodity—a form of connoisseurship that will allow him to stage the snuff fantasy that the passage depicts.[45]

While the boy's body is central to the staging of this fantasy (indeed it forms its key material substrate and support), it is finally treated with the interchangeability that all commodities are treated within the logic of avatar fetishism. While this rape and hanging is depicted as a visual spectacle, it becomes the initial moment of an orgy in which the original viewers of the spectacle stage the snuff act over and over again: "Boys by the hundred plummet through the roof, quivering and kicking at the end of ropes" (67). Of course, the serial multiplication of this sex act also suggests the logic of de Sade's texts. The seriality of the violence in the Sadean text can be linked, as Lacan points out, to the Enlightenment project of detaching reason from what Kant terms "pathological" concerns and thereby constituting "negation as a totalizing Idea."[46] In de Sade, seriality is linked to an idealist repetition that detaches itself from any specific "pathological" object and that produces, as Lacan describes it, its abjected double in the "raped and sewn-shut" body of the mother.[47] Repetition in Burroughs becomes a late-capitalist and explicitly thanatopolitical reworking of this logic, in which this idealist seriality is intimately bound up with the seriality of the commodity form and its promise of an immaterial body and produces as its abjected double materiality itself, including the material manifestation of the commodity—the boy, who is literally killed off to achieve this immaterial body. In this context, the specifically misogynist violence that Lacan locates near the beginning of modernity in the conceptual overlap between the writings of Kant and de Sade has become by the time of the late-capitalist moment that Burroughs writes a more generalized form of violence (although misogyny still represents one of its key manifestations) in which all forms of materiality can be reduced to the status of the abject real that serves as so much fodder for staging fantasies of transcendence.

Part of the force of the snuff scene, then, is the suggestion that in late capitalism consumption and predation are one and the same. And indeed, the line between consumption and predation, passive reception and active participation, is continually blurred in the "Hassan's Rumpus Room" and "A.J.'s Annual Party" sections. I have already indicated the way in which this blurring takes place, with the bourgeois spectators of the snuff scene becoming active participants in later iterations of the act. This blurring is also suggested by the porn film that is shown during A.J.'s party. In this film, as during the orgy, various consensual and nonconsensual sex acts are staged culminating with a snuff hanging and rape scene that echoes the ones earlier in the text. The difference between this scene and the earlier scenes is that this one is presented as part of the film, and the actors come on stage and take a bow: "Mary, Johnny and Mark take a bow with the ropes around their necks. They are not as young as they appear in the Blue Movies . . . They look tired and petulant" (87).

On one level, the differences between the two scenes seem to emphasize the difference between spectatorship and participation. While the boy in the earlier snuff scene has really been killed, at the end of this snuff scene, we meet the actors, who, in spite of the on-screen violence, appear tired from their affective and biopolitical labors but otherwise no worse for wear. Yet, on another level, the echo between these two scenes and the multiple repetitions of this snuff act in a primarily nonnarrative work of fiction in which the narrative certainty of any of the occurrences in the novel are equally called into question works to blur the line between spectatorship and participation.

Moreover, it is not merely the viewers of the film that are implicated in this blurring but the reader (and Burroughs as writer), as well; in reading *Naked Lunch*, we are in a sense assenting to the novel's sadism. Yet this assent is merely an echo of the kinds of sadistic assent in which we participate on a daily level in consuming commodities that are the product of exploitation and violence on another scene. It is in the context of such violence on another scene that we should understand Burroughs's ironic use of a form of reader address, "gentle reader," conventional to nineteenth-century romanticism and sentimental literature: "Gentle reader, the ugliness of that spectacle buggers description . . . Gentle reader I fain would spare you this, but my pen hath its will like the Ancient Mariner" (34). Burroughs, of course, does not spare us these scenes. Indeed he takes sadistic delight in relating them and thereby implicates the reader in her own investment (whether avowed or disavowed) in such sadistic scenes. The reference to Coleridge's long poem is apt in this regard, for, like the Ancient Mariner of the poem's title, Burroughs waylays us on our journey toward more bucolic pleasures, reminding us of what we would choose to forget.

In blurring the distinction between spectatorship and participation, Burroughs is not invested producing an idealist conflation of word and deed, representation and action. Rather, he is committed to demonstrating the material and exploitative underpinnings of the society of the spectacle, to use Guy Debord's contemporaneous formulation, even as he calls attention to the ways in which it has become increasingly difficult to disentangle materiality and image in the late-capitalist world.[48] Paradoxically, this inability to disentangle the two derives from occultation of the material produced by the fetishization of the image in the era of immaterial production. Thus the relay between film and deed in the snuff scenes suggests not the coincidence of image and materiality in late capitalism but rather the way in which the fetishism of the immaterial produces material effects on another, occulted scene. This other scene is, of course, the deregulated space of Interzone, with its violently exploited and reformed bodies, biopolitical and thanatopolitical commerce, and accumulation of waste made up of discarded and superfluous objects.

The Real of the Body and the Politics of Bare Life

Burroughs's emphasis on the economic dimensions of biopolitics and thanatopolitics marks the difference between his conception of biopolitics and those conceptions that merely emphasize it as a form of governmentality. Like Hardt and Negri, Burroughs emphasizes that the category of the biopolitical is an economic category as much as a political one. He also demonstrates the way in which the economic regulation and production of life is also bound up with thanatopolitical production, or the economic regulation and production of death. The economy of Interzone, with its exploitation of the corporeal and material real and its paradoxical fetishization of the immaterial, provides biopolitics and thanatopolitics with their objects and logic. The objects are of course bodies themselves, and it is to these bodies that are marked as expendable that we must look to find a locus of political resistance in the biopolitical and deregulated world presciently imagined by Burroughs's novel. The locus of this agency can be more precisely delimited by employing Giorgio Agamben's distinction between the life of the citizen and "bare life" (or, as he puts it, between *bios* and *zoē*). While Agamben is one of the theorists of biopolitics who tends to emphasize its political dimensions, the distinction that he makes between the life of the citizen and bare life is a crucial one for understanding the political-economic coordinates of life in the era of biopolitics.

The distinction between *bios* and *zoē* closely corresponds to the opposition between late-capitalist forms of citizenship and the forms of life that exist in extranational spaces such as Interzone. Bare life thus becomes the locus in which the violence of sovereignty is fully visible and can be enacted outside of the dictates of constitution, social contract, or law. Such spaces can also be termed, in Roberto Esposito's description, *thanatopolitical* spaces, in which certain bodies and subjectivities are deemed disposable and able to be killed. If, as Agamben argues, such states of exception are becoming the norm within which we all increasingly live in the biopolitical era, then the truth of the late-capitalist political economy resides in those locations in which the condition of bare life is most evident: the "free-enterprise zone" and other deregulated spaces of exploitation.

The emergence of the figure of bare life (or what Agamben terms *homo sacer*) as the truth of the late-capitalist political economy is concomitant with a shift in political agency: from the agency of the citizen to the potential for agency embodied in bare life. It is to this agency that Burroughs's text points in its depiction of the transformed and exploited and finally posthuman bodies of Interzone. While it represents a predatory figuration of the posthuman rather than a representation of exploited "bare life," the Mugwump is Burroughs's most striking metaphor for the emergence of such posthuman bodies: "Mugwumps have no liver and nourish themselves exclusively on sweets. Thin purple-blue lips cover a razor-sharp beak of black bone with which they frequently tear each other to shreds in fights over clients. These creatures secrete an addicting fluid from their erect penises which prolongs life by slowing metabolism" (46).

In this passage, the subjects central to the regime of biopolitical production have transformed well beyond the recognizably human. The economy of commodity addiction and the trade in the fragmented body produces a new flesh—one for which language can only designate catachreses, such as *Mugwump*. As a by-product of the unregulated and black-market forms of production and exchange that characterize Interzone, the Mugwump is one version of the posthuman that is produced in the extranational spaces of biopolitical capitalism. It is such reshaped figures that embody the new flesh of Burroughs's text. This flesh forms the real to the symbolic of late-capitalist commodity fetishism and biopolitical and thanatopolitical forms of governmentality.

The Way Out Is the Way In

While much of the emphasis on the production of the new flesh is on the novel forms of exploitation and violence, it is striking that Burroughs also characterizes it in terms of "human potential" (89). This description suggests that Burroughs presents the forms of biopolitical production characteristic of Interzone as holding resistant potential as well as being sources of exploitation. Some of this potential is suggested in the newly formed flesh of the Mugwumps. Thus the human potential of the new economy seems to point beyond the human itself, as we conventionally have conceived of it, toward a posthumanism that recognizes the centrality of materiality, including objects, the intransigently material aspects of late-capitalist production, and our transformed bodies, to any truly transformative politics of the present. And while the Mugwumps are represented in a largely negative light as an image of the most predatory forms of consumption, there is a suggestion in this new flesh holds generative potential as well.

This generative potential is perhaps best, if ambiguously, captured in the undifferentiated tissue that forms over the mouth of the carny in the novel's infamous talking asshole scene. The scene presents a Rabelaisian allegory in which a carny teaches his asshole to talk as part of a sideshow routine.[49] As the routine is regularly repeated, the asshole begins to talk on its own and finally suggests to the carny's mouth that it is unnecessary because the asshole could "talk and eat *and* shit" (111). It is at this point that undifferentiated tissue begins to form in the carny's mouth: "After that he began waking up in the morning with transparent jelly like a tadpole's tail all over his mouth. This jelly is what scientists call un-D.T. Undifferentiated Tissue, which can grow into any kind of flesh on the human body. He would tear it off his mouth and the pieces would stick to his hands like burning gasoline jelly and grow there, grow anywhere on him a glob of it fell" (111).

While the undifferentiated tissue has the potential to be read negatively, as the product of a process of potential devolution rather than evolution, it is described as radically productive and generative of new forms of embodiment. Indeed it is presented as almost preternaturally generative, creating new flesh wherever it falls. In its undifferentiated quality, the flesh refuses the stable differentiations of the symbolic; instead, it is the flesh of the real. As such, it represents the most basic product of the regime of bio-political production. This is the new flesh in its initial emergence—flesh that has no stable place in the symbolic and indeed exists in contradiction to it. It is the fleshly counterpart on the level of content to Burroughs's attempts to produce a language of the real on the level of style.

Burroughs suggests as much in one of his statements about the book in the "atrophied preface" that concludes the novel:

> The Word is divided into units which be all in one piece and should be so taken, but the pieces can be had in any order being tied up back and forth in and out fore and aft like an innaresting sex arrangement. This book spill off the page in all directions, kalei-doscope of vistas, medley of tunes and street noises, farts and riot yips and the slamming steel shutters of commerce, screams of pain and pathos . . . Gentle Reader, we see God through our assholes in the flash bulb of orgasm . . . Through these orifices transmute your body . . . The way OUT is the way IN. (191)

If there is any direct statement of intent in the novel, this is it. And indeed this passage pulls together all the different forms of materiality that I have addressed in *Naked Lunch*: from the linguistic, to the political-economic, to the bodily. The passage starts within the realm of the language of the real, where the signifiers seem to permanently exceed their signifieds. It then moves through the "steel shutters of commerce" to an invocation that directly recalls the talking asshole passage. This invocation admonishes the reader to "transmute your body" for the "way OUT" of the regime of biopolitical production is the "Way IN." In other words, the only way out of our current economy is by confronting its most abject, obscene, and stubbornly material products. This is also the locus of the new flesh that, in its generativity, represents the possibility of a new symbolic and biopoliti-cal order—one perhaps not predicated on exploitation.

The Literature of Materiality (Slight Return)

It is this emphasis on materiality, particularly the materiality of disavowed bodies but also the material underpinnings of the economy of so-called immaterial production, that distinguishes Burroughs's literary praxis from the forms of metafiction and purely linguistic invention that are often celebrated under the banner of postmodernism. This is a literary praxis in which language is central but one in which it is not coterminous with the world. Instead, language is central because, when employed against its routinized meanings and finally against itself, it can give us an indication of that which resists or exceeds symbolic coding and, even more centrally, our symbolic fictions of the world. What resists or exceeds our symbolic codings in Burroughs are bodies and other forms of materiality that are, at points, defined and shaped by language but also exist in a negative and resistant relationship to it.

In its engagement with the material, this literature of materiality suggests a form of political agency for the neoliberal era, for if, as Agamben suggests, in the late-capitalist era, the state of exception is becoming the norm, then we should look for a political resistance not so much in terms of those who occupy categories of citizenship but in terms of those who fall outside the protections of citizenship and those who exist in the bare life produced in free-enterprise zones and other spaces of transnational deregulation. Such a politics would involve an attention to those forms of materiality—especially those of the body—that have been most exploited and altered in the production of our sublime fantasies of material transcendence in the biopolitical era. Of course, such a politics would need a language, and to the extent that it produces one, it would claim a place in our transnational symbolic and thus leave the domain of the real. But such a symbolic language would be attentive to the disjunctions as well as the intersections between linguistic materiality and other forms of materiality. It would also recognize the limits of human fantasies of transcendence, even as it also attends to the way in which the human itself is increasingly reshaped by the biopolitics and thanatopolitics, producing new posthuman subjects. The posthumanism presented by Burroughs's novel thus not only is epistemological but, in Graham Harman's terms, is an "ontographic" mapping of "the basic landmarks and fault lines of the universe of objects."[50] It is about reorienting ourselves toward the material or, as Levi Bryant puts it, the "nonhuman and asignifying in the form of technologies, weather patterns, resources, diseases, animals, natural disasters . . . modes of transportation, and so on."[51] Yet it is also about recognizing the way in which biopolitics and biopolitical production have produced posthuman embodiments and forms of existence.

It is thus to such a political understanding of materiality that *Naked Lunch* points. The novel suggests that unless we attend to the material underpinnings of the economy of "immaterial production" in which we currently live, we will have no ability to imagine a more economically and symbolically just future. For all its infamous violence and transgression, it is toward such a future that the literature of materiality inaugurated by *Naked Lunch* finally points.

Given that Burroughs's novel and the genre of materialist writing it inaugurated speaks so powerfully to our neoliberal and biopolitical age, perhaps we are too hasty to consign the writing of the postmodern era resolutely to the past. While the search for new literary and cultural forms (and for a truly global conception contemporary literature) is both salutary and necessary, this search may draw more power from the recent past than we have allowed. If the status of the material is indeed one of the pressing questions of the age, then the literature of materiality, in contrast to its more celebrated metafictional brethren, still has much to teach us. While we are readying our scalpels for the dissection of the body of the present, the corpse we just finished with is rising zombie-like from the table—its flesh reformed and glowing with profane life.

CHAPTER 2

Vital Objects

Materiality and Biopolitics in Thomas Pynchon's *V.*

The picture of a temporal or extratemporal original state of happy identity between subject and object is romantic, however— a wishful projection at times, but today no more than a lie.

—Theodor Adorno, "Subject and Object"

Subject ≠ Object

Subject does not equal object in advanced capitalist life. This observation by one of the most celebrated of modernism's theorists can be understood, ironically enough, as one of the inaugural theoretical formulations of the era that we conventionally call postmodern and can also be characterized as the era in which biopolitics and its deathly double, thanatopolitics, migrate from the colonial periphery to the metropolitan center. If biopolitics is fundamentally about the direct shaping of subjectivity and life itself by power (whether conceived politically or political economically), then Adorno's formulation comes as a warning: we privilege the subjective and imagine the objective as subordinated to the subjective only at our own peril. Adorno's observations come from a late essay aptly titled "Subject and Object," which first appeared in 1969, right around the moment of the shift from Fordism to post-Fordism, and suggest the importance of attending to this disjunction as well as the "object's preponderance" for a political economy that is increasingly organized around fantasies of the object's manipulability and domestication.[1]

While much of Adorno's essay is concerned, in a manner that presages the object-oriented ontologies of the present, with the epistemological impasses presented by any attempt to theorize the two categories as adequate to each other, like most of Adorno's writings, it links these seemingly purely philosophical speculations to a historical and implicitly political-economic narrative. This narrative suggests that one of the dangers haunting the biopolitical present is a further disconnection between subject and object—one predicated on notions of the latter's effacement or transcendability by the privileging of the former or, more historically put, between the subjectivities of late capitalism and the object world they inhabit.

Published eight years before the appearance of "Subject and Object," Thomas Pynchon's *V.* presents seemingly the same diagnosis of the era of biopolitics as Adorno's essay. Focusing on the contrasting trajectories of its two main characters, Herbert Stencil and Benny Profane, Pynchon's novel charts the increasingly evident dissymmetry between subject and object in the history of the twentieth century. Stencil, the ultimate solipsist, understands history and the world he inhabits in purely idealist terms. Objects (including colonial populations conceived as objects) merely exist in order to be rigorously subordinated to the self-defining needs of subjectivity. He himself, existing primarily as a narratorial consciousness, is a figure for biopolitics. All the subjectivities and the forms of materiality presented in his narratives can finally be located as projections of his subjectivity; their very being is shaped and governed by his narrative reenactments. In contrast, Profane's subjectivity is defined as ancillary to and entirely contingent on the world of inanimate objects. His is a materialism without the possibility of subjective mediation or, in other words, an entirely brute and therefore finally meaningless materialism. By embodying different responses to the subject/object split, Pynchon's two characters also embody different versions of temporality. Profane's narrative, predictably enough, is situated in an open-ended, directionless present, while Stencil's narrative is one of historical retrospection and future anticipation. Indeed, in the sections of the book featuring Stencil, he is more often a narrator or auditor of past actions than a participant in present actions. As such, he is a parodic figuration of the historian or novelist—a point comically underscored by the fact that he "like small children at a certain stage and Henry Adams in the *Education*, as well as assorted autocrats since time out of mind, always referred to himself in the third person."[2] The different temporal trajectories represented by Stencil and Profane enable Pynchon to advance the historiographical critique that lies at the core of the novel.

This historiographical critique traces the prehistory of late capitalism and its increasing investment in biopolitics and biopolitical production, which Pynchon, like Adorno, presents in relationship to the effacement of the aspects of materiality that exceed subjective control and the increasing privileging of the subjective. Written during the postwar period that is often defined as a period in which a late modernism and early postmodernism overlap, Pynchon uses this moment of transition to reflect on the split between subject and object as it is shaped by the growth in industries such as robotics, plastics, biomedical industries such as plastic surgery, the auto industry, cybernetics, and the televisual industries.[3] These are all industries, in other words, that function by seemingly mixing or fusing subject and object in ways that promise more subjective control of the material world.

As Robert McLaughlin and Niran Abbas have pointed out, Pynchon's novel not only charts transformations in everyday life in the first world but also is critically engaged with the history of colonialism and its relationship to these first-world spaces.[4] This engagement is a historically retrospective one written precisely during the period of the decolonization (and decolonization struggles) of Africa and Southeast Asia. The novel's present is also set during the Suez Canal Crisis—a key moment in which national sovereignty is superseded by a global peace-keeping force and the logic of the state of exception, thus presaging what Hardt and Negri suggest is the shift from imperialism to what they term *empire* or from direct imperial possession to neoimperial forms of biopolitical and neoliberal exploitation. Thus Pynchon is charting not only the resistance to biopolitics and the production of what Agamben terms *bare life* in the space of the colonies but also the shift, in the metropole, from a state-administered biopolitics and thanatopolitics to a more economic-based (or neoimperial) regime of biopolitical and thanatopolitical production.[5] The uncanniness of Pynchon's text is marked by the return of the repressed, of those who have been rendered bare life (and thus been put under the sign of the subject who is object), and of the uncontrolled object world itself for those who imagine themselves as controlling subjects.

As this account of the uncanny in *V.* suggests, the novel also lends itself to psychoanalytic interpretation, though (as I will theorize more fully later) of a specifically posthumanist cast.[6] Thus the disjunction between subject and object can be theorized in a Lacanian register as the split between the symbolic and the real. And indeed, Pynchon's novel is rife with Lacanian resonances. Most central of these resonances is the figuration of the title "character," V., around whom the text swirls. V., the character (or characters) for whom Stencil ambivalently searches throughout the narrative, occupies the occluded center of the novel. Her narrative, if she and her narrative are indeed singular, is told in disjointed fragments, reconstituted through at least two and often three layers of narration. She is, in other words, the fetish that organizes the structure of desire and narrative in the Stencil sections of the novel. As such, she can be read as an avatar of the Lacanian *objet petit a*. Lacan defines his elusive objet as "that object which, in actual experience, in the operation and process sustained by transference, is signaled to us by a special status."[7] Derived in part from Melanie Klein's conception of the part object, the *objet petit a* is a little piece of the other or, more generally, to use Slavoj Žižek's formulation, a "little bit of real" around which transferential desire of the subject circulates.[8] It also represents that which threatens the consistency of the subject by promising to reintegrate it with the presubjective real that the subject has to renounce in order to gain entry into the symbolic. As such, it produces the ambivalent mixture of pain and pleasure, attraction and revulsion that Lacan terms *enjoyment*. It also can produce, as its correlate, the complex mixture of fetishistic devotion and violence that is captured in Lacan's famous dictum: "I love you, but, because inexplicably I love in you something more than you—*the objet petit a*—I mutilate you."[9] In sum, the *objet petit a* is a subversive reworking of both the Kleinian part object and the Freudian fetish—one that underscores the violent ambivalence that underwrites the logic of fetishism.

And like the Freudian fetish, the *objet petit a* is often embodied in an ordinary object or imagined object that takes on, via the fantasmatic logic of transference, extraordinary significance.[10] V., in all her manifestations, functions in precisely the same way in Pynchon's novel. She is alternately the cryptic name of Pynchon's novel, a meaningless signifier that becomes, precisely in its meaninglessness, the locus for all sorts of violent projections—a rat named Veronica that is the lover and convert of a Catholic priest living in the sewers during the Great Depression; the city Vheissu, a hidden country that manages to elude the colonial and cartographical reach of the British Empire in the early part of the twentieth century; Botticelli's Venus; Valetta, the Maltese city; and, most often (if they are the same person), Victoria Wren (a.k.a. Vera Meroving, a.k.a. the bad priest), an expatriate "fallen" British woman who is involved in various forms of international intrigue and whose organic body is slowly being replaced by inorganic machines.

As this latter description suggests, Victoria uncannily promises a new fusion of subject and object, even in the moment when the disjunction, or more precisely the impossibility of full dialectical mediation between the two spheres, becomes more apparent. This is precisely what all versions of V. promise as a fetish—the at least momentary reconciliation between subject and object, symbolic and real. It is striking, in this context, that V. is regularly and obsessively gendered feminine. As Stefan Mattessich has argued, this gendering is part of the novel's parodic critique and participation in a distinctively twentieth-century structure of misogyny—one that is bound up with its colonial-discourse-derived representations of race.[11] On the one hand, the novel parodically replays various fetishistic modernist associations that, as Andreas Huyssen has noted, link women with commodity culture.[12] On the other hand, the novel also draws upon contemporaneous tropes of colonial discourse that figure various nonwhite populations as feminized and more authentically in touch with the natural world than their white counterparts. Pynchon's midcentury parodic redeployment of these tropes suggests the way in which a constitutive misogyny underwrites fetishistic attempts to abolish the disjunction between subject and object that characterizes the period of late modernity and early postmodernity.

The violent ambivalence of the fetishism that V. signifies has Marxist as well as psychoanalytic resonances. The midcentury moment when Pynchon composes his novel marks an important transition point in the evolution of the logic of commodity fetishism within the more general movement from high to late capitalism. If the period of high capitalism, with all that it represents in terms of the production of the first wave of consumer goods and the concomitant emergence of mass-mediated culture, can be defined as the *locus classicus* of the conventional definition of commodity fetishism, then late capitalism has its own version of the concept—one that is part and parcel of the forms of "immaterial production" that Hardt and Negri have theorized as central to its development.[13] Whereas the object itself is the locus for the "grotesque ideas" that "transcend sensuousness" in Marx's classic account, in the late-capitalist version of commodity fetishism (what I term *avatar fetishism*), the object itself becomes secondary, degraded materiality to the transcendent and avatar-like subjectivity that becomes the locus of the fetish.[14] V. appears near the turning point of this shift. Written during the moment when Fordism had reached its apotheosis and the signs of post-Fordism had already begun to emerge, *V.*, as both novel and character, represents in some sense an attempt to engage the object of the fetish even as it is beginning to dematerialize. This dematerialization of the fetish, ironically enough, takes place as the object world becomes ever more determining of everyday life, demonstrating the further inadequation of subject and object in this moment.

Pynchon's narrative, then, is precisely about this disjunction between subject and object and the forms of fetishism that herald this split. While the organization of the novel pivots around this split, it also importantly points beyond it, presenting a materialist ethics that can be likened to what Sarah Ahmed describes as a different or queer orientation toward materiality and what Levi Bryant posits as a turn toward recognizing the (partial) autonomy of objects and materiality. Yet the ethics Pynchon articulates do not just presage Ahmed's and Bryant's arguments; they also supplement this attention to materiality and objects by suggesting that we need to attend to what he presents as the pain of those who are treated as objects and the imagined pain of the material world itself when subjected to biopolitical and late-capitalist forms of exploitation.

Pynchon's Materialism

Pynchon is often characterized as the quintessential postmodern writer. Certainly this is his status in that most canonical critical account of literary postmodernism, Brian McHale's *Postmodernist Fiction*, in which Pynchon emerges as the writer in which the postmodern "ontological" aesthetic of "world" construction has reached full realization.[15] In contrast to earlier writers of the transition from modernism to postmodernism that McHale takes up, including Samuel Beckett, Alain Robbe-Grillet, Carlos Fuentes, and Vladimir Nabokov, who are still partially mired in the "epistemological" issues of modernism (with its attempt to make sense of the world in which we live), Pynchon's *The Crying of Lot 49* presents a vision of the universe in which language presents the possibility of creating multiple worlds. Pynchon, in this account, becomes the metafictional writer *par excellence*, in which his fiction is about the possibility of fiction constructing worlds, each of which is as probable as any other. While such a reading may be possible for *The Crying of Lot 49,* I don't think it is a convincing reading of *V. V.* is too preoccupied with the intransigently material, with the stuff of the world in which we live, to be primarily focused on the possibilities of language to create multiple worlds. This engagement with the obdurately material is central focus of Pynchon's aesthetic in *V.* (not to mention in *Gravity's Rainbow*) and makes him part of the countertradition of the late-capitalist literature of materiality. This is a countertradition that demonstrates the material underpinnings and determinations of everyday life and of embodied subjectivity in an era of seemingly seamless biopolitical control and expanding biopolitical production. Materiality, in this tradition, is that which resists full integration into the life world produced by biopolitical forms of production and governmentality, just as it is also that which undermines postmodern theories, such as McHale's, that privilege the linguistic and the textual as able to fully account for the social. As Pynchon puts it in a passage in which he describes the violence done to the animate by the inanimate: "The world began to run more and more afoul of the inanimate" (290).

The object world in *V.* thus emerges as something dynamic and menacing—a locus of social transformation that biopolitical understandings of an administered life world fail to fully apprehend. It is also a world in which humanist forms of subjectivity, with their emphasis on individual human agency, appear increasingly inadequate in the face of a proliferating object world. This limitation of humanist forms of subjectivity is what gives Pynchon's novel it's characteristically antihumanist tone. Yet rather than antihumanism, which suggests a decentering of the human in terms of language or social structures, Pynchon can be more effectively read in terms of what Cary Wolfe has described as "posthumanism"—a decentering of the human in relationship to nonhuman otherness.[16] For Wolfe, as one of the founding figures of animal studies, this otherness primarily takes the form of the nonhuman animal; in my reading of *V.*, I want to suggest a version of posthumanism in which what is constructed as the human is decentered in relationship to a greater recognition of nonhuman material world as well as to those forms of life that have been objectified and rendered bare. What emerges, then, in the never fully congruent encounters between subject and object in Pynchon's novel, are various forms of subjectivity whose primary orientation is to the world of objects.

Uncanny Objects and Fetishistic Subjectivities

The changed status of desire and its relationship to the metastasizing world of uncanny objects and ever more subtle yet invasive biopolitical technologies that mark the postwar present of Pynchon's novel are captured in the infamous scene in which Ester becomes erotically transfixed while receiving a nose job. Plastic surgery is one of the biotechnologies of which Pynchon is interested in tracing the emergence in *V.* While Pynchon locates the initial emergence of plastic surgery in the aftermath of World War I, he presents a decisive shift in its functioning in the post–World War II period. This shift switches the technology from one of repair to one of biomedical enhancement. Plastic surgery emerges in the postwar period as a biotechnology that is part of the biopolitical "enhancement" of life, organized around what Foucault terms a *discourse of normalization.*[17] This shift from repair to enhancement presents postwar plastic surgery as an early manifestation of the larger shift, chronicled by Adele Clarke et al., from medicalization to biomedicalization that took place primarily in the last two decades of the twentieth century and continues apace in the twenty-first.[18] As Clark et al. have theorized, this shift is characterized in part by a reorientation of medicine from a paradigm of illness to one of wellness, where medicine's main purpose is less to treat the diseased body than it is to promote and manage physical, mental, and social hygiene. This emphasis on social hygiene corresponds to the emergence of elective plastic surgery as a means of maximizing a racialized, ethnicized, classed, and gendered conception of beauty (and minimizing it's abjected opposite— what the culture deems ugly or aesthetically/hygienically unappealing) and is part and parcel with avatar fetishism.

What is at stake in elective plastic surgery is an understanding of an idealized body in which the flesh itself is only so much inert, debased material. This conception of plastic surgery informs the scene in which Ester consults her plastic surgeon, Schoenmaker:

The first day Schoenmaker spent in pre-operative reconnaissance of the terrain: photographing Esther's face and nose from various angles, checking for upper respiratory infections, running a Wassermann. Irving and Trench also assisted him in making two duplicate casts or death-masks. . . . Next day she was back at the office. The two casts were there on his desk, side by side. . . . Schoenmaker reached out and snapped the plaster nose from one of the masks.

"Now," he smiled; producing like a magician a lump of modeling clay with which he replaced the broken-off nose. "What sort of nose did you have in mind?"

What else: Irish, she wanted, turned up. Like they all wanted.
To none of them did it occur that the retroussé nose is too an aesthetic misfit: a Jew nose in reverse is all. (103)

The social hygiene function of plastic surgery is detailed in this scene,
with the replacement of one undesirable ethnic trait, a Jewish nose, with
a fetishized one, its Irish equivalent. With its use of wartime metaphors
(Schoenmaker undertakes "reconnaissance" of the "terrain" of Esther's
face), the scene underscores the violence of this practice of social hygiene.
This violence is further indicated by the description of Schoenmaker
"snapping" the nose off and the description of the face castings as "death
masks." The passage's use of the language of warfare also underscores the
advance and growth of this technology during both world wars.

What emerges from this passage is the suggestion that the thanatopolitical violence of war is carried on in the postwar era but in ways "soft"
and subtle, if similarly sinister. If for Roberto Esposito the Nazi regime
is defined as the turning around of biopolitics into thanatopolitics, a
dynamic that the novel also locates in the logic of colonialism, what
Pynchon presents in civilian life in the postwar United States, then, is
a partially reversed dynamic (for those populations deemed worthy of the
protections of sovereignty): the turning of thanatopolitical technologies
of extermination into softer biomedical technologies of correction.

This reversal becomes Pynchon's version of Adorno and Horkheimer's
assertion that the social and political technologies of fascist Germany
were adopted wholesale by the allied powers in the aftermath of World
War II. Specifically, the genocidal Nazi obsession with social hygiene finds
ominous echoes in the softer technology of plastic surgery as a mode of
"racial correction." The novel presents warfare as social proving ground
upon which a range of biopolitical and thanatopolitical technologies are
tested. In this sense, war becomes, in Giorgio Agamben's terms, one version of the "state of exception," in which sovereign power can act outside
of the rule of law, a state of exception that then underwrites and forms the
uncanny double to the rule of law during times of peace.[19]

As the surgical scene continues, the violence of the operation mixes
in disturbing ways with a newly polymorphous conception of sexuality that is tied more to the interface between inanimate objects,
biopolitical technologies, and the subject rather than a relationship primarily between subjects. During her "corrective" surgery, Esther finds

herself masochistically aroused: "It was expected this would calm her down, but barbituric acid derivatives affect individuals differently. Perhaps her initial sexual arousal contributed; but by the time Esther was taken to the operating room she was near delirium" (104). This involuntary arousal becomes mixed with pain as the violence of the surgery becomes at once social and sexual:

> No one had told Esther that anything about the operation would hurt. But these injections hurt: nothing before in her experience had ever hurt quite so much. All she had free to move for the pain were her hips. Trench held her head and leered appreciatively as she squirmed, constrained, on the table. . . . A series of internal injections to the septum—the wall of bone and cartilage which separates the two halves of the nose—and anesthesia was complete. The sexual metaphor in all this wasn't lost on Trench who kept chanting, "Stick it in . . . pull it out" . . . and tittering softly above Esther's eyes. (105)

Pynchon's description, with its focus on the intersection of the syringe with septum and barbituric acid with Esther's libido, suggests that the coordinates of this sexuality are oriented around the relationship of a disjunctive yet ever more intimate relationship between subject and object.

At first, this intimacy between subject and object may seem to run counter to Adorno's claim of the growing disjunction between the two. The intimacy suggested by the surgical fetishism of this scene indicate that, if anything, the two categories grow more intimately bound together. Yet this increased intimacy is accompanied by a conceptual disjuncture. As the novel presents it, the object world of late-capitalist life mutates so fast, becomes so invasive, and has reached such a massive scale that the most immediate attempts at subjectification skitter off either into solipsism or into that partial reconstruction of the relationship between subject and object that we call fetishism. Thus while there are a number of distinct subjectivities foregrounded in the scene of Esther's surgery—Schoenmaker, the doctor; Trench, the smart-aleck assistant, whose name is another evocation of warfare; Irving, the professionally minded nurse; and of course, Esther herself—none of them appear to interact in any meaningful way. Instead, the most intimate relationship that each has appears to be bound up with an objective fetish. Thus while Esther's sexuality pivots around the invasive technologies of anesthesia and painful syringes, Trench is transfixed by the violence done to various material components of Esther's body, focusing both on her writhing hips and on the violent penetration of the syringe. Schoenmaker, on the other hand, appears fixated, both in his specific mediations on Esther's nose and in his more general musings upon his profession on the biopolitical management of less-than-desirable, racialized bodies (which at some point presumably included his own).

What emerges, then, from this scene is a representation of a fetishistic form of sexuality that is at once racial and sexual, broadly social and recalcitrantly solipsistic. Yet the representation of the intersections of machine and organism in *V.* represent an important counterconception of subjectivity in the era of biopolitics—one that crucially differs from Donna Haraway's much celebrated reconception of postmodern subjects as cyborgs. Haraway's cyborgs blur boundaries between nature and culture, organism and machine, animal and human, and the physical and the nonphysical and thus depend on a deconstructive textualization of such oppositions and reject the "dialogue between materialism and idealism that was settled by a dialectical progeny."[20] While Pynchon is equally interested in the intersections among these oppositions in the formations of biopolitical subjectivity, his vision is one in which the dialectical tensions between these different elements has not been textualized out of existence but rather one in which such tensions and the contradictions they produce are simultaneously heightened and rendered more global and more intimate. Haraway's theory finally remains focused almost exclusively on subjectivity, with the various extrasubjective or objectal elements functioning as fodder for the emergence of the utopian, posthumanist subject. Pynchon's vision, on the other hand, is both more materialist and more seemingly grim. The subject is reshaped by the object world, but it is the latter that dominates this process of transformation and that resists, in its inhuman obduracy, any full reduction or textualization to the realm of the subjective. This, then, is the difference between Haraway's and Pynchon's visions of posthumanism.

The domination of the subject by the object world in Pynchon's version of late capitalism is captured most memorably by the two test dummies, SHOCK and SHROUD, who come to life and speak to Profane while he works in a short-lived job as the night watchman at Anthroresearch Associates. As the name suggests, the company does research on the effects on humans produced by a range of contemporary technologies: "It did research for the government on the effects of high-altitude and space flight; for the National Safety Council on automobile accidents; and for Civil Defense on radiation absorption" (284). As this brief description indicates, Anthroresearch Associates rests at the intersection of a number of core industries of the postwar period, not only the industries associated with what Dwight D. Eisenhower described as the military-industrial complex, with their intricate interfaces between government and private corporations, but also the exemplary industry of the high Fordist era: the auto industry. And while these associations situate Anthroresearch squarely within the midcentury moment, Pynchon also gestures toward the emerging era of multinational capital by noting that Anthroresearch Associates is a subsidiary of Yoyodyne, Pynchon's fictional figuration of a multinational corporation in both *V.* and the later published *The Crying of Lot 49.*

SHOCK and SHROUD become different uncanny representations of the status of embodied subjectivity in Fordist (and emergent post-Fordist) biopolitics. An acronym for "synthetic human, radiation output determined," SHROUD is a transparent automaton: "Its skin was cellulose acetate butyrate, a plastic transparent not only to light but also to X-rays, gamma rays, and neutrons. Its skeleton had once been that of a living human; now the bones were decontaminated and the long ones and spinal column hollowed inside to receive radiation dosimeters. SHROUD was five feet nine inches tall—the fiftieth percentile of Air Force standards. The lungs, sex organs, kidneys, thyroid, liver, spleen and other internal organs were hollow and made of the same clear plastic as the body shell" (284).

With its "decontaminated" human skeleton and its fleshly body consisting entirely of that postwar wonder product plastic, SHROUD becomes a nightmare version of the posthuman. Rather than representing a promise of posthuman agency, his output is seemingly "determined" in advance. And while SHROUD's unexpected animation indicates that there is a ghost in the machine, one that isn't fully determined in advance, this ghost functions more as an index of the volatility of the object world in late capitalism than as a fully realized representation of human or even posthuman subjectivity. Indeed, it is as an anthropomorphization of the object world that SHROUD's voice functions as uncanny. His seemingly impossible voice speaks of the return of the repressed for subjectivity in

this midcentury moment—that the deep and full subjectivity celebrated by much canonical modernism, in its persistence in the late modern
moment, is predicated on the disavowal of an ever metastasizing object
world, one that resists subjectification and full discursive control. In this
sense, SHROUD's voice becomes the impossible voice of the real, speaking less as the material world subjectified, and more as the voice of that
self-same material world that eludes yet overdetermines the subjective
in late capitalism. The uncanny emergence of SHROUD's and SHOCK's
voices becomes one of the moments in which the ethical project of Pynchon's novel, to attend to the "voice" of the material and the objectified,
becomes manifest. Attending to the "voice" of the material and the objectified means to neither disavow their status as material nor fetishize it
but to begin to recognize and respect the vulnerability and power of the
material as an actant. It also means that we should recognize and affirm
the subjectivity and the material embodiments of those who are rendered
objects by biopolitics and thanatopolitics. As I will more fully articulate,
this is not yet a politics but an ethics—one that can provide the basis for
a politics.

SHROUD's materiality is largely humanly produced, but its human
genesis does not guarantee its control by human beings. Instead, much
like the ever expanding capitalist world market that enabled the United
States to emerge as the leading producer and exporter of the material
coordinates of postwar existence, these materialities may be humanly produced in their initial genesis, but they quickly exceed full human control.
Thus while SHROUD's synthetic body becomes a striking early image of
what Hardt and Negri term *biopolitical production*, in which subjectivity
and the body itself become sites of political-economic investment, it indicates that this site of production is not necessarily a locus of subjective or
symbolic control.

This absence of symbolic control is further emphasized by Pynchon's
depiction of SHOCK. SHOCK stands for "synthetic human object, casu-
alty kinematics," and as this full name suggests, his uncanny resemblance
to a human being is even more pronounced. Pointing toward the autoerotic sublime of Ballard's *Crash* that we will turn to in chapter 3, SHOCK
is an ultrarealistic crash test dummy: "SHOCK was a marvelous manikin.
It had the same build as SHROUD but its flesh was molded of foam vinyl,
its skin vinyl plastisol, it's hair a wig, its eyes cosmetic-plastic, it's teeth
(for which, in fact, Eigenvalue had acted as subcontractor) the same kind

of dentures worn today by 19 percent of the American population, most of them respectable. Inside were a blood reservoir in the thorax, a blood pump in the midsection and a nickel-cadmium battery power supply in the abdomen" (285).

Even more than his transparent brethren, SHOCK represents an uncanny figuration of the human in the era of the biopolitical. Here human biology has been synthesized right down to internal organs and blood, suggesting the ability of the state and the political economy in the biopolitical era to shape, control, exploit, and fabricate the body. Yet for all the discursive and political-economic control suggested here, SHOCK's function, to test the results of car crashes, points toward the continued contingency and what Levi Bryant has termed the democratic autonomy (I might say semiautonomy) of the object world and indeed of the constitution of the body itself, in the emergent biopolitical era. The object world and body are still governed, in part, by the forms of contingency that Žižek describes as one of the defining attributes of the real.[21]

The contingency of the real, and specifically the real of death, is further underscored by Profane's conversation with SHROUD:

"What's it like," [Profane] said.
Better than you have it.
"Wha."
Wha yourself. Me and SHOCK are what you and everybody will be someday. (The skull seemed to be grinning at Profane.)
"There are other ways besides fall out and road accidents."
But those are most likely. If somebody else doesn't do it to you, you'll do it to yourselves. (286)

Here the dialogue between SHROUD and Profane further emphasizes the role of uncanny double that the two mannequins play to Profane as the text's representative of hapless, prototypical humanity. And while SHOCK and SHROUD, with their synthesized organs and skin, become ironic embodiments of human beings in the emergent era of biopolitical production, their relationship to the midcentury, Fordist sublime of car crashes and nuclear annihilation suggests that there is a more intimate relationship between the era of post-Fordism and the Fordist era that proceeded it than many theories of the postmodern would allow. Indeed, Fordism literally produces the material world that post-Fordism takes

for granted and reshapes. Moreover, there is a specifically Fordist (governmental and administered rather than driven by neoliberal economics)
form of biopolitics. SHROUD's invocation of death (invoked in the acronym itself, including the contingent death of the car crash) indicates that
for all the ability to govern life and death suggested by the forms of biopower and biopolitical control that define late twentieth-century life, the
contingency of the material, including the contingency of death itself,
refuses to be completely calibrated. Instead of a world of pure administration and control, then, Pynchon presents the emergence of a biopolitical
world in which the rationalities of biopower produce, as Adorno and
Horkheimer prophesied, their dialectical opposite: productive irrationalities.[22] Similarly, this resistance is immanent to biopolitical forms of control
themselves: the object world and the world of bodies administered by biopower refuse to be subsumed into discursive control but instead continue
to exist in negative dialectical tension with the discursive realm.

Fordist and Post-Fordist Fetishism

One of the symptoms of this persistence of a negative dialectic is the posthumanist organization of desire in Pynchon's narrative. As we saw with
the organization of desire in relationship to Esther's nose job, Pynchon's
novel emphasizes the relationship between subjects and objects. And
while this object fetishism certainly takes on the coordinates of commodity fetishism as Marx formulates them, it partakes equally from the
psychoanalytic logic of fetishism, with its emphasis on the object as both
a substitution, in Freudian terms, for a lost relationship of desire and as
the object or little piece of the real, in Lacan's formulation, that promises
a restoration of a fantasized sense of subjective completion. Of course, as
Žižek has demonstrated, the Marxian and the psychoanalytic fetishes can
be productively theorized in relationship to each other.[23] Thus the object
as a substitution for a lost relationship that is the emphasis of the Freudian
fetish can be understood as parallel to the way in which the commodity
fetish substitutes a relationship among things for what was a relationship
of production between people. In this case, the value of thinking these
two forms of fetishism together lies in reconceptualizing commodity
fetishism as informed, as Žižek demonstrates, by the fantasmatic logic of
disavowal. This explanation, then, would be the psychoanalytic recasting
of the classic formulation of the commodity fetish central to the logic of

the latter's function within Fordism. The rethinking of commodity fetishism in relationship to Lacan's formulation of the *objet petit a*, on the other
hand, points toward the further dematerialization of the commodity fetish
that I have termed *avatar fetishism*. Here it is not so much the invested
object that is the final product of fetishism so much as the promise of a
transcendent and complete subjectivity that such an object promises
to provide. Thus the fetishized object itself is finally figured as inert and
degraded matter—merely a necessary correlate to the fantasized achievement of a complete and therefore completely solipsistic subjectivity. Of
course this promise, like all those provided by commodity culture, is, at
best, only momentarily and fantasmatically realized. The emergence, then,
of a post-Fordist logic of commodity fetishism is one organized around an
even further disavowal of the material underpinnings of existence—even
as those material underpinnings proliferate.

Both the Fordist and the post-Fordist dimensions of commodity
fetishism are highlighted in Pynchon's depiction of Rachel Owlglass's
obsession with her car. The Fordist dimensions of commodity fetishism
are made manifest in the sexual encounter that Rachel has with her car:

> "You beautiful stud," he heard her say, "I love to touch you." Wha,
> he thought. "Do you know what I feel when we're out on the
> road? Alone, just us?" She was running the sponge caressingly
> over its front bumper. "Your funny responses, darling, that I know
> so well. The way your brakes pull a little to the left, the way you
> start to shudder around 5000 rpm when you're excited." . . . She
> had climbed into the car and now lay back in the driver's seat,
> her throat open to the summer constellations. He was about to
> approach her when he saw her left hand snake out all pale to fondle
> the gearshift. (28–29)

Rachel's desire is here clearly marked as Fordist: that most Fordist of
objects, the automobile, becomes the locus of her adoration. The substitution of subject and object relationships for intersubjective relationship
becomes parodically manifest in this scene. Rachel's car is the true object
of her desires in a way that cannot hope to be replicated by any of her
human lovers, Profane included. Yet for all her eroticization of the objectal
dimensions of her car, the MG, her fetishistic desire for the MG renders
its materiality secondary to the sublime qualities it promises as a fetish. It

is the "in the MG more than the MG," to paraphrase Lacan, upon which she is fixated. As such, even this moment of high Fordist object fetishism points toward its post-Fordist incarnation, in which objects are rendered fully secondary the workings of avatar fetishism.[24]

The workings of avatar fetishism are even more pronounced in the scene when Profane first meets Rachel:

> [Profane] met her through the MG, like everyone else met her. It nearly ran him over . . . Profane kept walking, secure in a faith that burdened pedestrians have the right-of-way. Next thing he knew he was clipped in the rear end by the car's right fender. Fortunately, it was only moving at 5 mph—not fast enough to break anything, only to send Profane, garbage can and lettuce leaves flying ass over teakettle in a great green shower.
>
> He and Rachel, both covered with lettuce leaves, looked at each other, wary. "How romantic," she said. "For all I know you may be the man of my dreams. Take that lettuce leaf off your face so I can see." (23–24)

Here even the car in its materiality seems secondary to its function as an adjunct to Rachel's desire. The absence of her recognition of the car's materiality is comically (though ominously) captured in her complete disregard to the effects that it has on pedestrians. The passage presents the MG as functioning as a metonym for the more general workings of Rachel's desire. Profane in fact becomes another metonym having randomly come in contact with the car. For a moment, Rachel hopes that the random (and violent) conjunctions that have brought them together represent a moment of metaphoric desire in which her incipient avatar fetishism might be fulfilled: she half jokes that Profane may be the man of her dreams. The fact that his face is covered with lettuce while she suggests this indicates the entirely projective dimension of her fantasy. Her fantasy is about an idealized version of herself—one for which her true love (like all versions of "love at first sight") merely becomes a mirror.

The Imperialist Roots of Contemporary Biopolitics

If the parts of Pynchon's novel that are set in the present construct a world in which biopolitics are becoming the central form in which power is managed in the first-world metropole (or what we would later call the "global North"), then the historical chapters of the novel trace the roots of these forms of biopolitical control and thanatopolitical violence in the global history of European imperialism. As Achille Mbembe argues, the forms of biopolitical control that have become generalized within late capitalism have their roots in imperialism and modern forms of racism.[25] Specifically, Mbembe demonstrates the resonance of Giorgio Agamben's frequently invoked concept of bare life, or life that has been reduced to pure biology and thus has no claim to political representation and citizenship, for thinking about subjects under European colonialism. Indeed, Mbembe suggests that the notion of power over life central to the concept of biopolitics does not go far enough for thinking about power in colonialism—for it is not only power over life but power over death, what he terms *necropower*, that is central to the brutal logic of colonial domination: "Operating on the basis of a split between the living and the dead, such a power defines itself in relationship to a biological field—which it takes control of and vests itself in. This control presupposes the distribution of human species into groups, the subdivision of the population into subgroups, and the establishment of the biological caesura between the ones and the others."[26] While Mbembe uses the term *necropolitics* to talk about this administrative power over death, I prefer Esposito's term, *thanatopolitics*, because it locates the reversal of biopower into its opposite—the administration of death via the logic of immunity. Thus the killing of certain populations is justified in the name of maximizing other forms of life.

This conception of thanatopolitics suggests a different version of the subject/object split than the one I have been tracing in *V.*'s depiction of postwar existence. The objects in this context are the objectified bodies and subjectivities of the colonized who have been rendered, in Frantz Fanon's famous phrase, "object[s] in the midst of other objects," while the colonizers become the privileged "subjects" on the other side of the immunitary and racialized divide.[27] As Fanon and Homi Bhabha differently point out, this construction of the subject/object divide within the colonial context becomes organized by the logic of fetishism—for the colonizer becomes preoccupied with fixing the status of the racial other as object, yet the latter's subjectivity functions to uncannily disrupt this appellation.[28] Thus the colonized subjectivity functions as a return of the repressed in *V.*, as the undead subjects of a thanatopolitics that return to haunt the ostensibly immunized subjectivities of the colonizers. This return of the repressed takes on a particularly powerful resonance in Pynchon's novel, written as it is in the era of decolonization and when the technologies of biopolitics and thanatopolitics return to the metropole itself.

In *V.*, this specifically colonialist version of the subject/object split also gets mapped upon a more typical version of this split that is produced by the spatial and temporal dislocations that structure imperialism. In *Culture and Imperialism*, Edward Said argues that imperialism precipitated a crisis in novelistic representation.[29] This crisis is both spatial and temporal and is evident in the shift from realist to modernist aesthetic practices. Whereas realism imagines a social space and a temporal sequence that are continuous and navigable by the historical subjectivities depicted by the novel form, modernism constructs a world in which neither time nor space is easily represented or rendered continuous. Said suggests that, in addition to the cultural factors conventionally cited as influencing the emergence of modernism, imperialism's challenge to conventional representations of space and time need to be taken into account. Within the imperial landscape of the early twentieth century (a landscape, because of growing settler populations and the growth of colonial industries, that was markedly different from the nineteenth-century landscape that preceded it), the fragmentation produced by discontinuous, transcontinental spaces and temporalities finds its parallel in the fragmentary and disjunctive dimensions of modernist aesthetics.

Pynchon clearly agrees with Said's assessment. Indeed much of the historical portion of *V.* is taken up with an account of the growing disjunction between subject and object and the concomitant emergence of twentieth-century forms of biopolitical violence and control in various colonial locales. This colonial context also indicates the geopolitical underpinnings of the temporal and spatial jumps that characterize the novel on a stylistic level. Like Joseph Conrad's *Heart of Darkness*, which Pynchon clearly has in mind, the colonial context in *V.* is presented through two and often three layers of narration.[30] The outermost layer of narration in each of these sections is focalized through the subjectivity of Herbert Stencil, but in each case, it is further narrated via the memories, conjectures, and journals of a range of others: the journals of Stencil's father, Sidney, a British agent for much of the first half of the twentieth century, and Fausto Maijstral, a Maltese who lived through the siege of Malta during World War II; the memories of Kurt Mondaugen, a scientist in Southwest Africa who is told accounts of the Herero genocide; and the historical conjecture of

Dudley Eigenvalue, a New York City dentist with an interest in the history of prosthetics and particularly the case of Evan Godolphin, who is a pilot during World War I and the recipient of an early, unsuccessful attempt at surgical facial reconstruction using precious metals.

Yet even as Stencil presents these histories through two and three layers of subjective reconstruction and conjecture, he narrates all them via the same third-person point of view though which he narrates his own actions: "This helped 'Stencil' appear as only one of a repertoire of identities. 'Forcible dislocation of personality' was what he called the general technique, which is not exactly the same as 'seeing the other fellow's point of view'; for it involved, say, wearing clothes that Stencil wouldn't be caught dead in, eating foods that would have made Stencil gag, living in unfamiliar digs, frequenting bars or cafés of a non-Stencilian character, all of this for weeks on end" (62).

Here the appropriative logic of imperialism is reproduced on the level of narration. While Stencil's narration seeks to perform the omniscient narration characteristic of the realist novel, in which the writer seamlessly moves in and out of the consciousness of her third-person characters, what appears instead here is a kind of narratorial psychosis in which the alternate subjectivities of various third-person characters become effaced by Stencil's subjectivity writ large. This fantasy of third-person narration is represented in the text as coincident with the fantasy of imperialism— remaking the subjectivities of others in relationship to one's own image, a fantasy that literally becomes about possession of the other's subjectivity and rendering it another object to possess.

Third-person narration in nineteenth century runs counter to Stencil's mid-twentieth-century recapitulation of it. In realism, there is a recognition of both the common world shared by characters and the discrete subjectivities experienced by each of them. This representation of multiple subjectivities is on one level, of course, a lie—one of the "reality effects" that made realism the whipping boy of the kinds of textual avant-gardism celebrated by postmodern theory—but on another level, this ability to represent the interactions of multiple subjectivities both with each other and with a stable representation of the object world is what allowed realism to function as such a powerful map of nineteenth-century, metropolitan society. It is this cartographic quality combined with its agential representation of subjectivity that has enabled Georg Lukács and Fredric Jameson to differently theorize realism as a genre particularly suited to the representation of class struggle.[31]

Both the imagined adequation between subject and object and the belief in the ability to effortlessly represent multiple subjectivities are what begin to break down in modernism. As I have already discussed, the apprehension of the discontinuous spaces and subjectivities of imperialism are one reason for the breakdown of realist representation. Although Adorno probably did not have imperialism specifically in mind when writing "Subject and Object" and *Negative Dialectics*, the challenge to realist representation that imperialism presents in the twentieth century becomes one of the catalysts to the growing and ever more evident disjunction between subject and object to which he refers. Of course, imperialism itself is bound up with the exponential growth of the object world and of subjective atomization that is produced by the global expansion of capitalist production in the twentieth century, and it is to this that the disjunction between subject and object must be most directly related.

As Pynchon demonstrates, two subjective responses that emerge from this growing disjunction are, in the case of Profane, a metonymic giving over to the contingency of the object world or, it's opposite in the case of Stencil, writing your subjectivity large onto other subjectivities and onto the object world as an attempt at metaphoric subsumption and control. The latter then is the structure of Stencil's narration: omniscience as a form of psychotically erasing the difference of other subjectivities by writing yourself large upon the world. I describe this mode of narration as psychotic because in its most extreme manifestations it erases the distinction between internal and external perception—psychic reality and the reality of the object world.[32] Of course, this appropriative dynamic replicates the logic of imperialism in which the colonized is rendered an object among objects—ones defined in relationship to the appropriative subjectivity of the colonizer.

This appropriative dynamic defines not only the form of Stencil's narration but the content of what he narrates as well. Crucially though, here, those forms of subjectivity, bodies, and aspects of the object world that are constructed in opposition to the imperial subject are presented as productively resisting his attempts at control and definition. As I have already mentioned, the Stencil sections of the novel swirl around his search for the meaning and significance of the novel's titular character (or characters) who is known primarily by her initial V. V. in many ways becomes a metaphorical (and impossible) embodiment of the attempt to effectively merge subject and object.

Similarly, the narratives about her existence all stage allegories of biopolitical control. These allegories lie at the center of the book's history of
the twentieth century. If, as Giorgio Agamben has defined, the concentration camp is the *locus classicus* of the biopolitical in the twentieth century,
then Pynchon, like Mbembe, suggests that the technologies of violence
and control deployed in the camps had their initial genesis in various colonial contexts. Central to the colonial contexts depicted by Pynchon is the
attempt to affix the status of the colonized as bare life outside of the protections and political rights afforded by sovereignty. Central to the genesis of
bare life as Agamben theorizes it is the attempt to define certain classes of
people as political and biological objects without recognized subjectivities
yet subject to various forms of biopolitical and thanatopolitical violence.

While Pynchon's representation of the biopolitical parallels Agamben's
theorization of it in a number of ways, including the forms of violence that
the rendering populations as bare life authorize, it also crucially differs
from Agamben's account in one crucial respect. In contrast to Agamben,
Pynchon's allegories of biopolitical control finally demonstrate the impossibility of such forms of control. Just as V. eludes Stencil's attempts to
affix her meaning, the various subject populations in Pynchon's narrative
refuse to correspond to the fantasies of passive objecthood that the colonizer projects onto them. This elusive quality of the biopolitical "object,"
then, is part of the larger disjunction between subject and object that the
novel presents.

The elusiveness and resistance of the colonial "object" is most directly thematized in the novel via the elusive country Vheissu (one of the
many avatars of V.). Godolphin Sr., a British secret agent, narrates his
obsession with Vheissu to Victoria Wren while he is in flight from Italian authorities. All this is, of course, also narrated though the mediating
consciousness of Stencil. Vheissu is a country outside the cartographic
reach of any map and is only accessible by a weeks-long journey past dead
cities, swamps, lakes, a ring of mountains, and "hard blue ice" (169). For
Godolphin, above all else, Vheissu is a fetish: "He had been there. Fifteen
years ago. And been fury-ridden since. Even in the Antarctic, huddling in
hasty shelter from a winter storm, striking camp high on the shoulder of
some yet unnamed glacier, there would come to him hints of the perfume
those people distill from the wings of black moths. Sometimes sentimental scraps of their music would seem to lace the wind; memories of their
faded murals, depicting old battles and older love affairs among the gods,
would appear without warning in the aurora" (169).

For Godolphin, Vheissu is akin to the Lacanian *objet petit a*. While it is a material place he has traveled to, it is the "in-the-country-more-than-the-country" of Vheissu that haunts him. His fixation is made up of various part objects that stand in for the fantasmatic entity that is Vheissu: scraps of music, perfume, murals.

And just as the subject's relationship to the *objet petit a* is underwritten by the aggression that is the flip side of the impossible fantasy of romantic love as the merger of subject and (love) object, Godolphin's obsession with Vheissu reveals the violence that is the flip side of the colonialist fetish of otherness:

[Godolphin says,] "But as if the place were, were a woman you had found somewhere out there, a dark woman tattooed from head to toes. And somehow you had got separated from the garrison and found yourself unable to get back, so that you had to be with her, close to her, day in and day out . . ."

[Victoria responds,] "And you would be in love with her."

"At first. But soon that skin, the gaudy godawful riot of pattern and color, would begin to get between you and whatever it was in her that you thought you loved. And soon, in perhaps only a matter of days, it would get so bad that you would begin praying to whatever god you knew of to send some leprosy to her. To flay that tattooing to a heap of red, purple and green debris, leave the veins and ligaments raw and quivering and open at last to your eyes and your touch." (171)

Here the violence of fetishism and the fetishistic fantasy logic that underpins imperialism becomes frighteningly apparent. The language of the passage almost directly echoes Lacan's description of the "in you more than you," suggesting that the same violently fetishistic logic underpins the relationship of subject and object, self and other, in both the ideology of romantic love and that of imperialism. In thrall to this fetishism, Godolphin fantasizes reducing the country as woman to a mass of quivering veins and ligaments. This vision of genocide as misogynist violence emphasizes the forms of thanatopolitical violence that were central to the workings of imperialism in the late nineteenth and early twentieth century. Yet the passage also suggests that the fantasy of biopolitical control that such violence is predicated on is always undermined by the logic of fetishism that underwrites it. For all his attempts at inscribing a meaning onto the body of Vheissu once and for all, that little piece of the real that represents the "in you more than you" in her eludes any attempt at affixing its symbolic significance. While this piece of the real may be associated with some actual material fetish, such as the tattooed skin described by Godolphin, its fantasmatic significance exceeds this material dimension and eludes any attempt at capturing it. Thus, rather than resolving subject/object antinomy, the logic of fetishism only exacerbates it; for while the materiality of the object world and of people rendered as objects becomes violated material serving the ends of subjective fantasy, the subject can never fully control or master these objectified materials.

The Fetishistic Logic of Genocide

The relationship of fetishism and the subject/object antinomy to thanatopolitics is further explored in the sections of the novel that are set in German Southwest Africa during the Herero and Nama genocide. As David Olusaga and Casper W. Erichson detail, before the genocide, the Herero numbered 80,000 and the Nama 20,000 people.[33] Five years later, there were 10,000 Herero and 8,500 Nama left. Pynchon depicts this genocide through the narratives of the Germans, presenting it as a collective sadistic fantasy that has thanatopolitical effects—a fantasy underwritten by the logic of fetishism elucidated in Godolphin's account of Vheissu:

> Godolphin laughed at her [Hedwig Vogelsang, another possible avatar of V.] "There's been a war, Fräulein. Vheissu was a luxury, an indulgence. We can no longer afford the likes of Vheissu."
> "But the need," she protested, "its void. What can fill that?"
> He cocked his head and grinned at her. "What is already filling it. The real thing. Unfortunately. Take your friend D'Annunzio. Whether we like it or not that war destroyed a kind of privacy, perhaps the privacy of dream. Committed us like him to work out three o'clock anxieties, excess of character, political hallucinations on a live mass, a real human population." (248)

While the passage contrasts the genocide (the "war" in question) with Godolphin's early fantasies about Vheissu, it also suggests that both the private "dream" of Vheissu and the thanatopolitical violence of the genocide are motivated by the same fetishistic logic. Literally this fetishism is predicated on a "void" that needs to be filled with a fantasized "real thing." Echoing Lacan's near contemporaneous theorization of the Freudian "thing" in *Seminar VII* (an early theorization of the *objet a*), the language of the passage stages an opposition between a subjective void and a fantasized object (the fetish) that promises to fill that void.[34] In Lacan's discussion of *das Ding*, this thing is literally an object that insists on its status as real and thus is only imperfectly transformed into a signifier. The signifier still drips with the real, promising a unity with the real that can only ever be fantasmatically realized. The imperial subjects presented by Pynchon attempt to overcome the subject/object antinomy by constructing the colonial other as *das Ding*—as the impossible object of enjoyment that promises to restore the colonizing subject to an imagined sense of fullness. It also meets with the political, economic, and psychical resistance of the colonized, though Pynchon never details this in the novel. Instead, as Robert McLaughlin has noted, Pynchon is invested exclusively in the project (much like J. M. Coetzee at a later moment) of representing the paradoxes and the forms of fetishistic violence that characterize dominant forms of imperial subjectivity.[35]

While Lacan's formulation of *das Ding* may seem distant from the material dimensions of colonialism, if we attend to the way in which (as Eva Cherniavsky and Aníbal Quijano point out) imperialism was a political-economic enterprise that produced racialization as one of its core effects, the fantasmatic construction of *das Ding* can be used to understand the dimensions of racial fantasy that are intertwined with colonialism.[36] The fantasy of the other as possessing a special relationship to enjoyment is core to the form of racism that Žižek has termed *enjoyment theft*.[37] Central to most forms of Western racism is also the fantasy of the racial other as possessing a less mediated relationship to the body and bodily enjoyment and more generally to materiality as such. The colonizing subject then exists in a relationship of embodiment envy (the dialectical flip side to avatar fetishism) in relationship to the colonized. In other words, the fantasy stages the other as having greater access to embodiment and the fantasized real. Yet this attempt to affix and fully objectify the colonized meets with the impossibility of fulfilling such a desire. Thus the colonial other, if she can just be fixed as the impossible subject/object of desire, promises a resolution to the subject/object antinomy for the colonizing subject.

Within such a context, the thanatopolitical violence of colonialism can be understood as not only political and economic but psychosocial as well. In Pynchon's portrayal, the colonized body becomes the locus of the "in you more than you" for the colonizer, and the simultaneous demand for and impossibility of the colonized body to contain this enjoyment underwrites the aggression and sadism of the colonizer.[38]

This sadism is presented in graphic terms in the section on German Southwest Africa, when Foppl, a German army commander who is staging a "siege party" involving sadomasochism, cross-dressing, torture, and large quantities of food and drink, describes his participation in the genocide:

> But as they did this thing—and Fleische said later that he'd felt
> something like it too—there came over him for the first time an
> odd sort of peace, perhaps like what the black was feeling as he
> gave up the ghost. Usually the most you felt was annoyance, the
> kind of annoyance you have for an insect that's buzzed around you
> for too long. You have to obliterate its life, and the physical effort,
> the obviousness of the act, the knowledge that this is only one
> unit in a seemingly infinite series, that killing this one won't end it,
> won't relieve you from having to kill more tomorrow, and the day
> after and on, and on . . . It had only to do with the destroyer and the
> destroyed, and the act which united them, and it had never been
> that way before. (263–64)

In this passage, the parallels Pynchon constructs between the thanatopolitical violence of the colonial scene and the later forms of thanatopolitical violence that Esposito associates with the Holocaust are rendered almost explicit. Pynchon presents the colonial scene as part of the neglected history of the twentieth century. Indeed, if the holocaust becomes the *locus classicus* of biopolitical violence, one that ushers in the late-capitalist era in which forms of biopolitical control become ever more prevalent and routinized, then, as Pynchon demonstrates, the deadly carceral and corporeal technologies we associate with the Holocaust were already being perfected on the colonial scene in earlier moments in the nineteenth and twentieth centuries. Indeed, the passage with its genocidal equation of Hereros with so many insects in need of killing captures perfectly the logic of rendering whole populations as bare life or what Agamben also describes as "homo sacer"—members of a population that can be sacrificed or killed with impunity.[39] The retrospective dimension of Pynchon's historicism is captured by the description of the killing of the Hereros as serialized and as partaking of the midcentury logic of high Fordism. Their bodies and subjectivities become rendered as serialized objects in need of efficient disposal.

In contrast to Agamben and Esposito, Pynchon presents biopolitics and thanatopolitics not merely as aggressive forms of power that successfully attempt to bring various aspects of human life under greater administrative and political control but also as a defensive reaction of those in power to the growth of the subject/object antinomy and the forms of political-economic contingency produced by it. Indeed, he presents biopolitical fantasies of control as partaking of the forms of fetishism that emerge as a subjective response to the exponential proliferation of objects in twentieth-century history. This dimension of the biopolitical is indicated when Foppl discovers a fetishistic "unity" in the moment of murder. This fantasized unity, like the unity promised by other forms of fetishism, whether it is the moment the commodity seems to live up to its ineffable promise or the moment the erotic object seems to surge with the forms of displaced pleasure it contains, is fleeting and must be repeated ritualistically to try to regain the ever more elusive satisfaction.

This, then, is a very different version of biopolitics than that theorized by either Agamben or Foucault. Biopolitics, in this context, is a rationalized form of fetishism—a fantasy of disciplinary and political control that is inherently elusive and structured around a disavowal. The disavowal is of the irreconcilability of the object world and those who have been objectified in late capitalism to subsumption under the logic of subjective control.

V., the Elusive Subject/Object of Desire

The fantasy of biopolitical control as a reconciliation of the subject/object split is allegorized most forcefully in Stencil's search for V. Her name, in its status as a simple and meaningless signifier, promises a fulfillment that it also withholds—for initials usually have proper names for which they serve as shorthand. Similarly, proper names, in turn, hold the promise of an embodied subjectivity that they name and delimit. Yet the proper names attaching to V. are multifold, as are the conditions of

her embodiment, suggesting the impossibility of doing justice to or discursively controlling the subject/object thus named. In this context, the
period that always follows V.'s initial can be read as an index of the divide
that separates subjective domain from the metastasizing object world of
the mid-twentieth century.

The irreconcilability of these two realms is also captured by the forms
of mechanized embodiment by which V. herself is increasingly defined.
While the novel itself vacillates on whether V. is a singular person or a
signifier that attaches to multiple objects (or both), all the female incar-
nations of V. can be read as presenting different moments in the life of a
single person, who is named Victoria Wren when we first meet her. The
living tissue of V.'s body is being replaced with various prosthetic objects.
As a character, V. is presented as liminal, as being associated with the colonizers and the colonized, the axis powers and the allied powers, in equal
measure. She is both the amoral and aggressive subject of biopolitical
power and the feminized object upon which such power gets enacted. As
such, she seems to represent the greatest promise for the reconciliation
of subject and object in the novel. Yet even as she seems to embody both
subject and object in her very person, the opposition is still unreconciled
in her. This irreconcilability is perhaps most strikingly rendered in the
last scene we see her, in which she, who has been impersonating a priest
known as the "Bad Priest" in Malta during the bombing of the island in
World War II, is picked apart by the children of the war-scarred island. The
scene is described by Fausto Maijstral, whose "confession" written during
the siege of Malta is read by Stencil:

The woman did not seem to notice. Perhaps she could no longer feel.
But when they brought the feet to her head to show her, I saw two
tears grow and slip from outside the corners of her eyes . . .
I wondered if the disassembly of the Bad Priest might not go on, and
on, into evening. Surely her arms and breasts could be detached; the
skin of her legs peeled away to reveal some intricate understructure
of silver openwork. Perhaps the trunk itself contained other won-
ders: intestines of parti-colored silk, gay balloon-lungs, a rococo
heart. But the sirens started up then. The children dispersed bearing
away their new-found treasures [which include one of her mechanical eyeballs, her prosthetic feet, her sapphire bellybutton, her jeweled
teeth], and the abdominal wound made by the bayonet was doing

its work. I lay prone under a hostile sky looking down for moments more at what the children had left; suffering Christ foreshortened on the bare skull, one eye and one socket, staring up at me: a dark hole for the mouth, stumps at the bottoms of the legs. And the blood which had formed a black sash across the waist flowing down both sides from the navel . . . She began to cry. Tearless, half-nasal; more a curious succession of drawn-out wails, originating far back in the mouth cavity. All through the raid she cried. (342–44)

Here, instead of Haraway's cyborg, in which human and machine are seamlessly combined into a newly agential subject, we are presented instead with a representation of the subjectivity of V. and the prosthetic objects that make up much of her person as both intimately intertwined yet in irreconcilable opposition. A human version of SHOCK and SHROUD, her subjectivity both relies on its prosthetic embodiment and is not represented as integrated with it. In the violent mathematics of this scene, V.'s prosthetics are presented as separate and subtractable from her subjectivity, which is rendered powerless to do anything more than cry. And indeed in a fantasy of biopolitical control that echoes earlier ones in the novel, such as the skinning of a feminized Vheissu, the subtraction is imagined by Fausto as endlessly pursuable: one, he imagines, could skin V. and remove her mechanized internal organs. The scene also replays the logic of the fetish that informs fantasies of biopolitical control and thanatopolitical and misogynist violence: the fantasy of extending the biopolitical control further and further into the feminized subject/object in order to gain complete control even at the cost of death. Yet this promise of complete control is ever elusive.

A Recognition of Contingency

While the scene of V.'s dismantling appears to merely replay the irreconcilable oppositions that define Pynchon's novel, it also points to a different stance toward both subjectivity and the object world that does not merely replay the violent trajectory the novel details. While Pynchon's novel does not detail a politics of materiality, it does, as I have already suggested, indicate an ethical stance toward the material that positions the novel as more than merely the self-consuming object typically associated with postmodern forms of metafiction.[40]

This ethical position can be located the inchoate cry that V. utters during her dying moments, for in her cry, V., as the representative of the object world (including those forms of bare life that have been rendered objects by the workings of biopower and thanatopower in the twentieth century) gives unsymbolizable voice to the pain produced by biopolitical fantasies of control, the rendering of whole populations as marked for death, and whole domains of the object world that have been rendered merely inert and disposable. V.'s cry, then, represents the voice of that which has been excluded from the globally dominant symbolic imagined by the novel: objects and the objectified. In this sense, Pynchon's ethical position in this passage is also psychoanalytic: it is an injunction to tarry with and recognize that which has been disavowed or excluded from consideration by the privileged subject of Western modernity. In other words, V.'s cry can also be read as the cry of the real in psychoanalytic terms—as the emergence of the seemingly impossible voice of those populations and objects that have been abjected or rendered disposable or uncoded materiality in the formation of the first-world capitalist and biopolitical subject. The ethics articulated in this passage can thus be likened not only to Bruno Latour's injunction to attend to objects as actors but also to Said's Benjaminian injunction to read against the grain of imperial texts to attend to the forms of violence, exclusion, and exploitation that they both encode and disavow.[41] Such a perspective thus represents a different or, in Sarah Ahmed's terms, queer orientation to materiality and to the objectified—one that affirms the material and the populations who have been written under the sign of the material, rather than seeing them as fodder for first-world transcendence.[42]

This ethical injunction and the attention to the material and the objectified upon which it is structured is what locates Pynchon's novel as part of the late-capitalist literature of materiality. While a cursory perusal of V. may seem to indicate the novel is of a piece with the linguistic playfulness and self-consuming, metafictional qualities that have been associated with canonical postmodernism, a closer look reveals a novel that is about the violence and pain of the twentieth century. More cuttingly, it is about the pain underwritten by the kind of disembodied, imperializing stance shared by both Stencil and the authors of postmodern metafiction—a stance that renders the rest of the world degraded material for the working out of authorial desire and the concomitant fantasies of control that they underwrite.

It is striking that Pynchon advances this critique of imperial desire and fantasies of biopolitical control not only near the beginning of the era of high postmodernism but also during the middle of what Immanuel Wallerstein has termed the *Pax Americana*.[43] The history of biopolitical control that Pynchon traces in *V.* is one in which, as Giovanni Arrighi has demonstrated, hegemonic domination of the capitalist world system shifted from Britain to the United States.[44] In this context, postmodern metafiction can be read as the not-quite-triumphalist literature of this era—as a representative of the solipsism produced by a hegemonic positioning that fantasizes no resistance to the dominant subject's construction of the world. Thus Pynchon's engagement with the subject/object antinomy and its relationship to fantasies of biopolitical control comes as a warning about the danger of foregoing any kind of recognition of the object world and its difference from the subject. The latter thus becomes the dominant ideology of postmodern fiction.

Pynchon's ethical opposition to this ideology is given voice in V.'s cry. And it is less than coincidental that this cry comes at ground zero of one of the more brutal shellings of World War II—for this war not only marks the expansion of thanatopolitical forms of violence on a grand scale but also represents the limits of the fantasies of control that are central to this expansion. While the war may be the product of the West, it also represents the violent and implosive turning of the West in on itself. As such, it represents the contingency of political-economic and ideological forces that the West put into play in the twentieth century—a contingency that outstrips the fantasies of control associated with biopolitics. It is unsurprising that Pynchon returns in *Gravity's Rainbow* to World War II as the forge of what emerges as the political-economic logic of the latter half of the twentieth century.

Pynchon's ethical injunction in *V.,* then (and it is no more than an injunction because it has not yet developed into a political stance), is to side with bare life and the object world against the fantasies of a solipsistic subjectivity that writes the world in its own image (Stencil) or refuses any kind of historical or political understanding beyond the most immediate and thoroughly contingent (Profane). These are the twin poles of postmodern ideology, and it is against these two poles that the literature of materiality that I trace in this book wages war.

CHAPTER 3

The Late-Modern Unconscious

The Object World of J. G. Ballard's *Crash*

Nobody likes it when you mention the unconscious, and nowadays, hardly anybody likes it when you mention the environment. . . . Nobody likes it because when you mention [the unconscious], it becomes conscious. *In the same way when you mention the environment, you bring it into the foreground. It stops being the environment. It stops being That Thing Over There that surrounds and sustains us.*

—Timothy Morton, *Ecology without Nature*

Against the Linguistic Turn

Postmodernism and the linguistic turn are two concepts often thought of as deeply intertwined, if not in fact synonymous.[1] Whether theorized via the linguistic metaphors (such as discourse, textuality, simulation, narrative, and signification), privileged by poststructuralism, or as a cultural preoccupation with linguistic and the textual produced by shifts within the political economy that betoken post-Fordism, immaterial production, or late capitalism, language appears to be postmodernism's privileged object and medium.[2]

It is precisely this privileging of the linguistic that is challenged by J. G. Ballard's fictional aesthetic. Like the other authors considered in this book, Ballard's fiction of the early 1970s represents a challenge to the canonized version of the postmodern aesthetic, with its emphasis on metafiction and textuality. Instead, in the texts of what Martin Amis describes as his "years of mortar and steel," which include *Concrete Island*, *High Rise*, and the novel that this chapter will address, *Crash*, Ballard focuses on the late-modernist object world and built environment that forms the disavowed flipside to postmodern fantasies of the material's transcendence and of linguistic or discursive control, including the forms of discursive control associated with biopolitical forms of governance and production.[3] Ballard's is a late twentieth-century fictional aesthetic in which the soft, constructed, malleable world imagined by the linguistic turn and what Michael Hardt and Antonio Negri term "immaterial production" are systematically peeled away to reveal the hard-object world and obdurate infrastructure inherited from high Fordism.[4] It is precisely the latter that Crash posits as postmodernism's unconscious, as a location of both what Slavoj Žižek terms "obscene enjoyment" and the material domain that overdetermines the dominant narrative of postmodernity as an era in which the life world is endlessly malleable and understood most effectively in terms of linguistic metaphors.[5] Ballard's text thus engages what Theodor Adorno describes as the object's preponderance and Levi Bryant describes as the resistant "being of objects" over and against the "knowledge of objects," the objects in this case being the human-constructed object world of late capitalism itself.[6] Like Adorno, Ballard suggests that any accounting of subjectivity that wants to be more than merely ideological must attend to the object first, marking the ways in which subjectivity is shaped, limited, and enabled by its encounter with the world of objects. Such an engagement with the object's preponderance is particularly imperative in a social landscape that is increasingly imagined as malleable, textual, and fluid. And it is precisely such an engagement that Crash enacts, with its depictions of subjects whose desires are shaped and refigured by their encounters with the violent object world of car crashes.

The relationship the novel presents between the malleable surfaces of the postmodern and the resistance of the underlying built environment can perhaps best be understood in terms of a reconceptualized version of the classic Marxist infrastructure/superstructure distinction—one that allows us to further attend to the object's recalcitrance and preponderance. While this distinction has been regularly and rightly dismissed as a reductive account of causality in post-Marxist theory, cultural studies, and even much Marxist theory, I think it can be effectively rethought as a form of ideology critique that asks us to attend to the material underpinnings of culture precisely in a moment when culture wants to imagine itself as increasingly dematerialized, malleable, and all pervasive.[7] In this sense, Fredric Jameson's famous formulation about the fate of the infrastructure/superstructure (or base/superstructure) distinction in postmodernism needs to be rethought. Jameson argues that the economic and cultural "collapse back into each other" in the postmodern moment.[8] While it makes sense that the cultural becomes largely coincident with the economic in late capitalism, it is not clear that the reverse is equally true. I would suggest, instead, that the idea that the economic is reducible to the cultural (rather than the reverse) is one of the core ideologies of the postmodern era and a major limitation of theories, such of those of Hardt and Negri, of "biopolitical production."[9] In order to combat this ideology, I think the base/superstructure distinction can be rethought in ways that aren't so much about the privileging of the economic over the cultural but, to return to Marx's original metaphor in *A Contribution to the Critique of Political Economy*, attending to the *infrastructure* that both makes possible and is obscured by the most fetishized dimensions of the cultural. While the distinction has often been rendered base/superstructure, an alternate rendering of the German ("die Grundlage/der Überbau") is *infrastructure/superstructure*. It is this latter usage that I want to employ in discussing Ballard's *Crash*; the critique staged by Ballard's novel is not so much about the production of the cultural by the economic realm (although, in its attention to the built environment of high Fordism, the novel does dramatize the shaping of the former by the latter and vice versa) but by the way in which the infrastructural dimensions of late capitalism form the disavowed flipside to postmodern and biopolitical conceptions of culture and human embodiment as textual and endlessly malleable. In this usage of the infrastructure/superstructure distinction, it is not a question of the determination of one realm by the other but one of mystification: in the bright, shiny surfaces of culture, it is easy to forget the hidden aspects of the built environment and of economic production that help to create them. In this sense, I see the infrastructure/superstructure distinction more as a precursor to Marx's celebrated account of commodity fetishism than as a proscription for cultural or historical causality. The importance of the distinction lies in its insistence that we attend to what lies beyond that which appears immediately accessible, manipulable, and knowable as the realm of culture.

Crash, or the Persistence of the Material

The aesthetic practices of Ballard's 1973 novel, *Crash*, become a lot more comprehensible when understood within this rearticulated understanding of infrastructure/superstructure. Ballard's dystopian paean to the erotics of car crashes is not so much written in the dominant metafictional aesthetic of postmodernism as against it. (The text's lone metafictional moment is in naming its protagonist James Ballard.) It is written as an injunction to attend to the infrastructural dimensions of the late-capitalist built environment and the ways in which these structure both subjectivity and enjoyment.[10] The novel also reveals the material underpinnings of the forms of production that Hardt and Negri variously describe as biopolitical and immaterial. *Crash*, with its emphasis on the material built environment and the materiality of bodies as they intersect, often violently, with this built environment, can thus be read as a critique of the ideology of dematerialization that is central feature not only of late-capitalist life in the global North but also of so many of the theories that attempt to account for late-capitalist existence.

The built environment of late capitalism is emphasized everywhere in Ballard's novel. This built environment corresponds to accounts of the postmodern to the extent that nature and the natural world is nowhere present in it, except in the most mediated forms of landscaping. Thus it is a world, as Jameson puts it, in which "the prodigious new expansion of multinational capital ends up penetrating and colonizing" the "precapitalist enclave" that is "Nature."[11] Yet, on the other hand, this built environment is very much a product of Fordism, with its emphasis on modernist planning, large-scale construction, and forms of transportation, such as the airplane and that most fetishized of Fordist products, the automobile. And, of course, it is the "hard" technology of the automobile that careens violently and fetishistically through the heart of Ballard's novel. The hard geometry of this late-modernist built environment contrasts in marked ways with the fantasy of a "soft city" and of the plasticity and textuality of everyday life, with which David Harvey begins his description of postmodernism.[12] If Harvey sees Jonathan Raban's *Soft City* as exemplary of the change in sensibility and condition that he terms the postmodern, then Ballard's *Crash* underscores the late-modernist "hard city" that subtends the soft city of postmodernism.

For the dominant theoretical and novelistic epistemologies of postmodernism, the built environment is constructed and reconstructed as a malleable text or narrative, bodies are constructed by discourse, and the leading edge of post-Fordist production itself has become, in the words of Michael Hardt and Antonio Negri, both "biopolitical" and "immaterial."[13] Ballard's novel, in contrast, emphasizes the material built environment created by the high Fordist period that preceded post-Fordism; the insistently and vulnerably material dimensions of bodies, made up of flesh, blood, and bone, even when they fuse in posthuman ways with metal and plastic; and the dependence of the dematerialized imaginary of both postmodernism and immaterial production upon various disavowed forms of material production. *Crash* can thus be read as detailing a material unconscious that represents the dialectical flipside to the fantasies of material transcendence central to metafictional postmodernism.[14] Or, in other words, if metafiction, with its self-reflexivity and emphasis on the autotelic and the constructed, tends toward the autoerotic, then Ballard puts the *auto* back into the autoeroticism of postmodernism's unconscious.

Fordism, or Postmodernism's Unconscious

Ballard's infamously antihumanist and amoral novel can be read as making an important political intervention, asserting the dependence of the dematerialized world celebrated by postmodernism on the late-modernist built environment that we associate with Fordism. Aspects of this built environment—especially the most fetishized midcentury cultural product, the automobile—become the central components organizing the forms of desire detailed by Ballard's novel. James, the novel's narrator, is quite appropriately a highly paid member of an increasingly dominant class of symbol producers: he is a writer for an advertising company. As an adman he is one of the architects of the emergent regime of biopolitical production in which, as Hardt and Negri argue, subjectivity and life are directly shaped and produced through various forms of symbolic labor (including affective, service, financial, and intellectual labor such as the direct work with symbols that characterizes the narrator's job). Yet while James's job seems to place him firmly in the camp of immaterial production, the specific campaign he is working on for the Ford Motor Company suggests the return of the materialist repressed: "Catherine pulled a manila folder from her bag. I recognized the treatment of a television commercial I had prepared. For this high-budget film, a thirty-second commercial advertising Ford's entire new sports car range, we hoped to use one of a number of well-known actresses. On the afternoon of my accident I had attended a conference with Aida James, a freelance director we had brought in. By chance, one of the actresses, Elizabeth Taylor, was about to start work on a new feature film at Shepperton."[15]

The novel's mix of the dematerializing impulses of postmodernism with the late-modernist material substrata represented by Fordism is evident in this passage. If television is one of the privileged image-based technologies of post-Fordism and the forms of biopolitical production associated with it, it is here being used to market the titular commodity of Fordism. Similarly, while the cinema and advertising as twin modernist technologies precede the post-Fordist era, the blurring of the two into each other suggests a very postmodern commodification of image culture, indicating the two technologies reach their late-capitalist negative apotheosis when they become coincident. The linking of the very material commodity of the car with the immaterial figure of the star and the dematerializing technology of the commercial becomes a precise condensation of Ballard's representation of subjectivity in the late-capitalist era: while the postmodern subject imagines itself as increasingly dematerialized, as figured by various televisual avatars, it is subtended by and dependent upon the persistence of the material—a material that, as the rest of the novel suggests, becomes all the more violent, chaotic, and determining, the more it is disavowed. The passage thus suggests the specifically late-capitalist form of commodity fetishism that I term *avatar fetishism*, in which, rather than simply a relationship between things coming to replace the social relationship of labor between people, though this classical Marxian formulation still subtends the newer form of fetishism, a fantasy of subjectivity and the social world as fully simulated, constructed, and dematerialized comes to substitute for the material things represented by commodities themselves. Within the workings of avatar fetishism, commodities in their objectal form become degraded material for the achievement of the idealized subjectivity that they promise.

The material unconscious detailed by Ballard can thus be described as a late-modern unconscious. Of course this unconscious is not represented as unconscious in *Crash*; instead, it forms the conscious subject of the narrative and the forms of fetishism and enjoyment it details. This representation of the late-modern unconscious in the moment when the postmodern and the accompanying linguistic turn were attaining dominance is part of what can be read as the political praxis engaged by Ballard's novel. While *Crash* appears just when postmodernism was attaining ascendency (1973, as the moment of the dissolution of the international monetary standard, is a crucial year for both Harvey and Jameson), it suggests the partial continuity of the postmodern moment with the period of Fordism and late modernism that came before it. Yet this continuity is effaced by the ideology of postmodernism itself. Ballard's novel, then, is not retrospectively focused on the moment of late modernism and high Fordism when it was a dominant ideology. It instead insists on late-modernism's importance and persistence as the determining unconscious of the postmodern, representing all that postmodernism wants to repress in its fantasies of transcendence.

The Geography of a Critique

It is not accidental in this regard that Ballard writes this novel in England rather than at the epicenter of postmodernism, the United States. While the novel can be said to detail the workings of desire in relationship to the export cultures of late modernism and postmodernism, these cultures, while representing a new international style, are most forcefully associated with the United States as the hegemonic center of the postwar capitalist world system. Thus Vaughn's most sublime fantasy involves staging a fatal car crash with the Hollywood film star and international celebrity Elizabeth Taylor, and the fantasies of all the characters in the novel revolve around the products and built environments of a postwar international style that had the United States at its center. Writing from the slightly more peripheral vantage of England, a former hegemonic center of the world system, Ballard is able to view the ideology of postmodernism with a critical eye, underscoring that the "immaterial production" central to the emergent regime of postmodernism is predicated on the forms of material production and the material built environment that we more readily associate with late modernism and continue to be produced in other, increasingly peripheral, locations within the capitalist world system.[16] In this sense, Ballard demonstrates the continuity between what Immanuel Wallerstein has theorized as two parts of a Kondratieff cycle, in which the United States functioned as the hegemon of the capitalist world system. The first phase of such a cycle, which has characterized the rise and fall of each successive hegemonic power in the capitalist world economy, is aligned with the hegemon as a center of material production (in this case, the United States as the center of high Fordist production), while in the second phase, the hegemon becomes associated with financialization (i.e., post-Fordism), while material production moves elsewhere.[17]

By demonstrating the interconnectedness of these two phases, *Crash* implicitly challenges the epochal rhetoric of postmodernism's central theorists, demonstrating that postmodern or post-Fordist forms of production need to be understood as the products of one of the many waves of modernization that Enrique Dussel categorizes as "transmodern."[18] Such an understanding thus enables me to situate a writer like Ballard, due to his geographical location as well as the unevenness of the process of modernization itself, both within and partially outside the most recent wave of modernization that we call (or used to call) postmodernization, enabling him to attend to the forms that preceded it as well as cast a critical eye on its newly dominant features.

From the world-systems approach articulated by both Wallerstein and Dussel, then, postmodernism is not an entirely new era—one that represents a radical break from modernity—but rather a shift from one phase to another in a cycle that is a standard part of the successive waves of modernization that characterize the world system. It is not the emergence of a new era of postindustrial or biopolitical production on a world scale but rather the more limited emergence of these sectors within the core nations of the world system. Within such a context, the material is not so much superseded as repressed, forming the unconscious flipside to postmodern dreams of the eminent plasticity of the material and biopolitical fantasies of the complete socialization and discursive manipulability of life itself. The late-modern unconscious detailed by Ballard's novel, then, insists on the persistence and resistance of the material. It is such an unconscious that Ballard dramatizes in the forms of posthumanist desire and fetishism of the material that his novel chronicles.

The unconscious explored by *Crash* is one in which erotic investments no longer primarily attach themselves to intersubjective relationships between people but to relationships between subjects and fetishized aspects of the object world. Within such a context, Lacan's reworking of psychoanalysis becomes a crucial mode of mapping desire in late capitalism—for it suggests a way of attending to the fetishized objects (which in Ballard are crucially both fantasmatic and material) that structure desire and form the unconscious flipside to the fantasy of dematerialization that is central to avatar fetishism. As with all forms of the objectal real in Lacan, these objects only take on their fantasmatic significance in relationship to the organization of the symbolic against which they emerge.[19] Thus the subject's relationship and enjoyment of the fetishized pieces of the real becomes the novel's central preoccupation. This relationship is figured most disturbingly and alluringly in its depiction of a thoroughly posthumanist sexuality that emphasizes the intersections of bodily parts with auto parts in the staged and unstaged auto accidents—the "marriage of sex and technology," "a terrifying almanac of imaginary automobile disasters and insane wounds"—that are the novel's most notorious and obsessively repeated content (142, 13). In this sexuality, components of the late-capitalist built environment merge with the body imagined as thoroughly fragmented: "traces of smegma and vaginal mucus" marry "the splashed engine coolant of unexpected car-crashes"; "the jutting carapace of the instrument panel and the stylized sculpture of the steering column, reflect a dozen images" of "rising and falling buttocks"; and a "zodiac of unforgotten collisions" illuminate "a groin," to take just a few of the dozens of examples the text provides (29, 142, 201). What emerges from these descriptions, then, is a landscape of the body and the world in pieces that form the abjected detritus to the postmodern-dominated symbolic of late capitalism.[20]

Ballard's Poetics of the Object

The violence of Ballard's chronicling of the late-modern unconscious is offset by the novel's oddly affectless and clinical narration. While the novel is narrated in first person, focalized through the protagonist, James, the narration has a quality of detachment and photographic precision that is often more readily associated with the third person.[21] In this sense, we get little of the feeling of language straining against syntax as we do in some of the other writers considered in this book. Ballard's is no Burroughsian language of the real. It is instead almost classical in its economy, clarity, and precision.

A more descriptive account of his prose might term it *phenomenological*. Ballard's prose narrates objects as they are apprehended subjectively. While he often cites the surrealists as important influences, on the stylistic level at least, he is much more in debt to the line of objectivist or phenomenological poetics that runs from Gertrude Stein, Ernest Hemingway, William Carlos Williams, and Louis Zukofsky, through the writers of the *Nouveau Roman*. In Ballard's prose, there is an attention to the world of objects, as they impinge upon the subject. The narrator's subjectivity is decentered, functioning largely as an effect of the object world.

In contrast to the antihumanism typically ascribed to postmodern aesthetics, Ballard's aesthetic not only decenters the human subject a la antihumanism but also points toward those forms of materiality that exceed and impinge upon the subject. As such, I think Ballard's aesthetic is finally better described using Cary Wolfe's term *posthumanism*. Ballard's aesthetic suggests that control represents a final humanist (not to mention biopolitical) fantasy within the domain of the supposedly antihumanist. It is an attempt to ward off the contingencies and determinations of the object world and its intersections with the late-modern unconscious. The critique of control shapes *Crash*'s clinical tone. Rather than offering anti-humanist or scientific detachment as a kind of representational ideal, such a detachment is presented as a medico-scientific ideology that, as Sam Francis notes, is parallel to the amoral sexual proclivities practiced by the white-collar professionals who usually are his protagonists.[22]

It is in this sense that Ballard's prose style moves beyond classical phenomenology, with its emphasis on the apprehending consciousness as central, to marking the way in which this consciousness is overdetermined by the object world it reduces to perceptual qualities. Ballard's style can thus be aligned more closely with Graham Harman's reworking of Edmund Husserl's phenomenology as an object-oriented ontology in which objects exceed our apprehension of them and their qualities.[23] However, where Harman emphasizes the "withdrawn" (in the Heideggerian sense) nature of what he terms "real objects," Ballard, while recognizing this withdrawn or recalcitrant dimension of objects, foregrounds their impingement upon and violent intrusions into the space of the human.[24]

Ballard's aesthetic thus becomes organized around what Slavoj Žižek describes as various "answers of the Real."[25] Žižek posits such answers of the real as moments when the external world seems to correspond uncannily with our fantasies. Such moments regularly structure Ballard's fictions. In Ballard's version of the answer of the real, however, the uncanny occurrences usually do not fully correspond to the subject's fantasy. Like Vaughn missing Elizabeth Taylor's limousine by a few meters, Ballard's answers of the real seem to simultaneously answer and refuse to answer the subject's unconscious wishes, suggesting the way in which psychoanalysis itself, with its dismissal of the category of the "accident," is one more fantasy of control over the world of objects.

Vaughn's final accident is described as his "one true accident," and yet all the accidents in the novel carry a modicum of contingency and chance. Even as they are meticulously planned, they necessarily carry an element of randomness. For example, an accident staged by Vaughn to re-create a "multiple pile-up in which seven people had died on the North Circular

Road during the previous summer" turns into "a fiasco" that does not reproduce the accident in the slightest (85, 86). In this sense, Ballard's version of the answer of the real suggests that a lack of conformity of the material world to our fantasmatic constructions of it is at the uncanny heart of such encounters. His is a world organized around the subject's hysterical questioning and probing of a material world that refuses to provide the expected answers. The answer of the real is thus uncanny but uncanny in a way that reverses the psychoanalytic formula that locates it in a trace of the familiar within the unfamiliar.[26] In Ballard's world, it is the presence of the unfamiliar or uncontrollable in the familiar and predictable that represents the most disturbing aspect of the uncanny. This estrangement in the heart of things is what lies, in turn, at the core of Ballard's posthumanist aesthetic.

This emphasis on the contingency and intransigence of the material is visible on almost any page of the novel. Take, for example, the novel's description of the photographs that Vaughn takes of different accidents. The object world dominates these pictures, in which, "at first glance, no recognizable human figures appeared," suggesting the way in which the human body is presented as one object among many (96). While the representation of Vaughn as a photographer initially suggests the control of the man behind the camera, Ballard's prose consistently emphasizes the lack of full control that the subject has in relationship to the world of objects. Here the photos are taken with an "unsteady hand from a moving car" (96). They are "crude" and "blurred" (96). And even as the passage goes on to suggest that Vaughn can take the photographs with more precision and care, whenever he is photographing car crashes (which represents the core of his obsession), his pictures are necessarily shaped by the contingency and randomness of the car crash itself. The automobiles as material objects are the fetishistic focus of the photos, just as they are of Ballard's narration. This preoccupation with the automobile as a fetishized object is underscored by Ballard's use of the language of pornography to talk about the photographs: the shots take the form of "crude frontal pictures" and "close-ups" of impacted radiator grilles (96).

The Late-Modernist Built Environment

If the object world dominates Ballard's prose, disrupting the human-centered quality of most fictional narration, it literally towers over the landscape described by the novel, dwarfing the novel's human protagonists.

This is an urban environment in which the large-scale planning ethos of late-modernist architecture fills the entire landscape:

> For the past week, after being brought home in a taxi from the hospital, I had been sitting in the same reclining chair on the veranda of our apartment, looking down through the anodized balcony rails at the unfamiliar neighborhood ten storeys below. On the first afternoon I had barely recognized the endless landscape of concrete and structural steel that extended from the motorways to the south of the airport, across its vast runways to the new apartment systems along Western Avenue. Our own apartment house at Drayton Park stood a mile to the north of the airport in a pleasant island of modern housing units, landscaped filling stations and supermarkets, shielded from the distant bulk of London by an access spur of the northern circular motorway which flowed past us on its elegant concrete pillars. I gazed down at this immense motion sculpture, whose traffic deck seemed almost higher than the balcony rail against which I leaned. I began to orient myself again round its reassuring bulk, its familiar perspectives of speed, purpose and direction . . . I realized that the human inhabitants of this technological landscape no longer provided its sharpest pointers, its keys to the borderzones of identity. (48–49)

This is a landscape that is made up of the stuff of Fordist construction: "concrete and structural steel." Similarly, it is all but purged of what usually goes under the heading of nature. The only indications of greenery are the "landscaped filling stations and supermarkets," and even in this context, it is unclear whether the landscaping in question actually involves plant life or merely pleasantly shaped concrete. Indeed, the latter meaning is quite probable since words we normally associate with an unmodified nature, such as "island" and indeed "landscape" itself, are used here to describe the built environment of what Adorno terms a "second nature."[27] This second nature takes shape as ecology in the passage, with different aspects of the built environment functioning synergistically to support each other: the highway "shields" the supermarket and "flows elegantly" past apartments and houses that are reconceived as modular "housing units," and even the "anodized" balcony rail supports our narrator, who is dwarfed by the vast panoply upon which he gazes. Indeed, human life is rendered resolutely secondary in this concrete panorama. The humans in the landscape are detectable in the hive of activity that turns the highway system and airport into an "immense motion sculpture," yet even in this context, the focus is on the animate metal machines rather than the people themselves that make their activity visible. As James himself summarizes, "I realized that the human inhabitants of this technological landscape no longer provided its sharpest pointers, its keys to the borderzones of identity" (49). And, indeed, the key to the identity of this landscape is the built environment itself.

It is with this presentation of the built environment as a second nature that Ballard's fiction breaks with the dominant, metafictional aesthetic of postmodernism. Unlike the postmodern conceptions of the malleability and textuality of the social world, this representation of the built environment as a "second nature" suggests the inability of the subjects who inhabit this landscape to change or transform it at will. As with Ballard's style, then, his emphasis on the late-modern built environment disrupts the fantasy of control that lurks behind postmodern conceptions of textuality and performativity and biopolitical fantasies of the complete socialization of both life and work.

The emphasis on the textual and the performative characterize an investment in what Brian McHale has famously described as the "ontological" dominant of postmodern fiction—the emphasis on "improvising a possible world."[28] Yet such a conception leaves the author himself as the fantasized controller of the fiction, as the maker of worlds and of subjects. This is the humanist fetish that lurks behind postmodernism's ostensible antihumanism. Ballard's aesthetic in turn emphasizes the resistance of the object (even, or especially, the human-made object) to fantasies of individual human control. Ballard instead suggests that the object world is the product of collective human endeavor and, even in the case of such endeavor, such an object world often resists full human control. In this sense, McHale's ontology reveals itself to be an epistemology that disavows its status as such—it is a "construction" of an imagined world by a controlling subject (as much as the authority of this subject is disavowed). Ballard's aesthetic, on the other hand, emphasizes the intransigence of the object and of the extant world to conform to the fantasies of any controlling subject. In this sense, his fiction can be perhaps more closely allied with ontology or what Graham Harman describes as ontography—the mapping of the "basic landmarks and fault lines in the universe of objects"—than the metafiction that McHale celebrates.[29]

The resistance of the object world to human control is detailed in the novel's obsessive depiction of the effect of automobile accidents on the human body. *Crash* underscores the centrality of the body to our era of biopolitical production. The body, in Ballard's text, is simultaneously subjectively inhabited (a body ego, in the Freudian sense)—a material organism that resists full subjective control, a locus of what Judith Butler terms "vulnerability," and an organism saturated by Lacanian enjoyment in relationship to the larger world of objects with which it intersects.[30] This relationship between bodies and the larger, contingent object world is captured in a number of key spaces within the built environment mapped by the novel. One of those key spaces is the hospital, which is situated as a kind of processing plant for the larger built environment that surrounds it: "In this quiet terrain of used-car marts, water reservoirs and remand centers, surrounded by the motorway systems that served London Airport, I began my recovery from the accident" (26). The hospital is an integral part of the larger ecology of buildings, institutions, and transportation hubs that Ballard depicts.

Within it, the body is marked in various ways by the object world that impinges upon it. These objects are in part located in the hospital itself. James describes the objects in the hospital as reshaping the flesh with which they come in contact: "As they adjusted the harness around my legs, I listened to the aircraft rising from the London airport. The geometry of this complex torture device seemed in some way related to the slopes and contours of these young women's bodies" (27). The novel details the reshaping of human potential and the human body that is one of the key indices of the shift that was just getting under way at this time from medicalization to biomedicalization.[31] Yet the forms of microsurgery and noninvasive drug treatments that are central to biomedicalization in its current form were largely absent as technologies from the early 1970s hospital depicted in the novel. Rather than the soft, cyborgian technologies that permeate the technological sublime of certain corridors of the postmodern imaginary as well as of the microsurgical imaginary of contemporary medicine, the harness in which James's body is inserted is described as impinging upon the body with the violence of a torture device.

In contrast to the soft technology celebrated by the postmodern sublime, this "hard" technology impinges upon the body, leaving marks of pain in its wake. It would be a mistake to read this impingement of the material as merely a function of the relatively clumsy medical technology of the 1970s. Instead, Ballard's novel highlights the "hard" violence that lurks beneath the rhetoric of soft technology and the forms of human/ cybernetic interface that are promised by it. In underscoring such violence, Ballard's text is not rejecting technology and the benefits it can bring; it is rather underscoring the violence that often is an integral part of technological advance in late-capitalist society. Violence manifests itself as much in the forms of exploitation that produce such technologies as it does in their impingements upon various vulnerable bodies.

While the objects that Ballard portrays as impinging upon the body are partially the product the hospital itself, they are foremost the disjecta of the accidents that occur with statistical regularity on the freeways that form the arteries of the concrete ecology depicted in the novel:

> During the next week this rainbow moved through a sequence of tone changes like the colour spectrum of automobile varnishes. As I looked down at myself I realized that the precise make and model-year of my car could have been reconstructed by an automobile engineer from the pattern in my wounds. The layout of the instrument panel, like the profile of the steering wheel bruised into my chest, was inset on my knees and shinbones. The impact of the second collision between my body and the interior compartment of the car was defined in these wounds, like the contours of a woman's body remembered in the responding pressure of one's own skin for a few hours after a sexual act. (28)

This description, like the description of the harness, emphasizes the impact of hard objects on soft bodies. Indeed, the description itself very much appears to be an extension of Ballard's poetics of the object—for the body is literally branded by the material impingement of the various components of the car itself. Branding, in this context, takes on the double sense that Lauren Berlant has given it: it is both a violent inscription on the body and a marking of a "precise make and model-year" of the car as commodity.[32]

The Vulnerable Body

It is, of course, commonplace in many theories of the postmodern that the body is one of the crucial loci of transformation and change in the biopolitical era. Whether one considers Donna Haraway's articulation of counterhegemonic posthuman embodiment in her figuration of the cyborg or Hardt and Negri's articulation contemporary forms of immanent production and connectivity as a "living social flesh," the body in late or biopolitical capitalism is theorized as undergoing a thorough mutation— one in which it fuses in complex ways with technology.[33] While Ballard also emphasizes the transformations of the body in this era, the intersection between the body and the techno-economic is represented as more menacing and less seamless. In contrast to the performative and endlessly malleable bodies of postmodern theory, Ballard's bodies are distinctly vulnerable and marked by material limitations, even as they work to adapt to the technologies with which they intersect. Similarly, the interface between the technological and the bodily is simultaneously more contingent, more ill fitting, and more violent than is imagined through Haraway's cyborgs or Hardt and Negri's laborers.

It is tempting but much too easy to read Ballard's representation of the violent intersections of flesh and machine as merely a product of the technological limitations of the time in which he is writing. Such a reading would suggest that the intersections of vulnerable bodies with late-modernist hard technology are a product of the novel being written during the infancy of the technological revolution that would be initiated by the microchip, microsurgery, and other forms of computer-based microtechnology. Such a reading would argue that while Ballard's novel looks back toward the large-scale macrotechnologies of the Fordist era, it would take cyberpunk and the postmodern theorists of contemporary embodiment to fully explore the new interfaces created by the microtechnological revolution. However, such a reading overlooks the ways in which Ballard's novel actively resists the movement toward the microtechnological, the virtual, and the immaterial in its emphasis on the intersections of Fordist technology with both the real and imaginary dimensions of the bodies it depicts. It is not merely the body ego or the imaginary body that is transformed in these intersections but also the real body—the material aspects of the body that refuse the normativizing codings and technologies of medical intervention and egoic construction.

This emphasis on the violence of Fordist technology presents the earlier instances of the intersections of the body with macrotechnology as a moment of accumulation by dispossession (here dispossession of the body itself in its always historically uneven legal status as personal property) in the emergence of biopolitical capitalism: before the late-capitalist subject became fully acclimatized to these new intersections of technology and the body, the violence of this interface was more marked. It thus suggests the forms of violence that contemporary fantasies of the seamless interface of bodies and technologies seeks to disavow. Such violence resides not only in the initial moments of accumulation by dispossession but also in the increased invasiveness (and increased effectiveness) of microtechnologies as well as the continuing forms of industrial production that make such technologies possible. While this space of production is not directly represented in Ballard's novel, it is everywhere indirectly conjured by the built environment itself. It is also indirectly captured in the description of the branding of James's body.

The violence of the intersection between technology and bodies is perhaps most memorably captured in the novel's fetishistic representation of Gabrielle, a social worker whose body has been violently reshaped by an accident: "On her legs were traces of what seemed to be gas bacillus scars, faint circular depressions on the kneecaps. She noticed me staring at the scars, but made no effort to close her legs. On the sofa beside her was a chromium metal cane. As she moved I saw that the instep of each leg was held in a steel clamp of a surgical support. From the over-rigid posture of her waist I guessed that she was also wearing a back-brace of some kind" (94).

Far from Haraway's vision of an affirmative fusion of technology and the body, Gabrielle's body is violently transformed and constrained by her accident—an encounter that leaves her dependent upon the very forms of steel-based, hard technology that produced her wounds in the first place. In this sense, the car accident and the condition of technological dependency in which it leaves Gabrielle become a metaphor for the forms of accumulation by dispossession represented by Ballard in the novel. Her scarred and reformed body becomes a representation of the violence produced by the technologic-economic advances of biopolitical capitalism, suggesting what Mark Seltzer has described as the statistical casualties that accompany the advent of any new technology and become increasingly measured and predictable within the panoptic calculus of biopolitics.[34] Gabrielle's body becomes a figuration of the violence inflicted on bodies within biopolitical capitalism, whether this violence is an "accidental" yet statistically predictable product of consumption gone awry or whether it is an assumed cost of production, as with all the bodies painfully reshaped and "used up" by the production process itself. In both cases, the resistance and materiality of such bodies become the abjected real to the symbolic of biopolitical capitalism—a symbolic framework that wants to imagine our fusion with various prostheses as seamless and empowering. The text's description of Gabrielle's "gas bacillus" scars, with its play on gas as automobile fuel, suggests the intermingling of mechanical and biotechnological forms of violence. The technology of the automobile has literally penetrated her skin in the form of bacteria, leaving her flesh scarred and transformed.

Ballard's representation of Gabrielle is part the novel's erotic economy, which makes explicit the forms of obscene enjoyment in maimed and mutilated bodies that shape the fetishistic underside of the rhetoric of tragedy that usually attaches to car accidents and other technological mishaps. While fetishistic, Ballard's depiction of this erotic economy also marks the material violence done to certain bodies in the name of capitalist production and the reproduction of everyday life. Abjected within the symbolic coordinates of everyday life, such disabled bodies are not marginalized within Ballard's text. Instead they are fetishistically constructed as a locus and object of alternate forms of desire within the novel. *Crash* suggests the way in which the intransigent materiality of bodies and of the late-modernist built environment shapes, sets limits on, and opens up possibilities for the workings of desire.

Material objects thus become what Bruno Latour describes as "actors" in Ballard's text—ones that can't be metaphorized effectively in terms of discourse or textuality.[35] They are not merely the "backdrop to human action."[36] Instead they are active entities that intersect with each other and with the active, material body, as James notes in his description of the changes that take place in Gabrielle, captured in a series of photographs:

> In the later photographs the bruises that were to mask her face
> began to appear, like the outlines of a second personality, a preview
> of the hidden faces of her psyche which would have emerged only
> in late middle age. . . . The first photographs of her lying in the
> crashed car showed a conventional young woman whose symmet-
> rical face and unstretched skin spelled out the whole economy of a
> cozy and passive life, of minor flirtations in the backs of cheap cars
> enjoyed without any sense of the real possibilities of her body. . . .
> This agreeable young woman, with her pleasant sexual dreams, had
> been reborn within the breaking contours of her crushed sports
> car. (97–99)

Here Gabrielle is "reborn" via the material impact of the car crash. Like the human-technological births at the center of *Demon Seed* and other 1970s science fiction films, Gabrielle emerges from the car crash with a new subjectivity as well as a newly reformed body in the dimension of the real—what Ballard describes as the "real possibilities" that are produced by this composite of flesh and metal, technology and biology, which emerged over and against the symbolic scripts of both the larger culture and Gabrielle herself before the crash. Thus Ballard's prose emphasizes the reshaping of contemporary subjectivity and embodiment by the object world of late capitalism. This violent transformation of her body via cars, as actors that exceed human control, literally produces an altered subjectivity in which her bruises bring forth a "second personality" and her body becomes violently opened to its "real possibilities."

The passage suggests the changed temporalities and spatialities produced by the advent of biopolitical capitalism: the mask of Gabrielle's bruised face, calling forth the "hidden faces of her psyche which would have emerged only in late middle age," and Gabrielle's body, with its new prostheses and newly formed flesh, are respatialized in ways both violent and intimate. Thus the intersection of subjectivity and technology, body and machine, produce a literal speedup of Gabrielle's psychical and bodily age. This speedup suggests the speedups produced in other locations within late capitalism—from speedups that regularly and violently punctuate the labor process in Fordist and post-Fordist assembly lines and prematurely aging bodies, to the speedup of everyday life and fashion cycles, in which consuming bodies become ever more quickly outmoded and outdated with each passing fad, leading, in turn, to the widespread growth of age-defying techniques such as plastic surgery and biomedical interventions (for those who can afford them) to prolong health. These are the "real possibilities" opened up by biopolitical intersections of the technological and the bodily—possibilities that are condensed in Ballard's description of the post–car crash Gabrielle.

Rerouted Desire

While sexual interactions still occur between people in Ballard's novel, it would be a mistake to describe the sexuality as intersubjective. Instead, the sexuality depicted by *Crash* is represented as primarily turning on the relationship of subjects to objects. The most prevalent fetishized objects of the novel are of course cars and car parts, especially as they are deformed and reshaped by auto accidents: fractured windshields, errant steering columns, and dislodged door pillars are the repeated stuff of desire in the novel. Similarly, even the representation of the relationship of subjects to other subjects is organized in terms of the self and other as objects and detailed largely in terms of part objects: nipples, vulva, perineums, penises, and anuses are some of the novel's talismanically repeated body parts, or as Ballard summarizes at one point, "rounded sections of bodies interacting in unfamiliar junctions" (80).

It is the intersections and fusions of these two kinds of objects— "human, and non-human" as Levi Bryant provocatively puts it—that organize the movement of desire in the novel.[37] The object-oriented sexuality is captured in yet another photograph of Gabrielle: "The posture of her hands on the steering wheel and accelerator treadle, the unhealthy fingers pointing back towards her breasts, were elements in some stylized masturbatory right. Her strong face with its unmatching planes seemed to mimic the deformed panels of the car, almost as if she consciously realized that these twisted instrument binnacles provided a readily accessible anthology of depraved acts, the keys to an alternative sexuality" (100).

These representations of the intersection of bodily part objects with automotive part objects are indeed the keys to the sexuality imagined by *Crash*. This sexuality takes shape around the equivalence established between both sets of objects, an equivalence regularly reinforced by Ballard's descriptions in which bodily terminology and automotive terminology echo one another: the "planes of Gabrielle's face" echoing the "deformed panels of the car." Such descriptions proliferate throughout *Crash*, indicating not only the humanization of the automotive, a humanization that is produced by the force of desire chronicled by the text but also the objectification and componentization of the human.

It is important to recognize the way in which the novel's representation of desire is mediated at various points by the representational medium of the photograph. If Vaughn's book of photographs, as a perverse echo of the advertising campaign on which James works, can be read as a synecdochic figuration of the larger postmodern image culture within and against which the novel is written, then it is important to note that the "depraved acts" depicted in this book (and in Ballard's novel itself as a similarly depraved "anthology") are directly linked to image culture and the forms of visual addiction it underwrites. Yet even as the novel chronicles the depravity of these acts, marking the violence of the emerging biopolitical regime it depicts, I also want to take seriously its emphasis on the "alternate sexuality" imagined in this scene and other scenes like it, for it is within the context of this alternate sexuality that the novel's critique emerges most fully.

In order to fully apprehend this critique, it's necessary to understand the historical and fantasmatic dimensions of the form of fetishism depicted by the novel. A construction of human body parts as objects has always been central to psychoanalytic accounts of fetishism. Indeed, the Freudian fetish crucially turns on the relationship of a subject to an object. In Freud's classic account of fetishism, the fetish, as an object that is simultaneously fantasmatic and material, functions to ward off the unpleasant apprehension of a larger "truth" (i.e., the supposed "truth" of woman's castration).[38] This "warding off" takes the form of a disavowal rather than complete repression. Thus Žižek has read the Freudian account of fetishism as a the basis for a broader account of "ideological fantasy," in which the subject maintains her fantasized investment in the fetishized object in spite of knowledge to the contrary, leading to the classic statement of fetishistic disavowal, "I know very well, but nevertheless."[39] It is in this sense, as Žižek has pointed out, that Marx's account of commodity fetishism can be read as congruent with Freudian fetishism: the relation between things that defines commodity fetishism wards off the apprehension of the larger (and, for the capitalist subject, disturbing) truth of the social relationships among people that have produced these goods. The capitalist subject knows very well that commodities are really a product of exploited social labor, but nevertheless she experiences such commodities as entirely a product of an exchange between things (money, other goods, commodified labor, etc.). Both the Marxian and Freudian fetish, then, revolve around the substitution of objects for subjects: the subject's relationship to a fantasmatically weighted object wards off his recognition of a specifically intersubjective relationship. In both accounts, fetishism, as Žižek avows, functions as a form of ideology—as a warding off of a larger truth.

However, I want to suggest the opposite is the case in the forms of fetishism Ballard depicts in *Crash*; the fetishism of objects depicted in the novel works as a form of demystification rather than as a further mystification. In order to understand how this can be the case, it is important to recall my discussion of the shift that takes place in the structure of commodity fetishism itself in post-Fordism to produce the emergence of avatar fetishism. If in avatar fetishism the object has itself become degraded material—an adjunct to the generation of the avatar itself (as an immaterial substitution for an awareness of embodied subjectivity)—then the focus on objects in psychoanalytic fetishism can be seen as demystifying and insisting on a recognition of the material underpinnings of a society increasingly invested in the end products of what Hardt and Negri term immaterial production. Or, to put it another way, if the leading sectors of the capitalist world economy are indeed organized around immaterial production, then this ideological investment in the immaterial produces as its flipside what Bill Brown terms a material unconscious. It is with this material unconscious and the forms of object-oriented desire that structure it that the novel invites us to recognize, situating ourselves as objects among other objects in Levi Bryant's terms. This is not to say that we are not also subjects but that our subjectivity is an embodied one that is in a dynamic and often dependent relationship to organic and inorganic material actants. To do otherwise is to remain in the thrall of avatar fetishism.

It is not merely the Marxian conception of the fetish that changes with the changing historical and political-economic conditions of everyday life in the overdeveloped world but the psychoanalytic fetish, as well. In the sense, we can trace the shift from the Freudian fetish, to object relations, to the Lacanian reconception of the fetish as the *objet petit a* as an increasing emphasis on the importance of understanding the role of fantasmatic and material objects in the constitution of subjectivity. We can see this development of psychoanalysis as a product of the continuous advance of reification that Georg Lukács saw as part and parcel of the logic of Taylorism that becomes ever more developed within the logic of Fordism. What is central in Fordist reification is its emphasis on the subject's determination by various objects or in, as Kevin Floyd puts it, objectified states.[40] As such, while such an emphasis on the objective determinants of subjective states can, on one level, function as a form of ideology (as in classical commodity fetishism), on another level, it functions to demystify the emphasis on subjective self-determination that runs throughout capitalist ideology and becomes particularly marked in the era of avatar fetishism, with its desire to transcend the material. The increasing turn toward the object in midcentury psychoanalysis can be read partially as an ideological product of the further objectification and reification of everyday life produced by high Fordism, but it can also be read as continuing the anti-idealist force of psychoanalysis. The demystificatory

power of this psychoanalytic turn toward the object, then, becomes particularly pronounced when deployed to engage subjectivity in the era of
immaterial production.

In charting the objectal turn in psychoanalysis, it is important to attend
to the status of the object itself in psychoanalytic theory—for the psychoanalytic object is not merely or even necessarily material in a physical
sense. It is foremost a fantasmatic object that can be projected upon or
derived from material objects, but these objects only take on their significance for the subject through the logic of fantasy. In Lacan's formulation
of the *objet petit a*, his revisionary rewriting of both the Freudian fetish
and the Kleinian object, this paradoxical status of the psychoanalytic
object—simultaneously material and immaterial—is codified. This Lacanian reformulation resists the scientific reification of both the subject and
the object in psychoanalytic doxa. It decenters the subject by asserting its
determination by an eccentric object of desire; it similarly decenters any
fixation of this object by suggesting that the object itself only takes on its
status as fetish by the movement of fantasy as it intersects with the contingent world of objects. Lacan's refusal of the reification of both the subject
and the object (even as he draws upon the forms of knowledge that Floyd
associates with the emergence of such a reification) forces the interpreter
to reconstruct the symbolic, imaginary, and real (for the *objet a* is one of
the oblique indexes of the real) determinants of the moment of fetishism
and the logic of substitution upon which it turns. In this sense, while it
points to the importance of the object and the world of objects (as they
are saturated with fantasy and desire) in attending to late-capitalist subjectivity, Lacan's formulation echoes Marx in asserting the need to finally
work to reconstruct the larger social context out of which such a relationship between subject and object is constructed.

Queer Ballard

It is Ballard's representation of a material unconscious that forms the core
of the political critique enacted by the novel. This critique can be described
as queer but a queerness that is less about specific identities and bodies and
more about what Sarah Ahmed describes as a "queer phenomenology."[41]
Such a phenomenology functions as "a disorientation device"—literally a
turning away from the dominant and learning to see objects and subjects
differently.[42] This phenomenology is thus a perversion in the etymological

sense: literally a turning away from the straight or conventional. In working to explore an unconscious that remains a repressed or disavowed part of everyday life in the emerging era of post-Fordism, Ballard's novel turns away from either conventional depictions of intersubjective desire or metafictional versions of the self and instead works to desublimate the "invisible eroticisms" that remain latent in the late-modernist built environment. This desublimation is the queer phenomenological work performed by the novel, revealing the fantasmatic investments and entanglements in the late-modernist built environment precisely as cultural desires are being rerouted toward the malleable, biopolitical, and immaterial in the overdeveloped world.

The final sex scene between James and Vaughan needs to be understood (as do all the other sex scenes in the novel) in relationship to this queer reorientation and the landscape of automotive and sexual part objects that the novel depicts. While this scene depicts the novel's one explicitly realized act of homosexual sex (and it is important to recognize the refreshing absence of homophobia in this straight-identified author), it would be a mistake to read the depiction of anal sex between men as what is most queer about the scene. I want to suggest that this scene, like the novel's other sex scenes, can instead be read as staging a form of sexuality that is queerly oriented toward objects and bodies as they are reshaped both as and by objects.

What is emphasized in this scene is Vaughan's body as it has been altered by various car crashes and as it becomes a soft and vulnerable extension of the hard technology of the automobile and the highway:

> Yet Vaughan, for all his harshness, was a wholly benevolent partner, the eye of this illumination of the landscape around us. Taking his hand I pressed his palm against the medallion of the horn boss, an aluminized emblem which had always irritated me. I felt the indentation in his white skin, remembering the triton-shaped bruise in the palm of the dead Remington as he lay across my bonnet . . . remembering the exciting crevices and sulci of Gabrielle's crippled body. One by one, I moved Vaughan's hand across the glowing dials of the instrument panel, pressing his fingers against the sharp toggles, the projecting lances of the direction indicator and gear shift.

At last I let his hand rest on my penis, reassured by its firm pres-
sure on my testicles. I turned towards Vaughan, floating with him
on the warm amnion of illuminated air, encouraged by the stylized
morphology of the automobile's interior, by the hundreds of radi-
ant gondolas soaring along the motorway above our heads. . . .
I hesitated at finding myself wrestling with this ugly golden creature, made beautiful by its scars and wounds. I moved my mouth
across the scars on his lips, feeling with my tongue for those familiar
elements of long-vanished dashboards and windshields. (200–201)

I quote this scene at length not only because it demonstrates the queer
reorientation enacted by the novel and recapitulates, in one climatic (so
to speak) moment, all the differing obsessions charted by Ballard's novel
but also because it represents the moment in the novel that points toward
an escape from the dystopian landscape it depicts. The queerness of
this passage is apparent everywhere: normative midcentury sexuality is
replaced by a fetishistic sexuality that intermixes automotive objects, built
landscapes, and body parts. Moreover, the bodies and body parts that
are fetishized are nonnormative as well: scarred lips, crippled limbs, and
bruised palms.

The novel thus depicts a queer sexuality, but queer in a sense that goes
beyond even the subversion of the binaries of male and female, hetero
and homo, as important as such subversions are. Instead what is subvert-
ed is the conventional separation of the animate and the inanimate, the
human and the inhuman, human part objects and nonhuman car parts,
and vulnerable bodies and hard technologies. Yet this subversion of the
distinction between the two does not imply a seamless fusion. On the
contrary, Ballard emphasizes the damage, both accidental and structural, that accrues in bodies and inanimate objects themselves within this
regime. Indeed, Vaughan's car-ravaged chest is described as covered by
what seem like the "leaking scars of an unsuccessful transsexual surgery"
(201). As this description suggests, there is a sexual transformation here—
one in which the stubborn materiality of the body, and of the object world
more generally, resists the discursive and biopolitical scripts that are written for them. The scene thus emphasizes the contingency and resistance of
the real (here figured as resistant or uncoded materiality) to the symbolic
scripts written by culture.

For all the violence detailed by the previous scene, it also represents the text's lone hopeful or redemptive moment. A language of redemption or benediction seems to run through the scene, from the "illuminated landscape," in which the scene takes place to repeated descriptions of Vaughan's "benevolence" and "beauty," to the tender way in which much of the sex scene unfolds. Indeed, despite the early description of James and Vaughan as wrestling, there is a care and gentleness to this scene that contrasts starkly with many of the other sex scenes in the novel. While on one level we may want to comment on the misogyny that informs Ballard's other more violent depictions of sex (which almost inevitably take place between men and women, who are itemized as female body parts), on another level, the gentleness of aspects of this scene suggests that it is one of those moments in Ballard's oeuvre that Andrzej Gasiorek describes as pointing to a transformational grammar or aesthetic—a way out of the otherwise nihilistic worlds depicted in his novels.[43]

There is, of course, only a hint of such a transformation in Ballard's resolutely negative vision. Yet this hint should not be overlooked. The sex between James and Vaughn puts James in touch with a history of violence—a history encoded on Vaughn's body. In kissing Vaughn, he literally tastes and senses the "elements of long-vanished dashboards and windshields." Thus the body can be read as encoded with a history of violence that the symbolic of late capitalism wishes to cover over. It is striking in this regard that the scene begins with James pressing Vaughan's hand on "the medallion of the horn boss," which, one can guess, would indicate the manufacturer of the car. We move at the beginning of the scene from the commodity logo, with its implication of the forms of amnesia instituted by the commodity form itself, to the invocation of memory as inscribed on and enmeshed in bodies. It is this movement from a symbolic produced by commodity forms and dematerialization (one predicated on forgetting) to a process of attending to the history and materiality of bodies and the built environment that they occupy. This movement is perhaps best described as a process of re-membering as much as reorienting both a recalling of the history attaching to the material stuff of the world and an attention to the various "members" or objects that are the stuff of psychoanalytic fetishism—an attention that finally links these part objects to the subjectivities, bodies, forms of affect, and histories to which they belong.

Re-membering Bodies and Objects

While it is only briefly suggested in the sex scene between James and Vaughn, this process of "re-membering" is central to the political vision that runs quietly yet insistently throughout this infamously amoral and resolutely negative novel. Much of the politics of Ballard's novel can indeed be located in its negativity and refusal to affirm the world conjured by post-Fordism's dematerializing symbolic. It instead insists on the objects and bodies that resist, refuse, or (often accidentally) transgress that symbolic. It is this negativity itself that calls attention to the material unconscious that subtends this symbolic, emphasizing the late-modernist built environment and the vulnerable and damaged bodies that inhabit it. Such bodies, in turn, by giving the lie to the idea of endless malleability, performativity, and renewability and instead calling attention to the simultaneously structural and contingent violence of late capitalism, become indices of the resistantly material underpinnings and the forgotten material histories that form the flipside to a culture increasingly invested in avatar fetishism.

Paradoxically, it is the logic of the psychoanalytic fetish itself that allows Ballard's novel to challenge this structure of avatar fetishism, for it is the psychoanalytic fetish, particularly in its midcentury rearticulation via Melanie Klein and Jacques Lacan, that insists on the fantasmatic importance of objects that bear a partial relationship to larger structures of desire and meaning. Yet it is only through a positive hermeneutic that reattaches such objects to their larger social meanings that the work of demystification is completed. While Ballard hints at such a positive hermeneutic in the sex scene between James and Vaughan, it remains less than fully imagined in his novel. Yet his insistence on the object world and on the damaged, reshaped, and vulnerable bodies that populate the novel's dystopian landscape finally points toward a politics of tarrying with and attending to the material, particularly as the latter sets limits on post-Fordist fantasies of dematerialization and flexibility. In the next two chapters, we turn to texts that elaborate such a politics.

CHAPTER 4

Disinterring the Real

Embodiment, AIDS, and Biomedicalization in Dodie Bellamy's *The Letters of Mina Harker*

Writing can and should offer an emotional engagement with materiality. That engagement can be highly mediated or direct, but that engagement begins a politics, a morality of writing.

—Dodie Bellamy, "Body Language"

The Restive Corpse of Postmodernism

So postmodernism is no more.[1] We critics and theorist of contemporary culture gather around the open grave to say its last rights and perhaps to eulogize it (while we whisper our ambivalences about it to the mourners standing next to us), but mostly we throw dirt on the casket to make sure it stays buried. This dirt has taken many forms recently, from pronouncements that we have now entered into an era with a new cultural dominant, to arguments for a post-postmodern set of aesthetic practices in literary and cultural production, to assertions that postmodernism never really existed in the first place.[2]

Yet even as we turn decisively away from the grave toward the cemetery gates to exit the past and enter the promise of a world that is genuinely new, we hear the scratch of broken fingernails, the groan of the coffin lid being lifted . . . and we turn to confront the undead body of postmodernism, rising from the grave once more, the body beneath the grave clothes writhing with uncanny vitality.

The corpse of postmodernism refuses to stay buried, vampirically returning to haunt contemporary culture, thwarting our attempts to give ourselves fully to what Lee Edelman has described as the conscriptive political discourse of "futurity."[3] Nowhere is this haunting more apparent than in the claim that we are in the era of post-postmodernism, for if we are really in a new era (one not organized around the recursive postmodern logic of the "post-"), then surely it cannot be termed post-postmodern. Similarly, if there truly is a new set of aesthetic practices that have emerged as dominant, these too will have to have a less-tentative name than post-postmodernism. Indeed, the very proliferation of the concept of postmodernism in the work that attempts to bury it suggests the undead nature of this corpse. The desire for a genuinely new set of cultural and aesthetic practices is laudable. Indeed, one of the central premises of this book is the value of moving beyond theoretical postmodernism to engage those forms of theory grouped under the rubric of the material turn.

Yet the genuinely new would not want so much to bury the past as it would desire to engage the past and its undead qualities, in order to see what it could draw upon as well as what it needs to reject in crafting the syntax of the present. Rather than turning away or refusing to look behind us, we should perhaps turn sideways and, in the words of Slavoj Žižek, look at postmodernism awry,[4] for what we may find there may look very different from the canonical figure we expect. Instead, we may find that the subject of postmodernism has transformed in undeath and that the features that were so prominent in life have now receded or taken on less importance, while other originally obscured characteristics seem now to emerge, producing an uncanny visage. Rather than warding off this undead life in the name of futurity, we should perhaps turn to welcome this undead figure—for it is perhaps only by incorporating the dead, discarded, and insistently material that we can find the way forward.

The politics of attending to the undead, the abjected, and the material are central to Dodie Bellamy's 1998 experimental memoir/novel, *The Letters of Mina Harker*. As the title suggests, the novel/memoir is a rewriting of some of the central motifs of Bram Stoker's epistolary novel, *Dracula*.[5] Borrowing *Dracula*'s epistolary form, Bellamy's text willfully combines the autobiographical, the fictional, and the theoretical in order to explore issues of embodiment, sexuality, and death as they are figured both within and against the emergence of biomedicalization, neoliberalism, and the thanatopolitical dimensions of the AIDS epidemic, which, as Sarah Brophy puts it, holds "out the prospect of a position of safety and immunity to some, while tending to connect infection with moral corruption, deviance, and doom."[6] The AIDS crisis thus produced a specifically eroticized and biomedicalized version of what Roberto Esposito describes as "thanatopolitics," in which certain lives are rendered disposable or sacrificial in the name of immunizing the lives of those who are deemed morally and biologically hygienic.[7] The narrative counters this thanatopolitics on an imaginative level by embracing and affirming those who are marked for death by the larger culture and finally staging an erotic encounter with death itself. It suggests that it is only by turning to embrace the undead figure of the person with AIDS and finally by accepting and imaginatively incorporating the materiality of death itself that a political culture can be imagined that does not reproduce the logic of thanatopolitics. The way beyond thanatopolitics, the novel suggests, is paradoxically by tarrying with death rather than warding it off.

Focalized through the shifting point of view of its protagonist, Mina/Dodie, the narrative draws on popular cultural representations of vampirism in the horror and gothic genres, including but not limited to *Dracula* and its various film adaptations, in order to explore the relationship between popular narratives of sexual contagion, the material effects of the AIDS epidemic in San Francisco in the 1980s and 1990s, and the embodied experience of women and gay men marginalized by their relationship to a biopolitical and finally thanatopolitical discourse about sexual hygiene. Bellamy's narrative thus engages and reworks the conventional language of horror as a genre in order to reveal the forms of materiality, embodiment, desire, and violence that it both displaces and symptomatically reveals.[8] While the vampire genre may seem overworked in our post–Anne Rice and post-*Twilight* present, Bellamy uses the popular figure of the vampire precisely for its popularity. It allows her more theoretical and experimental concerns to be fused with a set of meanings that are inherent in the conscious and unconscious figurations of the vampire as a totemic figure in popular culture. Conversely, she also volatilizes this popular material by transmuting it via a prose that is at once experimental and fiercely materialist.

With its intertextual relationship to *Dracula*, it's metafictional self-consciousness, and its deconstruction of the lines between fiction and nonfiction, the popular and the experimental, and theory and literature, Bellamy's text seems, at first glance, to be exemplary of the metafictional postmodern aesthetic.[9] Yet the novel also breaks with this dominant aesthetic in crucial ways, proffering instead an alternate aesthetic organized around attending to the materiality of the body and other forms of abjected materiality that make up the flip side to the sublime promises of neoliberal commodity culture and the forms of biopolitics that accompany it. As such, Bellamy's novel can be allied with the countertradition of late-capitalist literature of materiality that we have explored throughout *Insistence of the Material*. Thus her novel may present to us a way forward for thinking about contemporary literature, but like the vampires she thematizes, this way forward takes a detour through what has already existed, reanimating the dead flesh of postmodernism in order to emphasize its more neglected yet undead materialist features. By reworking this counterpractice for the AIDS era, Bellamy crafts a vibrantly undead aesthetic.

Bellamy is one of a group of writers active in San Francisco in the last thirty years whose work has been described under the rubric of "new narrative." New narrative writing represents a return to narrative but a return that is informed by all the ways in which the category itself has been problematized by the work of poststructuralist theory as well as experimental fiction and poetry in the postmodern era.[10] New narrative writers such as Robert Glück, Kevin Killian, Bruce Boone, Sam D'Allesandro, and Bellamy herself both employ the descriptive, and indeed conscriptive, power of narrative to organize thought, imagination, and experience and attempt to complicate or subvert this power by continuously disrupting the naturalizing effects it conventionally produces. One way in which they achieve this disruption is by writing liminal narratives. Their narratives continuously defy genre expectations, gleefully combining the fictional, autobiographical, theoretical, poetic, novelistic, academic, and popular in order to produce texts that privilege instability. The new narrative return to narrative, then, attempts to maintain the critical force of deconstruction, particularly as it was actualized in the "Language" poetry of the 1970s and 1980s, while also moving beyond its hermetic negativity to reconnect language, however problematically, with the world.

Thus the writings of new narrative authors represent a form of contemporary writing that moves beyond (even as they draw on) the exclusively textual or linguistic preoccupations of much poststructuralist or postmodern theory to engage with the material underpinnings of everyday life, with particular emphasis on the intransigent materialities of the body. In contrast to Brian McHale's famous account of the ontological playfulness of postmodern metafiction that produces a plurality of possible worlds, new narrative fiction is engaged instead with ontological questions about our existence in a (singular) material world, even as it recognizes the epistemological limits of such queries. Its perspective on materiality can thus be aligned with what Graham Harman and Ian Bogost call "ontography"—"a descriptive alternative" to otology that abjures final claims to full knowledge of the material but rather maps materiality's presence, alterity, and insistence.[11]

The practice of late-capitalist literature of materiality as an ontographical aesthetic engages precisely the forms of materiality that are obscured by metafictional forms of postmodernism: the materiality of the body, the materiality of the object world, and the continuing materiality of key sectors of production itself. To the degree that the persistence of the material is a crucial (or crucially obscured) dimension of social life in the biopolitical era, this aesthetic practice represents an undead aesthetic for literature in the present.

Bellamy's novel thus insists on the recognition of the material and biological underpinnings of everyday life that continue to haunt our dreams of immaterial production and biopolitical control. Such material and biological underpinnings, *The Letters of Mina Harker* suggests, are the Lacanian real of late-capitalist life—a real that is disavowed with particular force in the era of the AIDS epidemic, in which the biological and the material are regularly conflated with death.

Biomedicalization, Thanatopolitics, and a Politics of the Real

As the epigraph at the beginning of the chapter suggests, Bellamy is particularly interested in articulating a politics and ethics of materiality in her writing. This political and ethical commitment manifests itself in *Letters* as a writing practice that works to attend to and ally itself with all those who have been marked for death in the thanatopolitical imaginary produced by the AIDS crisis in the United States and around the globe. This thanatopolitical imaginary is structured around the divide between those who are seen as deserving medical treatment and social investment (and thus are defined as having a right to subjectivity that transcends their embodiment) and those who are reduced to, in Agamben's terms, bare life, or life consigned to death.[12] The thanatopolitical imaginary emerges alongside what Adele Clark et al. have termed the biomedicalization of the U.S. health industry.[13] Indeed, specific thanatopolitics charted by Bellamy's novel can be likened to biomedicalization's underside: the abject product of its marriage of neoliberalism and biopolitics.

Clarke et al. define biomedicalization as a large-scale transformation of medical practices, industries, and discourses in the United States that has occurred over the last thirty years. They contrast it with the processes of medicalization that occurred roughly in the period between 1940 and 1990. The two processes should of course be considered partially overlapping and interpenetrating rather than absolute and discrete, with the decade of the 1980s, not uncoincidentally the decade that saw the emergence of the AIDS epidemic, as a crucial period of transition. In contrast to medicalization, which was organized around a paradigm of illness and the responsibility of health-care providers to treat it, biomedicalization is organized around a paradigm of the maximization of health and wellness, which is accompanied by the partial privatization and increasing commodification of health. It is also accompanied by an individualizing discourse founded on the notion of "human capital" in neoliberalism, in which "chronic illnesses are becoming individual moral responsibilities to be fulfilled through improved access to knowledge, self-surveillance, prevention, risk assessment, the treatment of risk, and the consumption of the appropriate self-help and biomedical goods and services."[14]

Clarke et al. chart the intersections of neoliberalism, biopolitics, and the emergence of biomedicalization; indeed the latter can be seen as one of the foremost expressions of neoliberal biopolitics in the context of the United States and increasingly around the globe. What remains less explored is the way in which the emergence of the AIDS epidemic in the United States also shaped the discourses and practices of biomedicalization that emerged alongside of it—both adding to and enabling the discourse of moral and sexual hygiene that made distinctions between those who deserved health and care and those who, by their taboo and "unhygienic" practices, could be left to die. Thus biomedicalization in the United States as it confronted AIDS was not only a practice of Foucauldian biopolitics, creating normativizing discourses that managed public health and directly shaped subjectivity, but also, above all, a form of what Roberto Esposito describes as thanatopolitics, in which certain populations are abjected, constructed as an unhygienic threat, and marked for death in the name of immunizing and maximizing the health of those populations that are deemed worthy of protection.

It is this history of the thanatopolitics as it intertwines with the AIDS epidemic and the inequalities produced by biomedicalization and neoliberalism that still shapes much of the fantasmatic construction of AIDS in the privileged corridors, medical centers, and condos of the global North and that hinders the response to it as a global epidemic. It is also this thanatopolitical history that shapes Bellamy's engagement with the materiality of the body and especially the AIDS ravaged body. In an echo of the thematics of avatar fetishism, for those on the privileged side of Esposito's immunary divide (those for whom a fantasy of disembodiment is already a form of privilege), AIDS is something more imagined than material. For those on the other side, on the side of the politics and economics of death (those who have been rendered as the walking dead or undead), it is something much more material.

Bellamy's novel thus enacts its politics and ethics of materiality in order to imagine a queer alliance of all those whose embodiment has been rendered all too material by the selective response to the AIDS crisis under biomedicalization. Thus her narrative is invested in attending to what can be described in Lacanian terms as the *real* of the body, of death, and of "the world of real, inanimate, nonhuman objects," in a moral, hygienic, and political-economic landscape that wants to imagine itself as transcending the material.[15]

The Lacanian real indicates all that is excluded from the domain of the symbolic. As that which is excluded from full signification in the symbolic, it can be used, as Lacan does in *Seminars VII* and *XI*, to talk about death, abjection, and trauma as sites where language fails.[16] Bellamy's narrative tarries with the real in order to articulate an explicitly feminist and queer politics of materiality and embodiment—one that affirms rather than recoils from aspects existence marked as abject, disruptive, and all too material. This politics allows her to challenge the thanatopolitical construction of certain bodies as marked for death within the AIDS crisis. It also allows her to challenge the emphasis on discursive construction more generally that we have inherited from the cultural turn. Indeed, Bellamy's text can be seen as proffering a distinctive theory of material embodiment that provides an important corrective to the more disembodying tendencies of poststructuralist derived theories of gender. For Bellamy, the body is both bound up with cultural signification (particularly the ubiquitous significations of popular culture in late capitalism) and irreducibly material.

The Vampiric Body

In order to fully understand Bellamy's theorization of embodiment and the challenge it represents to conventional poststructuralist theories of gender and sexuality, we need to unpack her operative metaphor of the vampire. The vampire for Bellamy represents a hybrid figuration that emphasizes the resistantly material as much as the discursively malleable. As Nina Auerbach and Laurence Rickels have differently argued, the vampire is a liminal creature, stalking the borderlands between life and death, technology and atavism, the biological and the cultural, and the textual and the material.[17] Bellamy's vampires occupy just such a borderland. If poststructuralist accounts of embodiment, such as Haraway's cyborg, Butler's performative subject, and even Braidotti's woman, have emphasized the malleable, technologized, textual, life-in-death side of these binaries, Bellamy's vampires lean toward the opposite poles: toward the biological, atavistic, intransigently material, and alien yet intimate presence of death in life.[18] To employ another poststructuralist formulation of being that draws upon the iconography of the gothic, if Derrida coins the term *hauntology* to describe the spectral dimensions of being, then Bellamy's vampires are the more substantial and necessarily bloodier undead cousins to Derrida's revenants.[19] They represent, in other words, a turn toward ontology and the ineluctability of material embodiment and the flesh of being. They are thus her metaphor for a more thoroughly materialist understanding of the gendered and sexual subject in the era of AIDS and biomedicalization.

Bellamy's vampires are not a return to the modern conceptions of embodiment marked by a strict separation of biology and culture, nor do they represent a complete break with the past. Instead, just as her metaphor of the vampire for contemporary embodiment is not itself distinct to the era of late capitalism but rather represents an adaptation of a modern and even premodern mythological figure to the specific exigencies of the present, her figuration of the contemporary body is both open to the hybrid and malleable possibilities we associate with the conventional postmodern subject and haunted by the material and biological limits that are more regularly associated with modernist figurations of the body. The body, for Bellamy, is marked by the distinct temporality of the vampire. The vampire is not only a mercurial figure, adaptable to the mythological and historical demands of whatever present she finds herself within, but also a figure that is conventionally associated with a past that is out of joint with the present and with an undead future that terrifies as much as it entices, representing a return of the repressed of the bodily and of death, rather than their transcendence.

It is important to attend to the specific vampire Bellamy rewrites: Mina Harker. Stoker's Mina, in contrast to Dracula, is a creature of modern technology; as the fictional author of most of Stoker's text and as secretary to the other vampire hunters, she employs up-to-date, turn-of-the-twentieth-century technology such as the typewriter and shorthand.[20] Similarly, Mina's turn-of-the-twenty-first-century reincarnation in Bellamy's text is the semifictional author of her text and master of the computer, VCR, and connoisseur of cable television. David Buuck describes Bellamy's vampire thus: "Over the course of the letters (written to person(a)s living, dead, and 'invented'), Mina chronicles the events of her (and 'Dodie's') colorful life as a writer living in San Francisco, as well as the ongoing (and playful) 'tension' between the 'author' Mina Harker and the 'character' Dodie Bellamy, whose body Mina sometimes inhabits."[21] The vampire in Bellamy's figuration represents a form of embodiment in which the biological is bound up with the cultural and the technological. However, in contrast to conventional postmodern constructions of a textual subject, this intermixing of the biological with the cultural and technological presents biology as neither comfortably integrated with nor reducible to culture or technology. Bellamy's figuration of the vampire thus marks those aspects of corporeality and social existence that fall away from the symbolic of contemporary commodity culture and biomedical fantasies of bodily control and transcendence: death, the biological, the animal, and the material.

Embodied Prose

The Letters of Mina Harker attempts the paradoxical: to write the body. As Bellamy puts it in an interview that I conducted with her, "Language and the body are never going to cross."[22] Yet, on another level, all of Bellamy's work and *Letters* in particular attest to the ethical and political imperative of attempting to write the body. Indeed, she characterizes Mina as an attempt to write about bodily boundaries and their porousness:

> I was thinking [about] issues of boundaries. For female sexuality penetration can be ambivalent. But I was also thinking of all sorts of other boundaries—there's always "dangerous" microbes penetrating the skin. It becomes the question of bulimia as well. There is this desire to devour the whole culture and have that penetrate

you, but at the same time there is this horror of boundaries being violated, which is a central motif of the horror films from which I borrow. So it's also that feeling of being invaded and wanting to keep things out.[23]

The question then becomes, how are we to understand this paradoxical injunction to both write the body and recognize the impossibility of doing so?

One answer to the question is the specific form of contemporary writing practice Bellamy undertakes, juxtaposing the theoretical and the intimate, the abstract and (representations of) the insistently material, to produce a discomfort that is simultaneously stylistic and affective. This production of affective discomfort in the reader marks the ability of language to impinge on the body and shape its meanings. In this way, language and the body in Bellamy's narrative are presented not only as distinct and discontinuous at certain moments but, at others, as interpenetrating and overlapping. Bellamy's disruptive juxtaposition of the language of theory and the language of the body thus becomes a stylistic correlate for this relationship between language and the body.

This disruptive juxtaposition is evident, to take just one example, in a passage in which Mina is writing a letter to her former lover, Dion, while she mourns the loss of her current lover, Quincy:

> I'm sorry, Dion, to objectify you, your hands your cock your name *what's private, what's public* I CAN'T STOP MYSELF *is there anything out there that isn't sexual* I'm a prisoner of jouissance *and then you pressed your thigh against mine and I thought of pistons churning, my intestines were slippery longing in their formlessness to consume an unusual external and yes I have a cunt and yes it was involved in all of this, "Dion" I murmured my lips of cool copper beckoning* HELP ME TURN IT OFF *I bang my metaphorical fists against the door of meaning* tell Tiki to pay no attention, stretch out your arms and yawn *Oh, that's just Mina being Mina, poor thing trapped in the midst of her literary conventions.*[24]

This passage juxtaposes theoretical concepts such as *jouissance* and analytical concerns such as literary conventions and the distinction between the private and the public with vivid descriptions of bodily organs and sensations. Thus theory is not divorced from sensation and the body but juxtaposed with them in a way that disrupts the former's claims to transcendence and the latter's passivity. Instead, the theoretical is presented as intimately bound up with the bodily and vice versa. Thus the passage's invocation of the concept of *jouissance* is juxtaposed with a description of Mina/Dodie's intestines as "slippery with longing to consume an unusual external." This juxtaposition brings together the concept of *jouissance*, which in its Lacanian definition denotes a kind of ecstatic enjoyment that is often tinged with as much pain as pleasure and invokes the death drive as much as the pleasure principle, with a kind of intestinal eroticism that is linked to two different forms of nonnormative enjoyment: a cannibalistic desire to consume the other and an anal sexuality that is often connected in the homophobic imagination with submission to a sadistic other and, in the era of AIDS, explicitly with death. Moreover, the cannibalistic image also invokes, by association, bulimia as a kind of enjoyment (one that Bellamy has suffered from) that functions as, as she suggests in my interview with her, a kind of narrative logic as well.[25] Moreover, the next sentence links these forms of enjoyment to vaginal enjoyment—through the invocation of the abjected term "cunt"—as a form of enjoyment that is similarly denigrated in our phallic culture. Thus *jouissance* as a term is immediately juxtaposed with nonnormative versions of its bodily manifestations. In this way, the meaning of the theoretical is immediately resignified in relationship to the body as much as the bodily is articulated by theory.

This juxtaposition of the theoretical and the bodily indicates and indeed enacts the theory of embodiment articulated by Bellamy's text. Bellamy presents the body and language as interpenetrating and partially mutually determining yet also as crucially distinct and discontinuous. In this sense, her conception of the relationship of language to the body can be refigured in terms of Lacan's theorization of the relationship between the symbolic and the real, particularly in the latter's definition as forms of coded and uncoded materiality that exist in tension and disjunctive juxtaposition with the symbolic and with imaginary mappings of the body. Bellamy's vampires represent just such a conception of embodiment.

This writing practice, with its refusal of generic categories and it's willful mixing of the abstract and the obscene, can productively be described as queer, albeit a queerness that is not merely about discursive resignification but rather the intersections of the discursive and the intransigently as well as dynamically material. This queerness extends to Bellamy's engagement with popular culture. Like much of the writing typically grouped under the banner of postmodernism, *Letters*'s intertextual references are drawn as much from popular culture as they are from so-called high or literary culture. Yet Bellamy does not reference popular culture in order to parody it or use it as so much inert material for the practice of pastiche. Instead, she takes it seriously, yet pleasurably, as a repository of collective fantasies about gender, sexuality, embodiment, and death.

Popular culture is something that is cannibalized and consumed in the narrative as the narrator allows it to penetrate her body and psyche even as she resignifies and retools its meanings. This process of cannibalizing and resignifying can be likened to what a vampire does with the blood she drinks; it is not only consumed but transmuted into a substance that can animate that which is beyond the grave. She thus vampirizes the popular, marking its entry into the body, even as such a process of incorporation becomes the locus of the popular's transformation. Thus Bellamy's text engages popular culture critically, but it does so without the distancing employed by most experimental borrowings from the popular. Instead the intellectual activity of critique is intimately bound up with the bodily affect produced by popular culture—the engagement with one necessitating an engagement with the other.

Bellamy's emphasis on affective immediacy also informs her choice of the popular forms with which she engages. In contrast to metafictional writers who borrow from the detective and fairytale forms, which are easily abstracted into a kind of formal narrative logic that can thus be engaged from a metafictional distance, Bellamy's privileged forms are horror and the epistolary novel, both of which are associated with the production of affect and emotion. Moreover, both forms have been historically privileged sites for the representation of female and queer desire and embodiment: the epistolary novel in its eighteenth-century heyday was primarily associated with women writers and the representation of female subjects, as was horror's older sister, the gothic. Moreover, as Judith Halberstam point outs, both the gothic and horror are often privileged genres in representing queerness.[26]

It is from within this (re)figuration of what is marked as monstrous within popular narratives that Bellamy's engagement with the real takes on its specific political charge. As she puts it in one of the aphorisms that periodically punctuate *Letters* early on in the text, "The monstrous and the formless have as much right as anybody else" (10). While couched in the language of humor, the aphorism invokes in all seriousness the paradigm of inclusion and exclusion that shapes neoliberal economics and the thanatopolitical construction of people with AIDS, with the division between those who are inside the sphere of immunity and those who are outside and do not count as fully human. Thus the aphorism succinctly captures the political gambit of Bellamy's novel: to indeed produce a discourse that can begin to do justice to the formless and that which is marked by the society as monstrous. The resignification of the monstrous is also suggested by another possible meaning of the sentence: that the monstrous have "as much right" (in the sense of a legal conception of "right") as those who are defined as having rights. Finally, there is an epistemological resonance to this aphorism: the monstrous and the formless have as much right in the sense of being correct in terms of knowledge as does the subject situated in the symbolic. This latter meaning is in fact the political truth of psychoanalysis: that the truth of the subject lies elsewhere than in its conscious discourse; it instead exists at least as much in that which remains unarticulated and in thrall to the unconscious and the real. This aphorism, then, marks what is at stake in Bellamy's use of popular culture and, more generally, with her engagement with the real and the way in which these open out to her larger political-economic critique of neoliberalism, the biomedical shaping of gendered and sexual norms, and the meaning of the AIDS epidemic.

The Vampire in the Neoliberal City

Bellamy's conception of the vampire, with what it restores to figurations of the postmodern body, becomes particularly apropos for conceptualizing the body in the era of AIDS. It is important to situate Bellamy's novel in its specific geographical and sociohistorical context when addressing its representation of AIDS and the forms of biomedicalization and thanatopolitics that were enacted around it. The novel is set in San Francisco in the late 1980s to mid-1990s, right after the first wave of AIDS casualties had decimated the city's gay and underclass communities. The scope of this decimation was in large part the product of a biomedical moral discourse that distinguished between "innocent victims" (such as poster child Ryan White, who received AIDS via a transfusion) deserving of medical care and those "high risk" populations (gay men, African Americans, Latinos, and intravenous drug users) who were constructed as less deserving of medical spending and care. Moreover, San Francisco itself in the eighties and nineties was near the end of a long transformation from being a Fordist city to becoming a post-Fordist or neoliberal one.[27] The transformation is most discernible in the changes that have occurred in the city's economic infrastructure in the last thirty years. As with many first-world cities, these transformations have entailed a shift from a largely industrial, shipping, and manufacturing base to an economic infrastructure organized around the electronic, service, and financial sectors of the economy.

This shift can be conceptualized as part of what Saskia Sassen has defined as a "new geography of centrality and marginality" in which what she terms "global cities" emerge as "major financial and business centers" over against a "vast territory that has become increasingly peripheral, increasingly excluded from the major economic processes that fuel economic growth in the new global economy."[28] In the case of San Francisco, the city has emerged from this process as a major international financial center (especially in the banking and investment arenas), a major center for software programming and design, and a key retail and service center that caters largely to the new urban bourgeoisie who are the beneficiaries of the first two developments. The shift in San Francisco's economic infrastructure has led to a concomitant shift in class formations, the exponential growth of the biomedical and biotechnological service industries (centered around University of California at San Francisco as one of the world's leading research hospitals), and the emergence of new social actors. As Sassen points out, these class formations can be understood both spatially and in terms of income differentials within the composition of the global city. They can also be traced biomedically in terms of the growing stratification of access within the largely privatized U.S. health care system.

All these shifts entail what David Harvey has described as the reassertion of "class power" by an increasingly global bourgeoisie, accompanied by the disappearance of large sectors of the middle class and the concomitant growth of a particularly disenfranchised underclass.[29] Accompanying this growth of class stratification is the more salutary emergence of new social actors. In the context of San Francisco, of course, one of the most dynamic and visible expressions of the new social actors was the gay liberation movement of the 1970s and the various forms of AIDS-related activism that had its heyday in the eighties and nineties but continues to the present day. Some of the lasting achievements of these various forms of activism has been to create a relatively empowered middle-class gay and lesbian community (a general culture that is more amenable to alternative sexual practices than is present in most communities in the United States) as well as class tensions (including those around affordability and access to health care) between the relatively empowered mainstream gay middle class and economically and symbolically more marginalized members of the queer community.

In order to understand the full resonance of *Letters*'s depiction of AIDS and embodiment, it is important to keep in mind the larger socioeconomic and geographical context I have just sketched. Bellamy's depiction of AIDS is intimately bound up with her representation of the changing public spaces of San Francisco. The transgressions and uncanny disruptions enacted by Bellamy's vampires are explicitly directed at this middle-class norm as it manifests in a biomedical morality about hygiene, bodily habitus, and the policing of sexual propriety.[30] In Bellamy's representation of AIDS and its impact on San Francisco, she is thus attentive to the construction of what Esposito terms *immunity* not only along the lines of gender and sexuality, but also in terms of class.[31]

In the larger geosocial and political-economic context I have just sketched out, AIDS takes on significations that are condensations of the political-economic and psychosexual, in which the construction of certain parts of the population as immune renders other parts of the population as disposable and already bodies-unto-death.[32] As Douglas Crimp has noted, forces of political and social conservatism in the United States used the emergence of AIDS as an epidemic in order to promote a political agenda that worked to roll back the hard-won sexual rights and freedoms attained by feminists and the gay liberation movement and reestablish a traditional morality organized around female sexual chastity and the pathologization and criminalization of homosexuality.[33] These associations produced what Lauren Berlant and Lee Edelman have differently described as the twin privatizations of citizenship and sex that has emerged as part of the hegemony of the new right.[34] These privatizations define forms of sexuality marked as queer or aberrant as public menaces that do not deserve the protections of privacy; at the same time, they articulate a new conception of citizenship centered on the privatized heterosexual family and the protected status of children. Finally, in the context of the uneven emergence of neoliberalism in urban spaces such as San Francisco, AIDS takes on a vampiric temporality in which it both mirrors the viral logic of the emergent future-oriented technological and financial landscape and, at the same time, invokes atavistic modernist associations with blood and the biological as material ground and limit.

All these associations are resonant in the vampiric work undertaken by Bellamy's text around the metaphorics of AIDS. The transgressions performed by Bellamy's vampires and her other undead creatures need to be understood in terms of this complex chain of metaphoric associations and substitutions. The transgressive work of Bellamy's undead is visible in a scene in which the vampire, Mina/Dodie, is fucking Dion in a parked car in San Francisco's Marina district:

> The following week Dion and I park in the Marina as far from streetlights as we can get, sailboats clinking in the foreground, we shift beneath the frosty windshield *ghostly inhabitants, elusive and unbelievable as certain ideas* I roll down my window to let the boats in *an atonal Japanese interlude* . . . Here in the dark I miss the fine lines under Dion's eyes that run to his ears, fissures in such a young face *something is coming apart* I'm having my period and Dion hasn't cleaned up from his day job—hauling around carcasses for eight hours his sweat is mingled with cattle ooze, his nails are caked with blood, he pushes his tongue down my throat as he pushes a finger up my vagina *all those discarded unsanitary world bits all that refrigerated death* . . . with every zooming headlight I stiffen: COPS? (51)

This passage constructs, in displaced form, a primal scene for the transmission of AIDS: fluid-on-fluid (here blood-on-blood) contact. Like all primal scenes, which are by definition retrospectively reconstructed, what is represented here is a product of displacement and revision.[35] This process of displacement alters what is often the culturally fantasized primal scene of AIDS: anal sex between gay male partners. Bellamy's rewriting of the dominant fantasy of AIDS in a primal scene enables her to resignify its fantasmatic components in a number of important ways. First, and most importantly, it refuses to give the reader the scene she expects. In doing so, it refuses the homophobic and thanatopolitical construction that imagines gay anal sex as the ground zero of AIDS transmission. The transmission of AIDS is *not* represented in this scene; neither Mina/Dodie nor Dion contract the disease from their encounter, nor is their sex particularly high risk in any way other than symbolically. While the blood-on-blood contact invokes the danger of AIDS in the cultural symbolic and in the culture's imaginary mappings of specific bodies, the dried cow's blood on Dion's hand represents no material threat of AIDS transmission. Instead, the scene invokes the specter of contamination while refusing to fix it within positive representation. In revising the scene in this manner, Bellamy thus presents AIDS as a traumatic kernel that in its status as real can only be misrepresented in the space of the symbolic.[36] Bellamy's text thus enacts what can be described as an ethical imperative in relationship to the representation of AIDS. Instead of trying to fix the meaning of the epidemic in terms of a positive biomedical discourse or morality, which produces thanatopolitics as its flip side, the passage suggests that the more ethical response is to acknowledge the disease's unrepresentability in relationship to its status as real and to instead attend to the metaphoricity of all representations of the disease (including scientific ones) as both generative yet catachrestic.

In pursuing the metaphoric resonances of the disease as it shaped the conception of sex and social space in the Unites States of the 1980s and 1990s, the previous passage, in addition to functioning as a primal scene, stages a defiant act of public sex. This public sex metaphorically enacts the possibility of what Lauren Berlant and Michael Warner have described as a queer counterpublic, which they theorize as a set of public sexual practices and contestations that articulate "the changed possibilities for identity, intelligibility, publics, culture, and sex that appear when the heterosexual couple is no longer the referent or the privileged example of sexual culture."[37] In order to fully appreciate the alternate public conjured by the sex act, it is important to recognize the location of the scene in the public space of San Francisco. Far from the bohemian, Latino, and working-class Mission district in which most of the novel is set, the Marina district is the heart of yuppie San Francisco. It is an area that is home to much of the professional class that oversaw the transformation of the city into a neoliberal urban space. While probably largely politically liberal in the case of San Francisco, this class is the prime beneficiary of what David Harvey has described as the neoliberal economic and social transformations produced by the new right.[38] Mina/Dodie and Dion's public sex act, then, becomes a literal *fuck you* to the sexual, biomedical, and class-based morality of this new professional class and its new right backers. This morality is organized around the privatization of citizenship and "acceptable sexuality" and a redefinition of public space as unhygienic and dangerous (full of "unsanitary world bits," as the passage puts it) and thus in need of constant policing, here symbolized by the literal threat of police interruption while Mina/Dodie and Dion are fucking.

This class is represented in the passage as literally disembodied— "ghostly inhabitants" who are metonymically represented by sailboats, a private luxury item par excellence. On one level, the description of the denizens of the Marina as ghostly might seem to ally them with Bellamy's vampires. However, their ghostliness is instead defined in diametric opposition to the enfleshed and embodied vampires. Here their ghostliness is not a sign of an allegiance with the dispossessed or the unjustly dead but rather the sign of the fantasized transcendence of the body promised by contemporary commodity culture. It also suggests the ghostly logic of the late-capitalist financial and electronic forms of immaterial production, in which money becomes increasingly dematerialized and embodied labor becomes less visible, shunted off to another scene, or disavowed in its relationship to the leading sectors of the economy.

Bellamy's vampires thus represent the return of the repressed body in this scene and indeed throughout the novel. In contrast to the ghostly inhabitants of the Marina, Mina/Dodie and Dion are profoundly embodied. This embodiment is both what Pierre Bourdieu describes as the excessive embodiment ascribed to the working class in relationship to middle-class definitions of comportment and the forms of uncanny embodiment that are ascribed to those who are defined as sexually aberrant.[39] Their embodiment embraces the very unhygienic forms of sexuality and public life that the morality of the new bourgeoisie is designed to ward off: rather than eschewing blood-on-blood contact, they embrace it; rather than locating the sexual union of their working-class and bohemian bodies in a private location on their side of town, they publicly fuck and do so right in the middle of a stronghold of yuppie, new San Francisco. Mina/Dodie and Dion also embody the nonsynchronous and uncanny temporality of the vampire. It is striking that Dion is defined in relationship to the manual labor of working at a slaughter house—one of the modernist industries disappearing from the neoliberal space of San Francisco. His blood-covered hand, then, becomes the return of the industrial repressed—a distinctly unhygienic return of that which has been banished from the sleek surface of the global city.

(Fuck You) Elegy

The logic of the return of the repressed also lies at the core of the cen-terpiece of *The Letters of Mina Harker*, Mina's posthumous letter to Sam D'Allesandro, a sometimes collaborator who died of AIDS in 1988. The let-ter is dated July 28, 1994, a good six years after Sam's death; it is written in part as an elegy, as an act of remembrance and mourning. As such, it func-tions as a text that, as Ross Chambers describes, renders the residuality of trauma (here the trauma of Sam's suffering and death at the hands of AIDS but also of AIDS itself as a traumatic kernel of the real) "liminally sig-nificant," producing a text that stalks the present-oriented temporality of culture in the United States, which, in relationship to the trauma of AIDS, is organized around the logic of forgetting.[40] Bellamy's undead characters function in precisely this space of liminality. Refusing to remain dead, they instead take on what Chambers, drawing on Peircean semiotics, describes as an indexical function, pointing to the beyond of a traumatic real that can only be catachrestically represented on the level of the symbolic.

While undertaking this elegiac function, Bellamy's novel is as much a *fuck you* to the very form of the elegy as it is a text that participates in this form. While the novel does participate in the practice of rendering trauma liminally significant as Chambers describes it, it also refuses the straightforward politics of mourning often associated with the elegy, for the process of mourning is also a process of re-membering in order finally to forget that which has been dismembered and defaced by trauma. Bel-lamy's text refuses this process of forgetting and the tone of depoliticized regret that is often associated with it. Instead the tone of the Sam letter, which in many ways serves as a condensation of the tone of the entire novel, mixes sadness and horror with celebration and affirmation. It refus-es to let the dead stay buried, disinterring and reanimating them in all their corporeality instead. In this way, it allies itself with the undead—those who refuse to be rendered unmourned and mutely dead by the workings of thanatopolitics.

This mixed tone is evident in a scene in which Mina/Dodie remembers a Halloween stage performance by Sam at a party: "You shuffled on stage wrapped in white gauze every inch of you *the real Sam was buried inside, a talented mummy* then came the dramatic unwinding, your bound mass flapping across the floor like a trout as an assistant reeled in yard upon yard of gauze, and out of the rubble of bandages you sprang up hurling plastic skeletons at the audience, I tucked one in the cleavage of my cami-sole *worm on the rose*" (168).

The tone of this passage is at once elegiac and celebratory, an acknowl-edgement of mourning and a refusal of its retrospective temporality. This passage turns Sam's death into a dark celebration, with Sam returning from the grave to perform a kind of danse macabre in which he tosses little bits of death in the form of tiny skeletons to his waiting audience. The skeleton Mina/Dodie catches becomes transformed into an erotic decoration as she tucks it into "the cleavage of her camisole." The eroticization of death becomes a way of both accepting death and refusing to be emotionally or psychically incapacitated by it. Death as eroticized refuses the thanatopo-litical logic that structures the dominant cultural constructions of sex and death in the era of AIDS. Instead of ideologically cordoning off "norma-tive sexual behavior" from the dangers of AIDS and the threat of death it represents, which then becomes relegated to the unsanitary behavior of those marked as deviant, the passage accepts the intertwining of sex and death as a condition of existence in the AIDS era. It articulates an ethics of macabre sexual celebration as a response that both accepts death's pres-ence in sex and refuses the negation of queer sex that this presence has been used to justify.

The continued existence and strength of San Francisco's queer commu-nity, even in the face of the intertwining of sex and death represented both by AIDS and by the homophobic and thanatopolitical practices that pre-vented effective measures to combat the disease, gives further resonance to Bellamy's figure of the vampire. Here the vampire becomes undead precisely through her complex acknowledgement and refusal of death. Moreover, the queer community itself becomes vampiric in relationship to the dominant thanatopolitical construction of AIDS: it refuses to stay dead but instead becomes an entity transformed through its encoun-ter with death, attaining a vitality and resistance beyond that which is ascribed to it by the dominant culture. Moreover, this resistance, such as Sam's danse macabre, works to transform and indeed vampirize dominant culture, rewriting its meanings in ways that affirm rather than reject queer sexuality, the materiality of death, and the body itself.

The body is also invoked in the description of Sam as a mummy. Yet the body in this description is figured either as a surface that endlessly peels away, like the mummy's bandages, or as "the real Sam buried inside," not representable within the space of the symbolic. This image records the disjunction between the symbolic and the real that is central to the figuration of the body in Bellamy's narrative. It also invokes a distinction that is particularly important to Bellamy's figuration of the body in the posthumous letter to Sam: the difference between the imaginary and the real body. What is represented by the endlessly peeling surface of the body is the body ego itself or, in other words, the imaginary body. The passage represents the imaginary body as that which can be figured but is finally insubstantial and the real body as that which is substantial but eludes representation. What death does, in part, is deform or peel away the imaginary body ego, insisting on the recognition, albeit indirect, of the real of the body and of death itself as that which resists such imaginary codings and attempts at discursive control.

The disjunction as well as overlap between the imaginary and the real of the body is highlighted in another scene from the posthumous letter to Sam—one that more directly figures the bodily ravages of AIDS. In the scene, Mina/Dodie's cat, Blanche, runs into the apartment of her neighbor, who is dying of AIDS:

He stands up, "Come on in." An attractive man in his early thirties, small features, lightish hair, a fine beige powder covers the lesions on his face *a visual ditto for what I've already heard* the talk of getting on disability outside my front door, his cough climbs the stairs a wheeze and rattle deep in the lungs sometimes a gurgle *spasms trail me through wooden walls, irreducible, obscene* AHHHHHHHH AAAHHHHHHHHH behind me on the toilet it sounds like he's jerking off then there's a fart *atonal bellow* then OHHHHHHHH OHHHHHHHHHH ... *his body made airborne, scraping my ears with raw emissions* Blanche skitters into his bedroom, striped tail twitching, "Bad cat!" I follow her ... the room is lined with mirrors, so many mirrors ... long strips lean against three of the walls, three irregular pieces are obtusely angled along the bay window— the only furniture in the room is a double mattress positioned on the floor dead center *the Real in every reflection.* (176–77)

Lacan's real is invoked directly in this passage, with its specific use in Lacanian discourse being signified by its capitalization in the passage. In the context of Bellamy's direct reference to Lacan, we can read the room with the multiple mirrors as a corresponding reference to Lacan's mirror stage.

However, while the real and the imaginary are both alluded to in the passage, the real is described as occupying the space of the mirror—the space usually reserved for the imaginary constitution of the body image. With the knowledge that Bellamy knows Lacan extremely well, the question becomes, how is the real "reflected" in the imaginary space of the mirror? I want to suggest that its reflection in this passage comes from the decomposition of the imaginary mapping of the body constituted in the mirror stage. If the mirror stage is the period or moment when our sense of bodily self is constituted through the "illusion of autonomy" that puts its "faith to the ego's constitutive misrecognitions," then what Bellamy presents in this passage is something like the reverse of that process.[41] The reflection of the neighbor's AIDS-ravaged body, as it is decimated and reshaped by disease, becomes an uncanny disruption or decomposition of his body ego. Indeed his reflection (appropriately never presented but invoked by the mere presence of the mirrors in the scene) can be likened to the grinning, anamorphic skull in Hans Holbein's *The Ambassadors*, a painting that Lacan analyzes at length in *Seminar XI*.[42] For Lacan, the skull is literally a hole in the symbolic of the picture—one that can only be accessed by, as Žižek puts it, "looking awry."[43] What the hole makes visible here is the real of death itself or, as Lacan describes it, "the subject annihilated."[44] Whereas the mirrors delineate the real of death in terms of the visual constitution of the subject, the resolutely nonlinguistic signifiers of pain that the neighbor utters suggest the embodied experience of the real of death, indicating both the decomposition of subjectivity and the slow decomposition of the body itself.

Fucking Death

The figuration of the body's relationship to death becomes one of the central concerns of the posthumous letter to Sam. This relationship is most spectacularly figured in the scene in which Mina/Dodie fucks Death. The scene, which Bellamy describes humorously as her "Bergman section" (after the scene with the knight playing chess with Death in *The Seventh Seal*),[45] is both wildly funny and profoundly disturbing, presenting Death as a yuppie who asks, "Do you have anything nonalcoholic?" and wears "lampblack Italian loafers" and the most menacing top there is:

Death always approaches from behind, I'm munching on a peanut butter cookie when I hear him faintly clicking in the distance

Captain Hook he snags me with his bony finger fists me nightly reaching his long arm up through my gut and camping my heart, he crawls in my brain boring straight through from one thought to the next, Death pins my outstretched arms like butterfly wings, starting at the back of my neck he works his way down biting so hard I feel he will chew me alive, *the skin on my hands and feet falls away . . . and then the nails . . . but beneath them new nails appear along with a fresh and vivid skin* . . . Death grabs his shirt from the floor and binds my wrists together his sweat embedding my pores, his hand tightens around my throat he does what he wants . . . *Sam I never dreamed that playing dead could make you feel so alive* Death has the biggest cock I've ever seen big and stiff as a stuffed musk-rat, I couldn't close my hand around it, couldn't imagine taking that taxidermic *Thing* into me, yet I did, stretching my lips around it taut as a rubber about to burst. "You need a larger mouth," he jokes. When we fuck the Thing scrapes away the wall of my vagina *in that rawness all categories explode.* (182–83)

I quote this passage at length because it dramatizes in the most explicit of terms one of the central dynamics of the Sam letter: the text's tarry-ing with the death drive and its use of it to challenge the larger workings of thanatopolitics in the context of the AIDS epidemic of the 1980s and 1990s (and that continues into the present). Bellamy presents a politics of embracing, materializing, and eroticizing death—one that refuses the logic of projection that underpins the thanatopolitical construction of the AIDS epidemic. This disruption of the logic of thanatopolitics takes place through the passage's eroticization of the death drive and the forms of jouissance associated with it. To draw on a distinction made by Alenka Zupančič, desire as it is figured in Mina/Dodie's encounter with Death does not function to ward off jouissance but rather to court it.[46] This jou-issance simultaneously betokens the annihilation of subjectivity and its potential renewal. Both these possibilities are figured in terms that are explicitly embodied: "*the skin on my hands and feet falls away . . . and then the nails . . . but beneath them new nails appear along with a fresh and vivid skin.*" What is most striking in this passage is the intermingling of Lacan's different registers so that the eradication and the rebirth of the imaginary body are mixed with the sensations and material violence experienced by the body as real. All this takes place in a context in which the symbolic is necessary to narrate these experiences yet the categories upon which this symbolic depends "explode."

This mixing of registers suggests that what the passage itself is describing is in part a traumatic encounter with the real—here the real of death—but also of the materiality of the body itself. It is in the traumatic "rawness" of Mina/Dodie's violently fucked body that "all categories explode." The real is figured not only in this rawness but also in Death's cock, which is described, with what I suspect is another nod to Lacanian terminology, as "the Thing." Lacan glosses Freud's notion of *das Ding* (the Thing) in *Seminar VII* as an object that stubbornly refuses symbolic dialecticization and remains fixed in the "dumb reality" or mute materiality of the real.[47] It is not that the object cannot be named in the symbolic (Death's cock is clearly named in the passage); it is that any symbolic name clearly remains inadequate to the "in itself more than itself" attraction of this object that has refused the dematerialization that usually accompanies accession to the symbolic. The precursor to Lacan's later formulation of the *objet petit a*, *das Ding*, exerts a powerful force of both attraction and revulsion in the subject, producing a jouissance that in its mixture of pleasure and pain threatens to overwhelm the subject.

The passage thus stages an encounter with *das Ding* and in doing so proffers an ethics of embodiment in relationship to death and the death drive—for *das Ding* is also bound up with death, both symbolic and literal. It represents the possibility of the momentary abolition and subsequent refiguring of the symbolic as well as the final cessation of the opposition between the symbolic and the real, or what Freud describes as the complete cessation of tension, that occurs in material death.[48] Rather than warding off death by thanatopolitically projecting it onto supposedly deserving or vulnerable others as does the dominant middle-class, heterosexual culture, Mina/Dodie literally courts the death drive by allowing death to violently enter her and masochistically both accepting and transforming the embodied meanings produced by this encounter. In this sense, the passage articulates an ethics of masochism in which the very affect and imaginary composition of the body is transformed through submission to and acceptance of death. The real of death is thus recognized and incorporated rather than disavowed, and this incorporation transforms the affect and composition of the body: death clamps the heart and bores through the brain. What emerges from this encounter is the vampire herself, undead in the sense of now symbolizing death within, existing in an embodiment that has incorporated a bit of the real of death within her very constitution. Bellamy suggests that it is only from such an incorporation and embodiment that the noninfected, nonabjected subject can begin to ally himself (without conflating his voluntary position with the nonvoluntary position of the person with AIDS) with those who are infected and indeed abjected by AIDS. Moreover, Bellamy's novel suggests a more general ethics of embodiment that can begin to imagine political connections among all those whose position is abjectly and often painfully embodied in relationship to the dominant thanatopolitical symbolic constructed by new-right social relationships and neoliberal commodity culture.

An Ethics and Politics of the Real

Bellamy's novel thus proffers an ethics and a politics of the real.[49] This ethics becomes one pole of a complex ethical position articulated in the narrative. At the end of the posthumous Sam letter, Bellamy posits an ethics of looking. If the ethics articulated in the sex with Death passage is one of liminality and, finally, transitivity—of imagining a connection and a shared relationship between bodies differently situated—the ethics of looking presented here by Bellamy is the dialectical flip side of that, marking the impossibility of knowing the other's experience: "Your eyes will remain unreadable to me, will never 'reveal'—but that's not the point is it—the point is to look, not in horror not in pity or even in compassion, but to look as precisely as possible at the ever-wavering presence right in front of one—this is the closest beings as imperfect as we can come to love" (195). This is a powerful statement of the ethical imperative to recognize the fundamental difference and unknowability of the other's subjectivity. Such a recognition is a central part of Lacanian ethics, with its emphasis on the unknowability of the other's desire even (or especially) in the context of the sexual relation. In positing such an ethics, Bellamy is particularly invested in critiquing the forms of paternalist "understanding" proffered by liberalism as one of the dominant forms of morality advanced by the privileged in Western societies: "Yes, [I was advocating] a politics of recording or even just looking. Again, I really have problems with the whole notion of understanding. And, for me, it's part of a critique of liberalism. As soon as you understand, you're projecting. How can you possibly understand? There's something amoral about taking the stance of understanding. What's moral is to say no I'm never going to understand you, but I'll look at what's there."[50]

Central to the ethics that Bellamy articulates in *The Letters of Mina Harker* is the refusal of the liberal politics of projection. The latter is fundamentally a fantasmatic politics of mastery: the liberal subject both appropriates the experience of the other by projecting aspects of her own psyche and experience onto the subjectivity of the other and inscribes, in the very act of paternal understanding, the fundamental superiority of her own position vis-à-vis the other. Such a position of mastery is finally a position of comfort in which the real of the jouissance saturated body and death is safely ascribed to the poor, suffering other. This ideology of liberal charity, then, is the slightly more appealing flip side to the new right ideology of free-market competition and sexual purity: we should have pity for those poor souls who did not exhibit enough virtue to wind up winners in the economic and sexual markets, even as we recognize that the fault is their own.

Bellamy rightly asserts the bankruptcy of this ideology and marks the dangers of the assimilation of the position of the other to that of one's own. Instead, she advocates a politics of looking. This politics of looking can be aligned with what Sarah Ahmed describes as a politics of queer disorientation, in which we disorient ourselves from our conventional psychosocial maps of the world and begin to reorient ourselves as embodied subjects to queer subjects and objects.[51] Such a reorientation produces a very different understanding of space and collectivity than the one underwritten by liberal tolerance. With its politics of queer disorientation and reorientation, then, Bellamy's text does not abandon a larger commitment to either ethics or politics. Subjectivities may be discontinuous but aspects of the subject's relationship to the real can produce a transitivity and commonality that can be the basis for a collective conception of ethics and politics. Bellamy herself asserts this possibility in the epigraph that begins this chapter.

I have already described one version of the transitivity that enables an intersubjective, emotional "engagement with materiality" in my discussion of the sex with death section of the novel; as my closing example, I want to offer Bellamy's invocation of the biomedical space of the hospital as another such moment—one that suggests the possibility for a collective politics of materiality.[52]

The section of the novel in which she writes about the hospital (also in the posthumous Sam letter) invokes this space as the killing floor of AIDS—the thanatopolitical space in which the abject and disavowed bodies of people with AIDS undertake the agonizingly slow process of decomposition:

I walk through a room lined with lightboxes chilly *blur of white-white black-black* negatives large as life map hands skulls stomachs *a flat and squishy world where matter has no substance* everywhere I turn bodies are hooked up to or duplicated by metallic contraptions *with all these edges the potential for bruising is tremendous* a woman says to a man who is scrubbing his midriff, "If you're going to get slop on you it's better to get gastric slop instead of blood"... People are in transit here pushed through antiseptic aisles, IVs jingling beside them *appendages of alien lifeforms* plastic bladders drip day glo green rootbeer brown, ambulatory subjects pull their own IVs, the bags of candy-colored fluid hanging from metal racks set on wheels. (188–89)

Bellamy alternates these descriptions with descriptions of other bodies in various states of medical distress ("the only thing left intact on the woman's head are her ears") and, most strikingly, of Mina/Dodie's medicalized body in the hospital: "a homunculus lives in my right ear he says jump off and run *sweetness drips through my exposed plastic veins* I am tired of his nonsense *it's as if I'm some escaped idea that accidentally fell out of someone, someone who has voice has visibility has embodiment* in the blue room they will insert a catheter in my thigh and push it along the 'major pathways' until it reaches my brain" (188, 191).

These passages set up a series of correspondences, even as they carefully mark the differences among people dying of AIDS, a woman undergoing (either elective or nonelective) plastic surgery, and Mina/Dodie undergoing a medical procedure. The point of these correspondences is not that the experiences of those depicted are equally traumatic or materially equal. Clearly the slow death of somebody with AIDS is not comparable on a material level with undergoing a procedure that one survives. However, the point of these passages is not the equation of different experiences (a la liberal "understanding") but rather imagining the possibility of an alliance between embodied subjects engaged in a traumatic encounter with the real.

This encounter with the real applies to not only those who encounter the real of the body and death in the space of the hospital but, more generally, those in our rapidly globalizing world who experience (perhaps merely once or sometimes with miserable daily regularity) the experience that Mina/Dodie, rewriting a phrase from D'Allesandro, describes as feeling *"as if I'm some escaped idea that accidentally fell out of someone, someone who has voice has visibility has embodiment"* (189); what Bellamy is describing here is the experience of all those who feel that they have fallen out of the fetishized grid of the socially dominant symbolic. This is a neoliberal and thanatopolitical symbolic that organizes not only our social relationships (of race, gender, and sexuality, among other things) but our economic ones (of class and production), as well. Central to such a symbolic is the logic of avatar fetishism, through which privileged subjects get to imagine their transcendence of and symbolic control over materiality— especially the materiality of their own bodies. Bellamy instead imagines an ethics and the beginning of a politics that is predicated on an orientation toward and embracing of the material body and the material limit of death itself. It is only by symbolically accepting our relationship to bodies and to forms of materiality that exceed and set limits on, even as they partially intersect with, our subjectivities that we can begin to imagine a way past the thanatopolitics of the present. Such a way forward is predicated on a politics of materiality.

Conclusion: The Promise of the Vampire

These, then, are Bellamy's vampires. They not only haunt dominant culture but return forcefully to drain it of blood and transmute its "immunary logic" into something more just and collective. Their undeconstructed materiality also marks them as different from that other famous figuration of late-capitalist subjectivity, the cyborg. Like the postmodern cyborg, they may have bodies that are made up of "exposed plastic veins" and are "hooked up to or duplicated by metallic contraptions," but they are also bodies that know the intransigence of the "squishy world" of "slop and blood." Moreover, their privileged genre is not science fiction but horror. In their undead resilience, they seem to suggest that it is only in tarrying with the undead creatures of horror, even as we importantly hang on to our science-fiction-derived utopias, that we can begin to imagine the potential for a more ethical and politically responsible future. Such a future necessitates a recognition of the materiality of the body, of the world of objects, of the political-economic realm, and finally of death itself. Only through such recognitions can we produce a positive form of biopolitics, including a political economy of medicine—one that is not tied to fantasies of social immunity and divided by a neoliberal logic of winners and losers.

These recognitions are central to Bellamy's artistic practice. This is a practice not simply about metafictional language games; it is one that employs an experimental aesthetic to indicate that which language cannot fully describe: the forms of materiality and embodiment that underpin late-capitalist existence. It is in this liminal realm between the symbolic systems within which we speak and dream and the mute material strictures that circumscribe yet enable our existence that Bellamy's vampires become disinterred and writhe with very material life. It is perhaps to their (our) half-articulable stories that we can turn in order to imagine a space beyond postmodernism and the forms of neoliberal exploitation to which it is tied.

CHAPTER 5

Almanac of the Living

Thanatopolitics and an Alternative Biopolitics in Leslie Marmon Silko's *Almanac of the Dead*

Things congeal as fragments of that which was subjugated; to rescue it means to love things. We cannot eliminate from the dialectics of the extant what is experienced in consciousness as an alien thing: negativity, coercion, and heteronomy, but also the marred figure of what we should love.

—Theodor Adorno, *Negative Dialectics*

Transmodernity and Silko's *Longue Durée*

Leslie Marmon Silko's *Almanac of the Dead* is a book for our time.[1] At first glance, this claim may seem strangely anachronistic. After all, Silko's novel appeared more than twenty years ago, and certainly the world has changed in ways both hopeful (the growth of counterglobalization movements, the growth of fourth-world forms of resistance such as the EZLN, resistance partly modeled on Silko's almanac, and the emergence of the anti-austerity and Occupy movements) and not so hopeful (the continuing scourge of neoliberalism, the exponential growth of environmental degradation on a global scale, and the open-ended war on terror and the permanent state of exception it entails) in the intervening years.[2] Indeed, *Almanac of the Dead* was written long enough ago to be categorized as part of the literary production of another era—that of the postmodern. Leaving aside for one moment the very real problems with applying the signifier postmodern to third-world, fourth-world, and Native texts, Silko's text never fell comfortably within the dominant aesthetic coordinates delineated by that term,[3] nor is it easily characterizable by the even more fraught (but currently trendy) signifier, post-postmodern. Indeed, the latter signifier seems to mark a generational divide or a self-lacerating recognition of the aesthetic and ideological exhaustion of postmodernism from within the metropolitan, first-world circles that generated the term in the first place, rather than the emergence of a genuinely new or more global aesthetic. Instead, Silko's almanac insists on a set of geographical and social displacements and reorientations that reveal the postmodernism/post-postmodernism debates to be at best limited in their general applicability and at worst unconsciously racist. As such, Silko's novel is better understood as part of what Enrique Dussel has termed "transmodernity."[4] In contrast to the first-world bias of the term *postmodernity*, Dussel's transmodernity describes populations and subjectivities that are situated simultaneously inside and outside the histories of modernity. While Dussel's concept can be applied to all the novels examined in *Insistence of the Material*, it is particularly used to describe the complex spatial and temporal experiences of Indigenous, fourth-world populations in relationship to the dynamics of modernity. As such, it is applicable to the complex spatial and temporal positioning of Silko's novel, which addresses the spaces of both the metaphorical global North (including the parts of the global North that are in the global South) and the metaphorical global South (including parts of the global South that are in the global North).[5] Thus the novel represents both a transnational business class who move between spaces such as San Diego, Tuxtla Gutiérrez, and Buenos Aires and dispossessed classes who occupy spaces such as the Sonoran desert, the jungles of Chiapas, or the economically abandoned sections of cities such as Tucson and Mexico City. In providing this representation, then, the novel engages modernity and late capitalism yet represents Indigenous forms of subjectivity and political community that cannot be completely reduced to the space and time of modernity.

Almanac of the Dead's spatial and social reorientations are mirrored by the temporal reorientation that it enacts.[6] This temporal reorientation enables it to be a text engaged with the present. The present, for Silko, is part of a *longue durée* that is linked with the ancestral past and the Indigenous history of the Americas, of which the almanac is a partial record and for which the conquest of the Americas is a recent event—one whose end is foretold. This sociopolitical temporality is echoed by the form of ecological time deployed by the novel. In this ecological time, the violence done to the earth and the ancestral lands of various Native peoples through the exponential growth of capitalist exploitation and the forms of genocidal displacement that have accompanied it in the last five centuries represents a relatively recent challenge to the Indigenous occupation and steward-ship of the lands, the history of which is much longer and the power of which is much more enduring than the five hundred years of "Western" occupation that is detailed in the almanac.

Yet this ecological and sociohistorical temporality intersects with other forms of temporality depicted in the novel, for unlike some of the most praised and taught texts grouped under the rubrics of "Indian" or "Native American" literature or, more broadly and reductively, "multi-cultural literature," Silko's text doesn't merely focus on Native contexts or Native life, nor does it posit a model of easy and comfortable multi-cultural coexistence. Instead Silko's almanac is oriented around two different axes: one is a transnational Native and subaltern world as it has been shaped and changed by a five-hundred-year history of imperialism, and the other is the overdeveloped urban spaces of the global North and certain parts of the global South, where the poisonous fruit of neoliberal-ism and contemporary biopolitics (as they morph, in Roberto Esposito's terms, into thanatopolitics) are fully on display.[7] The environmental deg-radation and forms of hemispheric and global exploitation produced by these practices have only grown in the period since the publication of *Almanac of the Dead.*

It is for this reason, in part, that I suggest that *Almanac* is a text of our time, for Silko's narrative, with its depictions of the black market in bioma-terials, the transnational drug trade, and the hemispheric traffic in torture films and in torture itself, could be describing our present and recent past. Even if the locations of torture have changed from Argentina to Guanta-namo Bay and Abu Ghraib, the violence of the drug trade has come to manifest itself most immediately in Juarez and other border cities, and the process of what Adele Clarke et al. have termed biomedicalization, with the attendant legal and illegal trade in biomaterials, has grown exponen-tially in the twenty years since the almanac's first publication.[8]

In engaging these biopolitical products of late-capitalist life, Silko's text can be defined as part of the trajectory of the late-capitalist literature of materiality that I have been tracing throughout this book. Like Ballard, Burroughs, Pynchon, and Bellamy, Silko details the cultures of exploita-tion and violence that are central to biopolitical capitalism. Indeed, Silko claims Burroughs as one of her heroes, and many of the sections of *Alma-nac* that are set in the global North are Burroughsian in their intentionally amoral depictions of economic and bodily violence.[9] Silko represents San Diego, Tucson, and other urban centers of the global North as locations in which industrial production has receded and what emerges in its stead are legal and illegal forms of biopolitical production, including affective labor, such as Seese's work as a stripper; symbolic labor, including Lecha's work as a psychic and a translator of the almanac and David's photographs; the trade in biomaterials and biomedical products, including Trigg's blood and organ bank; and all the various legal and illegal industries in which Beaufrey is involved, including drugs, torture tapes, guns, infants, and so on. As this description indicates, for Silko, the forms of biopolitical production detailed by *Almanac of the Dead* are bound up with what Roberto Esposito has described as a thanatopolitics. For Esposito, biopolitics—the politics of the direct production and management of subjectivity and life—are always bound up with thanatopolitics, or a politics of death waged in the name of life. The transformation of biopolitics into thanatopolitics occurs through the logic of "immunity."[10] For Esposito, in the name of achieving (an always impossible) immunity, communities and nation-states underwrite murderous violence toward those internal or external enemies who are defined as threats to those who are immunized.

Thanatopolitical Production

For Silko, however, the production of thanatopolitics is an economic process as much as it is a political one. Thus we can talk about thanatopolitical production in *Almanac of the Dead*. This thanatopolitical production is both distinctive to the neoliberal present in the novel, in which the central biopolitical technologies it depicts are all underwritten by death on another scene, and bound up with the entire five-hundred-year history of the European occupation of the Americas and the long history of capitalism to which it is tied. In this sense, the colonization of the Americas can be read in both economic and political terms as a thanatopolitical project. The political dimensions of this project can be understood in terms of politics of religious and racial immunity that were core to European imperialism and the forms of community established in the so-called new world. While the economic dimension can be understood in terms of the exponential growth of capitalist production in the Americas starting in the "long sixteenth century" and continuing up to the present, with its genocidal accompaniment produced in the name of acquiring ever more resources and ever greater access to the land.

Silko, like Aníbal Quijano, presents capitalism as central to the whole history of the colonization of the Americas.[11] In Quijano's world system account, capitalism predates both wage labor and industrialism; it is instead organized in its initial formation around the transnational agricultural market and the market for raw materials, as well as the forms of slave labor that produced and procured materials for these markets. In such a context, wage labor itself was marked as a racial privilege (a designation that continues to haunt the politics of both race and class in the Americas) and a "systematic racial division of labor was imposed."[12] This early capitalism fueled European colonization and the forms of "accumulation by dispossession" that accompanied it.[13] Through its complex, recursive temporality, the novel links these founding moments of accumulation by dispossession in the Americas with the reemergence of the same dynamic as central to the "restoration of class power" under neoliberalism. From a Native perspective, the novel suggests that the "return" of accumulation by dispossession as a central dynamic of neoliberalism is merely the shifting of a dynamic that is a perpetual part of capitalism from the periphery, where it has been central to an ongoing process of settler colonialism and resource appropriation, to the core or metropole, where it reappears in the forms of financialization, austerity measures, corporate welfare, and the elimination of Fordist forms of social infrastructure in order to appropriate the earnings of a once protected and immunized middle class.

In this way, *Almanac of the Dead* demonstrates the political-economic applicability of Esposito's notion of immunity. It also suggests the relevance of its political vision for the global North as much as the global South. Esposito conceptualizes immunity as tied to the biopolitical organization of the nation-state, determining which bodies count and are protected or granted immunity on the level of citizenship and which can (and sometimes must) be eliminated in the name of immunization. This dynamic of immunization and the forms of nation-state constitution to which it is tied can be understood more broadly as a political-economic process—one in which, as Quijano and Eva Cherniavsky differently note, class formation and racialization are contrasting processes for differently situated laboring populations. Class defines those laborers who are exploited through wage labor and are constructed as a subordinated population that is internal to the nation-state, while race denotes those whose labor and possessions are expropriated by direct force and who are constructed as a population that is external or supplementary to the nation-state.[14] In high capitalism, accumulation by dispossession was generally applied only to racialized populations. What is happening under neoliberalism, then, is that dynamics that were originally applied to racialized populations or expropriated to the global South are returning with a vengeance to the formerly immunized populations of the global North. The forms of thanatopolitical production and appropriation that have been central to the five hundred year long war (and war is a thanatopolitical-economic dynamic par excellence) emerge then in the cultural and economic practices of the cities of the global North; this is the culture of death that Silko presents.

In this sense, Silko's novel depicts the situation that Chela Sandoval describes as the crucial link that late capitalism produces between newly uprooted and proletarianized first-world populations and the already dislocated and hyperexploited populations of the internal and external third world.[15] This link is crucial in understanding the novels political vision. As a number of different critics and readers (including the EZLN's subcomandante Marcos himself) have noted, Silko's text is part political manifesto.[16] The novel articulates a revolutionary vision of the five-hundred-year Indian war to reclaim tribal lands (thereby reversing the incursions of accumulation by dispossession). Indeed this is part of the reason for the novel's *longue durée* to chart the forms of what Gerald Visenor has described as "survivance" and struggle that are ongoing and, within the ecological time presented by the novel, relatively recent.[17] What Silko's almanac does, then, in its representation of the spread of the dynamics of the accumulation by dispossession to the global North, is suggest articulations for new forms of insurrectional and revolutionary struggle—ones that recognize but finally reach beyond the racialized categories produced by the history of such accumulation to challenge its more generalized form in the present. Thus while political struggles depicted by the novel will produce the "disappearance of all things European" (as foretold in the novel's titular almanac), the multiracial coalition imagined by the novel, the Army of Justice and Retribution, which includes not only the coalition of Native nations lead by the twin brothers but also the army of the homeless lead by Rambo and Clinton as well as multiracial urban populations, suggests that this disappearance of things European refers more to political-economic structures and forms of domination rather than populations defined as European.[18]

Rethinking Political-Economic and Ecological Struggle

This complex revolutionary vision is tied to the almanac's refiguration of Marxist theory. The novel dynamically refigures and transforms Marxist theory, hybridizing it with various forms of Native knowledge and fourth-worldist critique in order to produce a theoretical framework adequate to the material struggles around accumulation by dispossession as well as the epistemological struggles the novel depicts around temporality and the definition of historical actors. The refiguration of Marxism is part of the conscious theoretical work done by Silko's almanac. It addresses one of the theoretical lacuna central to Marxist theory: how to account for forms of resistance in the periphery and from various fourth-world spaces in a body of theory that champions the industrial proletariat and the processes of modernization that creates it.

One of the more recent and fruitful attempts to think through this lacuna, one that dovetails in important ways with the work done by Silko's text, is Michael Hardt and Antonio Negri's theorization of the multitude in *Empire, Multitude,* and *Commonwealth.*[19] In the trilogy, Hardt and Negri suggest that one of the positive developments of the emergence of biopolitical production as the leading edge of the global economy is that it creates both new, potentially revolutionary social actors and new forms of organization for social life. Because biopolitical production is organized around various forms of immaterial labor (intellectual, affective, and service), all social actors are viewed as equally, if singularly, productive within such a regime.[20] Neoliberalism, in this conception, becomes (as it is for David Harvey as well) not so much a form of economic production but a regime of accumulation—one in which the products of biopolitical production are appropriated by the dynamics of accumulation by dispossession. Within such a regime, alliances are possible between subjects (including those who used to be perceived as partially or fully outside of the circuits of labor, such as the homeless, the underclass, and various fourth-world populations) of the global North that were only possible with much more difficulty before.

In contrast to such forms of appropriation, Hardt and Negri posit what they term the "commons" or alternately the "commonwealth": the domain of the collectively owned that exists in opposition to the privatizing logics of neoliberal economics on the one hand and the "public" appropriations of the state on the other.[21] The revolutionary transformation that Silko presents in *Almanac of the Dead* can be understood as articulating a similar conception of collective ownership that rejects these twin forms of appropriation. Yet Silko's presentation of transformational struggle in *Almanac* doesn't merely parallel Hardt and Negri's accounts but also diverges with them in important and indeed crucial ways.

Biopolitics and Materiality

One of the crucial ways in which Silko's text breaks with Hardt and Negri's vision is around questions of materiality. With the exception of the materiality of bodies, Hardt and Negri tend to background the status of materiality in their accounts of contemporary biopolitical production. For them, the material transformation of everyday life is at the heart of the earlier regime of modernist industrial production—one that has been surpassed or rendered secondary by the emergence of biopolitical production as the leading edge of the capitalist world economy in late modernity. For them, biopolitical production is organized around what they elsewhere term "immaterial production," with intellectual, affective, electronic, and service work becoming the leading edge of the global economy and earlier forms of production, such as agricultural and industrial production, becoming remade via the logic of immaterial production (via the integration of computing systems, new genetic technologies, etc.). This account of "immaterial production" constructs a historiographical periodization in which the production of material goods is conceptually rendered secondary and in which materiality itself, while recognized, is relegated to the background of their theorizing.

Hardt and Negri's emphasis on the immaterial runs counter to the political and epistemological valuation of materiality that is central to Silko's text. Hardt and Negri's trilogy can thus be understood as organized around a disavowal of the material—one that is organized around a notion that all forms of political and economic struggle can be understood on the level of the symbolic and the subjective, without any encounter with the resistance and insistence of the material or what Levi Bryant describes as "the non-semiotic or non-representational differences [of] nonhuman objects."[22]

In opposition to the form of biopolitics proposed by Hardt and Negri, which emphasizes, in drawing upon Foucault's account, the fully discursive construction of subjectivity and the social itself, Silko presents an oppositional form of biopolitics that is grounded on a subjective recognition of and respect for the intransigence as well as the malleability of the material. This is a biopolitics that is oriented around Native ecological practices that emphasize sustainability and the respect for the ecological and political economic. It is also organized around an epistemology that recognizes what Adorno describes as the preponderance of the object to any just and nonimperializing conception of the world.

Indeed, Silko produces not only an alternate representation of political economy in *Almanac of the Dead* but an alternate representation of what Bruno Latour and Jane Bennett describe as political ecology. This alternate economic and ecological conception vision is recognition that, as Bennett, Latour, and Bryant argue, matter itself can function as an actor—one that can work in asymptotic ways to human actors.[23]

It is this alternate conception of biopolitics, a biopolitics built on the recognition of the resistance and actions of the material and on a respect for all living things, which lies at the heart of Silko's revolutionary vision in the almanac. Such a biopolitics provides a way out of the cultures of thanatopolitical production that are central to life in the global North. Rather than a biopolitics organized around governmentality (with its dynamics of discursive control of both life and subjectivity) and the neo-liberal calculus of human capital (with its determination of those who are capitalized and those who are disposable), Silko's biopolitics presents an account of subjectivity that is organized around a collective conception of political-economic production that, like Hardt and Negri's concept of the commons, is separate from both private corporate ownership and the public ownership of the nation-state and a recognition of the material insistence of both bodies and the natural/object world in our globalized present. This, then, is Silko's almanac of the living: an epic narrative that moves through late-capitalist spaces of death and toward a revolutionary conception of sustainable and just life.

The Materiality of the Almanac

At first glance, Silko's narrative seems to be the odd woman out in the collection of novels addressed in this book. While all the other texts, from Burroughs and Pynchon to Ballard and Bellamy, have impeccable experimental credentials and indeed can be seen as core texts in any account of late twentieth-century experimental fiction, Silko's narrative would seem to be more easily categorized as realist and placed within the countertraditions of either Native American/American Indian literature or multicultural literature.[24] While I do not want sever *Almanac*'s ties to these two latter traditions, I want to suggest that the novel is written against the ghettoization that often occurs between experimental fiction, on the one hand, and Native American/American Indian fiction on the other. In this regard, while emphasizing her work's relationship to forms of Laguna storytelling and to pan-Native concerns more generally, Silko refuses to think of her texts as separate from global fictional currents.[25] Like the hemispheric and finally global vision put forward by the novel, Silko's writerly practice is also global, having as much to do with postcolonial and anticolonial fiction and the textual disruptions of experimental fiction as it does with a specific tradition of Indian or Native American writing.

In a similar vein, I want to suggest that Silko's text is written against the forms of reception that are conventional to the marketing of multicultural fiction. With its graphic representations of torture films, drug use, and violent sex, as well as its refusal of conventional forms of humanist warmth, the text is forcefully written against the liberal structures of feeling that conventionally attract the upscale and white readership that is a key demographic for multicultural literature. In this sense, the novel itself enacts on the level of content and genre the guerrilla tactics that it represents as part of the global struggle against European and capitalist hegemony. Thus the text not only depicts transgressive acts but enacts generic and stylistic transgressions as well.

It is on this level—the level of formal and stylistic transgressions—that the relationship of *Almanac of the Dead* to the tradition of experimental fiction that I have been analyzing throughout the rest of this book should be obvious. The fact that this isn't readily apparent says more about the forms of barely submerged racism and Eurocentrism that attaches to the signifier "experimental" than it does to the specific qualities of Silko's prose that characterizes geographically and culturally diverse writing practices. In other words, *Almanac* should be located as part of the tradition of experimental fiction—the late-capitalist literature of materiality that I have been tracing throughout this book.

On the level of content, Silko's text echoes the transgressive violence and dark humor of writers such as Ballard and Burroughs. She, like the other authors I have considered in this book, emphasizes the centrality of materiality, especially forms of intransigent, resistant, and discarded materiality, to the workings of biopolitical capitalism. Silko's novel is quietly yet powerfully experimental on the level of form as well. The novel's realism is only surface deep; a more careful reading of the text reveals the myriad ways that it breaks with conventional realism and even with the magical realism that is associated with the Latin American experimental tradition and with writings by women of color in the United States.

This break with realism is not as evident on the sentence level (though it is present here, particularly in the narrative's complex mix of past and present tense) as much as in relationship to organization and structure. As a number of critics of the novel have noted, the structure of the text really is that of an almanac, with theory and history wedged side by side with the stories of individual characters.[26] The Mayan and pan-Native almanacs, which Lecha, Zeta, and Seese are in the process of translating as the novel unfolds, are not only the novel's subject but the novel itself. The novel is one of the almanacs. Thus the novel cannot be read as reproducing the contained and retrospective narratives that characterize conventional realism—for both the stories and their implications for the events narrated by the novel are radically open-ended (as is indicated by Silko's strategic use of the present tense). This open-ended quality shifts the history being told by the narrative from the retrospective to the continuous and proleptic. *Almanac* resists and breaks with the settled contents of historical narratives by attending to that which is excluded from them or exceeds them. Silko's text thus enacts rather than just records history, breaking with its codification by emphasizing the open-ended and still generative quality of the events it depicts.

The open-ended quality of Silko's text is bound up with the *longue durée* it depicts. For the revolutionary fourth-world populations that the novel presents, "the Indian Wars have never ended in the Americas" (15). The five-hundred-year imperial occupation of the Europeans represents merely a small period of time in relationship to the long historical and ecological times that are central to the relationship of Indian cultures to their ancestral lands.[27] Within such a conception of geography, culture, and time, past, present, and future are bound together, part of a *longue durée* that is still unfolding. Or as La Escapía, one of the leaders of the novel's Army of Justice and Retribution puts it, blending the words of Marx and tribal elders, "They must reckon with the past, because within it lay seeds of the present and the future. They must reckon with the past because within it lay this present moment and also the future moment" (309, 311). This description perfectly captures the novel's complex temporality and its radical reworking of the tropes of realism.

This emphasis on the open possibility of the future indicates that the novel is invested not just in representation but in enactment, in intervening in the present to produce a future event. All this is captured in Silko's use of the term "almanac," which, in its twin definitions as a manual that charts the material changes of the weather and as a book of prophecy, suggests that it is a guide to producing as well as recognizing material changes in the world.

It is a text that works to be more fully adequate to the object world (just as almanacs do that attempt to predict the weather or describe the most fortuitous seasons for planting), while at the same time recognizing the inability of language to ever be fully adequate to the objects it describes. Thus Silko's almanac represents what Bryant describes as the "intransitivity" of objects and what Alain Badiou describes as the nonpredictability of the revolutionary event within the structure of being that precedes it.[28]

Like an almanac, the novel is made up of heterogeneous materials, history, theory, individual and collective stories, theology, accounts of revolutionary praxis, and so on. Moreover, in its use of language, it attempts to push beyond the merely subjective and linguistic in order to produce a form of language and storytelling that begins to be adequate (while recognizing that it cannot be fully so) to the world of materiality and material struggle. The text's related attempt to move beyond the merely subjective is one of the sources of its posthumanism; its notorious coldness is a product in part of trying to write a history of the Americas from the perspective of the ecological and geohistorical temporality of Silko's *longue durée*. Within such a frame, individual lives are subordinated to the larger movements of history and of the earth itself.

Imperialism and the Historical Roots of Biopolitics

Central to Silko's engagement with questions of temporality and materiality is what Ericka Wills has described as the novel's critique of contemporary biopolitics and specifically a critique of the forms of biopolitical production linking the global North and the global South in the novel and in everyday life in the present.[29] Silko, like Pynchon, links the emergence of the biopolitical economy in the present to the use of biopolitics and their dialectical counterpart thanatopolitics in the context of imperialism and slavery. Indeed Silko, like Achille Mbembe, presents imperialism and the forms of slave labor instituted by it as the site of the original emergence of biopolitics and what Mbembe terms *necropolitics* (what Esposito renames *thanatopolitics*).[30]

Both the biopolitical and the thanatopolitical dimensions of imperialism are tied to the processes of what David Harvey terms *accumulation*

by dispossession. In Silko's almanac, this process is depicted in all its ruth-
lessness in the sections of the text that record Yoeme's narrative. Yoeme
is the Yaqui grandmother of Lecha and Zeta and remembers the events
vividly that transpired during the appropriation and exploitation of Yaqui
ancestral lands (in and around present day Potam in Sonora) by Mexican
mining companies and the Mexican government itself: "They had been
killing Indians right and left. It was the white men coming to find more
silver, to steal more Indian land" (117). The use of Indians as slave labor
for the mining of silver was central to this expropriation process, rendering much of the Yaqui population in the area as "bare life," in Agamben's
terms.[31] Constructed simultaneously as outside the state and yet central
to its political-economic processes, the Yaqui, like other Native populations, are presented here as directly subject to the power of the state and
the corporation, while situated outside its institutions and the discourse
of civilization. Their subjectivity and very biological being are thus shaped
by the power of the state and the economy as they function outside the
mediation that notions of citizenship or rights would provide. Such formations (central to the simultaneously subjectifying and objectifying
logic of imperialism) are almost textbook definitions of bare life as Agamben defines it. As Yoeme's injunction, "It was war," suggests, it would be
a mistake to equate the bare life experienced by the Yaqui with political
quietism or submission. The novel depicts slavery as existing in tension
with the continuous war that is being waged between the Yaqui and the
Mexican government, which is in turn one front within the five-hundred-
year war for the Americas. *Almanac of the Dead* thus clarifies an aspect
of Agamben's theory of bare life that remains ambiguous. In the novel,
biopolitical "bare life" is not so much a condition of subjective destitu-
tion leading to powerlessness (as it sometimes seems in Agamben) as it
is a conflictual relationship of a population with a state and/or a political
economy—one that is organized around what Agamben terms a state of
exception, in which populations are racialized and deemed as outside the
purview of legal jurisprudence and life managed directly by political, mili-
tary, and economic power.[32]

    If imperial rule and enslavement (i.e., direct, unmediated political and
economic rule over life) represent one face of the biopolitical coin, then
the war that Yoeme invokes represents its other face. It is here where the
thanatopolitical dimensions of biopolitics are most evident. The thanatopolitical dimensions of biopolitics are multiple. As Mbembe suggests, the

"power over life" that is central to biopolitics also immanently contains the "capacity to dictate who may live and who must die."[33] This, then, is the threat of death that is always immanent within any state of exception, suggesting that the threat of death is always needed in order to manage those who have been rendered bare life, who, in turn, continue to struggle against this condition. Building upon Mbembe's conception, Esposito posits the logic of immunity as central to the intertwining of biopolitics and thanatopolitics. In the name of protecting and nurturing the life of those who are granted the immunity of citizenship and racial inclusion, genocidal war is waged against all who fall outside the auspices of the state and are presented as a racialized and often biological threat to those who are granted immunity. It is precisely such a genocidal imaginary that animates the imperial violence of the Mexican and U.S. forces both in the work of accumulation by dispossession and via the state of exception.

Yoeme's story about the cottonwood trees provides a brilliant condensation of the thanatopolitical violence that rests at the heart of imperial conquest in the Americas. Yoeme begins the story of the trees by noting the violence of their very placement within the landscape of the estate owned and run by Guzman, Lecha, and Zeta's Mexican grandfather and Yoeme's former husband, who is long dead at the time of the story's telling:

> The fucker Guzman, your grandfather, sure loved trees. They were cottonwoods got as saplings from the banks of the Rio Yaqui. Slaves carried them hundreds of miles. The heat was terrible. All water went to the mules or the saplings. The slaves were only allowed to press their lips to the wet rags around the tree roots. After they were planted at the mines and even here by this house, there were slaves who did nothing but carry the water to those trees. "What beauties!" Guzman used to say. By then they had no more "slaves." They simply had Indians who worked like slaves but got even less than slaves had in the old days. (116)

The status of the Indian slaves as bare life is rendered painfully apparent via the hierarchy of being established in this passage, in which the trees and the mules merit more water than they do. This rendering of the slaves as subordinate to animal and plant life recalls Agamben's account of bare life as zoē—life that is constructed as purely biological without any access to citizenship or political status. Here, however, the situation is,

if anything, even more extreme: not only are the slaves rendered equivalent to animals and plants and understood as biological objects that can
be dominated, but they are constructed as beneath both in the hierarchy
constructed by Guzman and the other Mexicans. Indeed the hierarchy created by the whites (a category that the novel extends to white-identified
or Spanish-identified Mexicans) is a violent inversion of the pan-Native
ethic of respect for and valuation of all living things that Silko articulates
at other points in the novel. Rather than all beings being afforded respect
and valuation, all beings are rendered as objects to be accumulated and
disposed of by those who count as subjects. The ecological violence of
this construction is further suggested by the transplantation of the trees
from their natural habitat to a landscape in which they need to be kept
artificially alive.

The passage marks the violence not only of accumulation by dispossession but also of the regimes of production and accumulation that follow it.
Slave labor was, of course, used not only for mining and other processes
of extraction but as a central feature of agricultural capitalism, here hinted
at metonymically by the name of the trees themselves—cottonwood, with
cotton being a central cash crop of eighteenth- and nineteenth-century
agricultural capitalism. Yet the passage also invokes the history of wage
labor that was central to the transformation of agricultural into industrial
capitalism, indicating the transformation of slave labor into wage labor
within both the agricultural sector and the extraction sector under industrial capitalism. And just in case we were to see wage labor as an advance,
Silko underscores the continuing violence of biopolitical exploitation
under "wage slavery," noting that the Indian laborers were even more
exploited with the advent of wages and that their biological being was just
as much directly shaped by the market as it had been shaped by slavery.

The intertwining of thanatopolitics with the biopolitical dimensions
of imperial conquest and exploitation is made explicit in the next part
of Yoeme's story, in which she relays that the cottonwood trees became
the site of a mass lynching. This intertwining is perfectly captured in
the image of the cottonwood trees being transformed from a principle
of life (one that functions as an actor in "suckling like a baby and talking to the water") to one of death, from which Yaqui resisters, warriors,
and rebels are hung (117–18). Thus the very political ecology (one that
in the transplantation of the trees is partially engineered) is used by the
colonizers against the Indigenous inhabitants of the land. This image of

mass lynching of course has significance beyond the immediate context of the scene that Silko depicts; indeed, the centrality of lynching as a disciplinary tactic within the plantation economies that characterized most agricultural production in the Americas in the eighteenth and nineteenth centuries gives this image a pan-American resonance—one that is central to the transnational political vision of Silko's narrative. The fact that the trees line the path to the mine as well as surround the plantation house suggests that death is a central product not only of the plantation economy but also of the labor of resource extraction that is key to the process of accumulation by dispossession. Thus what emerge from this scene are a political ecology and a political economy of death, indicating the centrality of thanatopolitics to the history of imperial conquest and capitalist development in the Americas.

Thanatopolitics and the Emergence of Biopolitical Production

While much of *Almanac of the Dead*'s critique of thanatopolitics and biopolitics is focused on the emergence in the late twentieth century of what Hardt and Negri term *biopolitical production*, in which affect, embodiment, and subjectivity are the core economic products produced by the leading edge of the economy, the novel takes pains to underscore that the emergence of such a form of production represents in many ways a generalization of conditions that were long experienced by fourth-world populations within the context of Euro-American imperialism and accumulation by dispossession. What the emergence of biopolitical production and neoliberalism has produced, then, is the generalization of the condition in which subjectivity is no longer primarily tied to citizenship, with the rights and privileges this entails, but rather directly produced and managed by the marketplace and the forms of technology central to present-day production. As Chela Sandoval has suggested, this creates a context in which there is a possibility of alliance between first- and third-world subjects because of a newly shared experience of subjectivity, and this is clearly captured in Silko's novel where the homeless in the global North (those newly dispossessed by neoliberalism), alienated intellectual workers such as the hacker Awa Gee, eco-activists, and even new-age spiritual seekers in the global North become allied with the Army of Justice and Retribution made up of fourth-world Native populations and other dispossessed populations of the global South (290).

In presenting the possibility for such alliances, Silko does not erase the differences between such populations—differences that are marked by class, race, and national inclusion. In the economic transactions mapped by the novel, Silko demonstrates the circuits of biopolitical and thanato-political production that link the global North and the global South, even as they reproduce and intensify divisions between an increasingly transnational elite and similarly transnational working and underclasses (or, in other words, producing the global South in the global North and vice versa). These circuits of biopolitical and thanatopolitical production include the movement of illegal drugs; plasma, organs, and other bioma-terials; torture and death videos; arms and other weaponry; and insurance for private corporations and for governments that will guarantee profits in times of social unrest as well as the private armies that enforce such guarantees. In each of these examples, the technologies in question are directly implicated in the production of privileged forms of immunized life that are dependent upon a much wider political economy of death for those who are rendered disposable or seen as a threat to this immunized life. What emerges from the movements of such forms of biopolitical and thanatopolitical production, then, is the large-scale political-economic and political-ecological production of death—what is known in the Indig-enous movements depicted by the narrative as either the reign of the "Death-Eye Dog" or the reign of the "Fire-Eye McCaw": "Some knew it as 'The Reign of the Fire-Eye Macaw,' which was the same as saying 'Death-Eye Dog' because the sun had begun to burn with a deadly light, and the heat of this burning eye looking down on all the wretched humans and plants and animals had caused the earth to speed up too—the way the heat makes turtles shiver in a last frenzy of futile effort to reach the shade" (257). The description of this reign, which corresponds to novel's violent present, underscores the ecological as well as economic costs of thanatopolitical production, with its references to global warming and the threatened death of not only humans but plants and animals as well.

Death inflects the realm of culture in *Almanac* just as much as it informs processes of political-economic production and political-ecological dev-astation, demonstrating the interpenetration of the two realms in the era of biopolitical production. As T. V. Reed aptly puts it, "The embeddedness of European and U.S. cultures in the logic of the Death Eye Dog is appar-ent in everything from sexual to aesthetic to political practices—all are reduced to the economic nexus."[34] This culture of death is captured most vividly in Silko's depiction of David's photographic exhibit that takes the suicide of his former lover Eric (who kills himself, in part, over David) as its subject: "Death had not been any more peaceful for Eric than his life had. The extreme angles of Eric's limbs outlined the geometry of his despair. The clinched muscles guarded divisions and secrets locked within him until one day the grid work of lies had exploded bright wet and red all over. . . . David had focused with clinical attachment, close up on the .44 revolver flung down to the foot of the bed and on the position of the victim's hands on the revolver" (106–7).

In a section mordantly titled "Art," Silko goes on to describe the sensation that David's photographs of Eric cause in the art world: "Later the critics dwelled on the richness and intensity of the color. One critic wrote of the 'pictorial irony of a field of red shapes which might be peonies—cherry, ruby, deep purple, black—and the nude human figure nearly buried in these 'blossoms' of bright red. The core photograph was a close-up of the face or what remained of it" (108). Echoing Ballard's clinically detached and geometrically precise descriptions of car crashes as well as the art world's ambiguous fascination with figures like Damien Hirst, whose instillation work with animal carcasses was just gaining international renown at the time of *Almanac*'s publication, the passage depicts a culture of death. The forms of thanatopolitical production that the novel details thus link death to despair, not only for those on the losing side of what Esposito terms the "paradigm of immunization" that is central to thanatopolitics, but also for those ostensibly protected by such acts of immunization.[35] The *geometry* of despair figured by Eric's body thus becomes a singular condensation of the *geography* of despair as it is mapped throughout the novel as a whole—a geography produced by thanatopolitical production and the neoliberal policies of structural adjustment that devastated Mexico and other Latin American states during the period of *Almanac*'s composition and the dismantling of the welfare states in the United States and other nations of the global North.

For the bourgeois denizens of the latter, as the description of the fascination of the art world suggests, death functions as a return of the repressed. As in Bellamy's narrative, death may be disavowed, but as a dimension of the real, it always returns and returns with a vengeance the more it is disavowed. This structure of disavowal, in turn, produces the complicated mix of hygienic containment and fetishistic fascination that characterizes cultural constructions of death in for the global bourgeoisie in late capitalism.

Yet the description in the passage of Eric's death photography cuts both ways, for Silko reveals not only the culture of thanatopolitical production but her text itself, with its tales of death and torture and its apocalyptic pitch, also participates in it. In presenting Eric's photographs, Silko is not articulating an individualist condemnation of certain art or certain artists (to think otherwise is to miss the rigorously posthumanist and collective dimension of her narrative address). Instead her representation of David's art can be best understood as a symptomatic reading of the status of art in the era of thanatopolitical production, including her own. Within such a context, art needs to address the workings of thanatopolitics, even at the cost of becoming symptom of the very process it criticizes. This, I think, is what is at the heart of Silko's admiration of Burroughs and what, along with her engagement with materiality, ties her book to the tradition of transgressive fiction that *Insistence of the Material* addresses. What is different about *Almanac of the Dead* is that it points, more fully than the other texts I have considered, toward collective solutions to neoliberal biopolitics and the political economy of death.

Biomaterials, Torture Videos, and the Political Economy of Death

Before turning to those solutions, however, I want to chart more fully the novel's depiction of forms of neoliberal biopolitics and the forms of thanatopolitical production that they underwrite. As Ann Brigham points out, "The novel's most disturbing articulation of the extraction paradigm is that of the human harvest. This new technology of extraction sustains a population of white, middle-class imperialists by mining the worker's body for new parts."[36] This intimate technology of bodily extraction can be defined as a core part of what Clarke et al. describe as the growth of the "biomedical technoservice complex."[37]

Biopolitics are central to the workings of neoliberalism in two distinct ways: first, through, as Foucault demonstrates in *The Birth of Biopolitics*, the use of the market as a direct and efficient means of shaping and managing subjectivity and the living being's potentiality (what neoliberals term the *maximization of human capital*), and second, through the direct investment in and commodification of the stuff of life and especially the stuff of the body. It is this latter dimension of neoliberal biopolitics that is central to the workings of biomedicalization, which Clarke et al. define, in part, as "a new biopolitical economy of medicine, health, illness, living, and dying which forms an increasingly dense and elaborate arena in which biomedical knowledges, technologies, services, and capital are ever more co-constituted."[38]

With her usual prescience, Silko captures the workings of bio-medicalization in its moment of emergence in her depiction of Trigg's "Bio-Materials Inc." enterprise: "Biomaterials! Biomaterials—the indus-tries 'preferred' term for fetal brain material, human kidneys, hearts and lungs, corneas for eye transplants and human skin for burn victims" (387, 398). While, as we have seen, a similar commodification and instrumen-talization of the body accompanied the biopolitical forms associated with imperial conquest and colonialism, with their uses of slave labor and the slave trade, in the neoliberal version of biopolitics, the commodified body is no longer a tool of labor (traditionally conceived) but one commodified and appropriated end product of the production process itself. This dis-tinction is captured in the difference between the embodied subjectivities produced under slavery versus the fragmented body parts that are the final product of Trigg's industry.

And as with older forms of imperialist biopolitics, the thanatopolitical dimensions of this form of biopolitics becomes disturbingly manifest. No longer satisfied to "harvest" the dead and those "inessential" body parts and bodily substances, such as blood and kidneys, with which the living can safely part, Trigg starts to kill his largely homeless clientele in order to meet the international demand for his product: "Trigg blames the homeless men. Trigg blames them for being easy prey. . . . They were human debris. Human refuse. Only a few had organs of sufficient quality for transplant use" (444). Trigg's enterprise is thus the novel's central image of thanato-political production and its intimate connection to neoliberalism. While the lives of the global bourgeoisie who are the recipients of such biomate-rials are enhanced and prolonged (and enhancement of health, including the moral imperative to maximize wellness, is a key feature of biomedical-ization as described by Clarke et al.), this is at the cost of the lives of the "human refuse" who are worth more dead than alive. The homeless are on the losing end of this divide and thus are literally human waste products of the thanatopolitical economy. The neoliberal imperatives that organize who falls on which side of this divide are nicely captured in Trigg's contempt for the homeless, in which he blames them for their own victimization.

Silko represents the international market for torture videos and snuff films as another key thanatopolitical industry—one that points prescient-ly toward the dialectics of virtuality and embodiment in our televisual and electronic age. These videos, when not faked by the pornography industry, are often taken from interrogation footage (like the filmed torture that is part of the interrogations that take place in Tuxtla Gutiérrez) or footage of surgeries (botched and otherwise) and late-term abortions. Early in the novel, Beaufrey, who deals in both the art market and the underground video market, reflects on the demand for such videos:

> The real weirdoes became even more obsessed with the "real thing"—they claimed they could detect fakes—an utter lie since Beaufrey had yet to sell an actual "snuff" film. Beaufrey had got a good laugh out of the "real thing" freaks who paid him hundreds or even thousands of dollars. The queers couldn't get enough of those flicks of the steel scalpel skating down the slope of the penis tip, a scarlet trail spreading behind it. . . . The demand for films of ritual circumcisions of six year old virgins had doubled itself every year. There were waiting lists of creeps who got weak at the mention of hairless twats and tight little buds. (103)

In this passage, the thanatopolitical dimensions of late-capitalist culture present themselves in the form of a sadistic desire for death or, if death is not available, for pain, torture, and suffering. Central to this sadistic formation is the obsession with the "realness" behind the televisual image. As Gilles Deleuze theorizes, sadism proper (as opposed to the theatrical sadism demanded by masochism) is obsessed with the "realness" of the violence it produces or witnesses.[39] This drive for realness becomes particularly complicated in an age of media simulation and saturation, in which the line between staged media event and recorded actual event has become ever more blurred. Central to this blurring is the increasingly murky distinctions between pornography (which ostensibly is theatrical in nature—even when real acts are depicted), documentary, and snuff. Thus documentaries of ritual mutilation and sex change surgeries are circulated as part of the snuff market, and pornography increasingly insists on its realness, even as "the real thing" of snuff is increasingly difficult to distinguish from faked versions.

This blurring of the line between the real and the theatrical is captured most chillingly in a scene in Tuxtla-Gutierrez in which makeup is used to make the filming of police interrogation and torture more vivid for the video market:

The police chief complained to Vico, his wife's brother: the
Argentine interfered and often interrupted interrogations. The
Argentine had persuaded them to use lipstick and makeup on the
genitals so they might show up better on the video screen. All
the Argentine talked about was "visual impact" or "erotic value."
Making a little on the side selling the tapes—that was one thing,
so long as police work was not hindered. The chief was delighted
to make money from the filthy perversions of thousands hope-
lessly addicted to the films of torture and dismemberment. . . .
Vico was no better than the Argentine. They both only cared
about a "quality product." (342)

Here the lines between fake and real, pornography and torture film,
collapse. And this collapse is not to the benefit of those who are on the
embodied end of the torture. Rather than theatricality somehow mitigat-
ing the violence, instead real violence increasingly informs and undergirds
theatricality. And Silko's text presents this torture scene as a condensation of the larger political economy of exploitation and death depicted by
the novel. Neoliberalism is presented as a large-scale version of Deleuze's
sadistic scenario, in which the pleasure of the global bourgeoisie is instan-
tiated in the realness of the suffering of exploited global working classes
and underclasses.

The Dialectics of Embodiment

This condensation has even more resonance in our own present, in
which the exponential expansion of so-called immaterial production
and neoliberalism has produced a context in which consumers and those
connected with the financial and electronic sectors are the privileged
who get to be relatively disembodied and experience the embodiment
of others through the mediation of the computer screen, while service
workers (such as sex workers), affective laborers, factory workers, and
agricultural laborers are imprisoned in a degraded embodiment that
suffers for the pleasure of the privileged. This divide suggests that the
dialectics of fantasized disembodiment (i.e., the ability to mediate one's
embodiment) and painful immediate embodiment are one of the axes
around which global class formations are structured in the present. The
division intersects, via the racialization, sexualization, and gendering of

the contemporary global workforce, with other axes of difference, and the division may be articulated and experienced primarily through any of one or more of these divides.

This oppositional structure around embodiment suggests that for the global bourgeoisie, who are increasingly invested in avatar fetishism, there is a corresponding compensatory fantasy that the real and the material exist somewhere else, in the global South or among the underclasses of the global North—all those who live in conditions that do not allow them to abstract from the experience of immediate embodiment. In such a context, the sadism Silko depicts as underwriting the interactions between the privileged and the exploited seems to be more than merely a product of neoliberal economics, with its neo-Calvinist morality of praiseworthy winners and contemptible losers, though it is certainly this as well. It also seems to be underwritten by a structure of embodiment envy that is the flip side to the ideology of avatar fetishism. Like the paradoxical forms of racial and class envy that commentators such as Eric Lott and myself have attributed to middle-class whiteness in the early to middle of the twentieth century, embodiment envy constructs those who are disempowered by the global economy as having a paradoxically privileged relationship to embodiment, precisely because they are not allowed a regular transcendence of the body's demands.[40] This embodiment envy, then, is organized around a sadistic desire to punish those who seem more embodied as well as demonstrate the "real thing" that is their embodiment through increasingly spectacular scenes of violence.

Silko's Revolutionary Vision

Since a number of other critics have already written brilliantly on the text's innovative articulation of the forces of revolution, I will only briefly sketch out the originality of Silko's vision and instead move relatively quickly to the hints of a postrevolutionary vision of a different social and natural order that the text articulates. As Kimberly Roppolo, Chanette Romero, Eva Cherniavsky, and Shari Huhndorf have differently articulated, Silko posits a vision of fourth-world alliances and political-economic struggle— one that represents an important counterarticulation to the domination of the field of Native American studies (or American Indian studies) by notions of nationalism.[41] This emphasis on nationalism represents a powerful response to the wholesale destruction of cultural traditions and national territories that accompanied the genocidal violence practiced by the United States and other forces of Euro-American imperialism. It also represents an important counterresponse to the liberal and new age commodification of distinct Native cultural practices to produce a wrongly unified and reductive understanding of Native American traditions. Yet, as Huhndorf suggests, this nationalism also produces its own political limitations—limitations that not only are bound up with the nation form itself but also are tied to the way in which it can set limits to the production of pan-Native alliances and forms of resistance. She argues, "Confounding the nationalist paradigms that have dominated Native literary studies, *Almanac* rewrites the history of the Americas from a transnational perspective that unites imperialism, slavery, and class struggle in a single ongoing story of land conflicts and it attempts to negotiate a collective revolutionary identity based on histories shared by Native peoples across cultural and national boundaries" (141). This revolutionary rearticulation of Native identity is what Huhndorf, after Silko who is, in turn, rewriting Marx, terms "tribal internationalism."[42] As powerful as this pan-Native articulation is, the novel's revolutionary vision, as T. V. Reed, Ann Brigham, and Laura Shackelford differently articulate it, reaches beyond the bounds of race to articulate a wide array of social actors.

Ericka Wills offers a reading of Silko's revolutionary coalition as a vision of what Hardt and Negri call the *multitude*. Hardt and Negri coin the term to move decisively beyond the limitation of conventional understandings of class formation as it is articulated within the Marxist canon, with its proletariat (or working class) proper and what Marx terms the "lumpen proletariat," or the dangerous, out-of-work classes. Marx sees revolution and labor as the product of the wage-earning working class and presents the lumpen proletariat as a decadent threat to revolution.[43] Hardt and Negri argue that such a distinction probably never had much use and is particularly limiting in a context in which biopolitical production has become the leading edge of global capitalism.[44] In biopolitical production, it becomes clear that all forms of social production (intellectual production, electronic production, affective production, cultural production, symbolic production, nonwaged work, etc.) are forms of labor and contribute directly to the generation of everyday life. Furthermore, since, as Quijano points out, "from the very beginning of the colonization of America, Europeans associated nonpaid or nonwaged labor with the dominated races because they were 'inferior' races," the paradigm of the multitude is particularly productive for rethinking a revolutionary politics that can include Indigenous populations as the center rather than the margins of struggle.[45]

While paralleling Hardt and Negri's vision in a number of ways, Silko's account of revolutionary praxis is distinctive in its emphasis on the negative as necessary to such forms of revolutionary struggle, not only internally, by enabling differently situated groups to come together only by working through their negativity (e.g., in the scene in which the Barefoot Hopi discusses what is needed to unify prison populations separated into distinct racial camps), but also externally, by articulating a force strong enough and resolved enough to negate the violence of what is. It is the negative that Silko depicts in her account of thanatopolitics throughout the text and in the forms of revolutionary struggle that are needed to dislodge it that make her vision more than just a more inclusive form of multiculturalism. It instead informs the almanac's vision of the "disappearance of things European" (570).

Silko's novel is dialectical about the meaning of this phrase, and it is important to attend to the specific wording of this prediction—for it doesn't predict the disappearance of people of European descent (indeed they are included in the book's vision of a revolutionary collective) but rather *things* European. This suggests that what is at the center of Silko's revolutionary vision is not only revolutionary struggle and the forms of negative and positive articulation central to it but also a postrevolutionary praxis that transforms the human relationship to things themselves—to the material world that we inhabit. The ambiguous resonance of the term *European* in this passage is also worth considering, for it suggests a change in epistemological orientation as much as a necessary transformation of what is. For example, computer technology is included as part of the revolutionary struggle, suggesting that it is not so much the technological dimensions of Euro-American dominance that is being challenged as it is the Euro-American and capitalist understandings of and uses for such technology.

Silko's Politics of Materiality

Silko's postrevolutionary vision is centrally articulated around an altered understanding of materiality—one that is based around, though not fully reducible to, pan-Native understandings of the relationship between language and materiality. This understanding of materiality, in turn, is central to the novel's articulation of a political economy and a political ecology that balances the human with the nonhuman. Jane Bennett and Bruno Latour both use the phrase *political ecology* in their groundbreaking work on science, ecology, and the nonhuman. Their conception of political ecology echoes the concept of political economy as it is used in Marxist theory: political ecology in this sense suggests a sustainable system of dynamic interactions between the human and the nonhuman as well as a different way of understanding this political relationship. Both dimensions of the term are relevant to the altered understanding of materiality articulated by *Almanac of the Dead*.

This altered understanding is articulated most forcefully by Calabazas, a Yaqui Indian and smuggler, whose knowledge of the Sonoran desert around Tucson is detailed, as becomes clear to his two employees, Root (a white man) and Mosca (a fellow Indian):

> Once Root remarked that he thought one dull grey boulder looked
> identical to another dull gray boulder a few hundred yards back.
> Calabazas took his foot off the accelerator, and Mosca had tried to
> save Root by adding quickly, "Maybe in the dark they look alike."
> But that had not prevented Calabazas from giving them one of
> his sarcastic lectures on blindness. . . . "I get mad when I hear the
> word identical," Calabazas had continued. "There is no such thing.
> Nowhere. At no time. All you have to do is stop and think. Stop
> and take a look. . . . Survival had depended on differences. Not just
> the difference in the terrain that gave the desert traveler critical
> information about traces of water or grass for his animals, but the
> sheer varieties of plants and bugs and animals." (201–2)

Central to Calabazas's critique of Euro-American perceptions of the desert is a critique of identity and the notion of the identical upon which it depends. Paralleling Adorno and Horkheimer's critique of identity as the logic of capitalist and Western hegemony in *Dialectic of Enlightenment*, Calabazas critiques the forms of instrumental rationality that would turn the qualitatively distinct materialities present in the desert into so much quantifiable and interchangeable stuff—the indifferent identity of an endlessly repeating desert landscape.[46] It also suggests the way in which such a logic of identity obscures the ways in which, as Graham Harman puts it, "objects are units that both display and conceal a multitude of traits."[47] The qualitatively distinct and, in Harman's language, "withdrawn" qualities of objects instead fall into what fellow object-oriented ontologist Levi Bryant terms an "unmarked space" and thus can be treated as exchangeable and exploitable stuff.[48]

It is this latter attitude that allows Leah Blue, the novel's figure of a rapacious real estate broker, to see the desert and the specific ecology it embodies as wasteland upon which she can build her "city of the twenty-first century, Venice, Arizona" (374). As its name implies, Blue's dream city is designed to re-create Venice in the desert, complete with canals, fountains, and golf courses—a huge appropriation and waste of the desert's most precious resource, water. Central to the novel's critique of identity, then, is the recognition of the irreducible particularity and qualitative dimensions of the material world—dimensions that are destroyed when the object is reduced to the logics of identity and seriality.

The difference, of course, between Adorno and Horkheimer's critique of identity and that of Calabazas is that the former are articulating this critique from somewhere near the center of Euro-American imperialism, while Calabazas is located in a position of what Walter Mignolo describes as "exteriority" of coloniality.[49] This exteriority is not a position outside colonial dynamics but rather a position situated at their subaltern edge. Such a position enables Calabazas (and Silko) to see the value of Native practices for imagining a way beyond the limitations of Euro-American capitalist modernity. It is here where Enrique Dussel's notion of "transmodernity" is crucial—for it posits modernization and postmodernization as dynamics that do not obliterate what went before but instead intersect with differently situated subjects in a way that transforms them while granting them access to what came before and to the possibilities of what comes next. For Dussel, the subjects who inhabit the postmodern present are not fully cut off from forms of historical knowledge that proceeded it or future possibilities that bisect it, precisely because the postmodern is not a cultural totality in the progression of linear history but a dominant ideology in a system that is made up of an array of interlarded histories, modes of production, and locations within the world system. Thus Silko, writing from the subaltern edge of Western modernity, is able to articulate a critique of the logic of identity that becomes part of a larger politics and theory of revolution and postrevolutionary possibility in her novel.

Like Bryant and Harman's object-oriented ontology, Silko's revolutionary vision is grounded in an understanding of the difference between our
names for things and the animate and inanimate objects or materialities
(including people and animals) so named. As Calabazas further meditates,

> The tribal people here were all very aware that the whites put great
> store in names. But once the whites had a name for a thing, they
> seemed unable ever again to recognize the thing itself.
> The elders used to argue that this was one of the most dan-
> gerous qualities of the Europeans: Europeans suffered a sort of
> blindness to the world. To them, a "rock" was just a "rock" wher-
> ever they found it, despite obvious differences in shape density,
> color, or the position of the rock relative to all things around it. The
> Europeans, whether they spoke Spanish or English, could often be
> heard complaining in frightened tones that the hills and canyons
> looked the same to them, and they could not remember if the
> dark volcanic hills in the distance were the same dark hills they'd
> marched past hours earlier. To whites all Apache warriors looked
> alike, and no one realized that for a while, there had been three
> different Apache warriors called Geronimo who ranged across the
> Sonoran desert south of Tucson. (224–25)

Calabazas, here, stages a critique of the equivalences produced by
language and the blindness to the qualitative material differences that language effaces. Such equivalences have not only ecological consequences
(one rock is just like any other rock) but racist social consequences as
well (one Apache warrior is just like another one).

Recognition of these qualitative differences involves attending to the
specific agency or action exerted by matter. Both Latour and Bennett
posit the importance of attending to the agency of matter, such as the
work done by ecological processes of erosion and mineral creation, bio-
chemical processes that shape the composition of life, the movements of
electrical currents, the transformations produced by pollution and radiation, and so on. In this emphasis on the agency of matter, both thinkers
are, in effect, radicalizing Timothy Morton's crucial assertion "nature is
history."[50] For both Bennett and Latour, nature is not only historical but
made up of social actors (although these actors need to be understood
as operating in a way that is distinct from our notions of human agency).

This recognition of the agency of materiality or materiality as an actor thus becomes part of the creation of a different political ecology—one that attends to the political stakes at work in human interactions with matter and the material world.

Silko's narrative, with its articulation of the winds, rain, snow, and earth itself as political actors presents just such a vision of an alternate political ecology: "The old-time people had warned that Mother Earth would punish those who defiled and despoiled her. Fierce hot winds would drive away the rain clouds; irrigation wells would go dry" (632). While Silko's vision of these forces is distinctly anthropomorphic, with its conception of Mother Earth and the various spirits that represent different natural forces, this vision emphasizes the agency of material forces in a way that Euro-American instrumental approaches to nature do not. Moreover, when this conception of matter as actant is combined with Calabazas's meditations on the heterogeneity of the material world, what emerges from Silko's text is an injunction to recognize and attend to the forms of materiality that exceed, delimit, and shape our cultural constructions of the world.

Silko's Political-Ecological and Political-Economic Vision

What Silko helps us see here is the limitations of social construction—and the linguistic and cultural turns upon which it is based—for a just and sustainable political-ecological and political-economic vision of the global future. Calabazas's understanding of the heterogeneity of the material world and it's irreducibility to identity, whether these be linguistic or otherwise, points us toward a different understanding of the relationship between the human and the nonhuman and the constructed and the material.

Such an approach is an alternate epistemology that becomes what Graham Harman has described as "ontography" or a "mapping" of "the basic landmarks and fault lines in the universe of objects."[51] Such an ontography represents a mapping of being and its difference from human access and human significations, rather than a hard and fast ontology (since such an ontology would suggest full access to or knowledge of being). Central to the most politically minded versions of such an ontography is Bruno Latour's insight that the political and the natural are coconstitutive rather than separate realms. Thus part of a sustainable

political ecology and political economy is about recognizing the political import of the nonhuman and the material, whether this recognition
involves an awareness of the animal and plant world as differently situated beings (as Calabazas articulates it, "the sheer varieties of plants
and bugs and animals," even as he understands the useful dimensions
of plants and animals for humans); a recognition of the qualitative
materiality and irreducibly material genesis of the resources we use in
constructing our late-capitalist imagescapes (no matter how much the
rhetoric of virtuality tends toward obscuring such a material genesis);
or a recognition of the forms of action exerted by all these nonhuman
beings and materials.

This recognition can be articulated as part of what Hardt and Negri
theorize as the commons. They posit the term as a way of distinguishing
the immanent productivity of the social in the era of biopolitical production from notions of either the public (which implies a state) or the
private (which implies private property and capitalist ownership). Calabazas, in meditating on the history of the Yaqui people in the Sonoran
desert, articulates just such a collective relationship to the land and to
productivity: "We don't believe in boundaries. Borders. Nothing like that.
We are here thousands of years before the first whites. We are here before
maps or quit claims. We know where we belong on this earth. We have
always moved freely. North-south. East-west. We pay no attention to what
isn't real" (216). Here, Calabazas articulates an understanding of the social
and its relationship to the material landscape that corresponds closely
with Hardt and Negri's understanding of the commons—a collective relationship that remains distinctly outside of definitions of either public or
private. Moreover, while this vision of the commons is articulated within
Calabazas's Yaqui epistemology, the novel presents it as part of the larger postrevolutionary vision that the text advances. The almanac's vision
of the commons is thus finally coterminous with the transnational alliances it imagines: the coalition of first-, third-, and fourth-world peoples.
Similarly, this commons is made up of not just human actors and human
technologies but plants, animals, material processes, and the land itself
as participants in an enlarged conception of both political economy and
political ecology.

Yet Silko's vision involves not only the affirmation of the commons but
also giving the negativity represented by both objects and subjects its due.

The text insists on the object's preponderance and irreducibility over and against any simple sublation of it. Moreover, it insists on the value of social negativity for challenging the forces of the late-capitalist present and for producing the equality and democracy of what is to replace it. A positive biopolitics of the commons—one that moves us out of the orbit of the forms of thanatopolitics that continue to haunt it in our present—is paradoxically only achievable by giving the negative its due.

Tarrying with the Material

Production thus creates not only an object for the subject, but also a subject for the object.

—Karl Marx, *The Grundrisse*

To (Not) Conclude . . .

This conclusion takes the form of a series of propositions. These propositions are not meant to be binding or definitive but rather speculative and generative. In the spirit (so to speak) of Hegel's preface to *The Phenomenology of Spirit*, which meditates on the impossibility of writing a preface, this will be a conclusion that doesn't conclude.[1] Instead, I borrow my form in this conclusion from the writers and theorists who have been central to this project. It is no accident that these writers and theorists are known for their formal discontinuities, whether it is Bellamy, with her radicalization of the epistolary form; Burroughs, with his attempt to produce a language of the real; Silko, with her almanac of different voices and materials; Adorno, with his aphoristic style; or Lacan, with his punning, disruptive style designed to speak to the unconscious as much as to consciousness. In each of these cases, and even with the seemingly more conventional styles of Pynchon and Ballard that produce similar effects in the ways in which each of their accounts of objects and materiality disrupt the forward movement of their narratives, the style recognizes the impossibility of the text mastering its objects. This then leads to a first proposition.

1. Theory and critical thought should work to disrupt their fantasies of mastery while still attempting to be as adequate as possible to their objects.

This contradictory double imperative is easier to invoke than maintain. As I delineated in the introduction, one of the strengths of the linguistic turn has been to build epistemological self-consciousness into the very structure of academic inquiry. This is the force of deconstruction and of much of the powerful discursive work done by new historicism as well as discursive theories of gender, class, race, and sexuality. However, when the linguistic turn takes language as its end point, it begins to do violence to the very heterodoxy of the material world that its self-consciousness was designed to forestall. Similarly, theory that treats language and the object world as if they are unproblematically related, either through straightforward referentiality or through a notion of language as *equally* material as the objects it describes, also effaces the heterodox dimensions of the material world. In making this argument, I am not refuting or bracketing referentiality. Indeed, the referential function of language is the crucial way in which the materiality of language intersects with other forms of materiality and attempts to be adequate to them. One of the problems with the linguistic turn was its insistence, following Saussure, that referentiality should be bracketed.[2] What I am resisting instead is the notion that the referent can be fully adequate to that which it refers. The writing styles of both Adorno and Lacan in different ways engage this double movement toward reference and away from any notion of its straightforward transparency or adequacy.

Adorno's aphoristic style is produced from two conflicting imperatives: (1) the importance for Marxist and Marxist-derived theories to map the totality of social and political-economic relationships and (2) the recognition of the will to mastery that informs both the attempt at totalization and attempt by theory to fully account for its object. Adorno's solution to this contradiction, particularly in a text like *Minima Moralia*, is to write aphoristically—to both theorize the totality of political-economic interconnections that compose the exploitative structure of industrial capitalism in the moment of the text's composition and to indicate formally the impossibility of giving a full account of that about which he writes.[3] The gaps in the text then—literally the spaces—in between theoretical moments become full silences, acknowledging that which is present that the text can only gesture to in its absences. They underscore the epistemological violence done by any theory to its objects.

The double imperative then becomes a version of the negative dialectical relationship between the universal and the particular that has been rearticulated by Slavoj Žižek and Fredric Jameson in recent years.[4] In the rearticulation of this dialectic, the tension between the two positions is never resolved. Moreover, the universal here should be understood either as a version of ideology and its universalizing claims (Žižek) or as the movement toward an attempt at being adequate to the totality of political and economic relationships in late-capitalist life—particularly as these relationships are obscured or rendered opaque on the levels of the local and immediate (Jameson). At its most careful, then, the practice of negative dialectics does not produce a universalizing synthesis or an eradication of difference; it instead attempts to attend to the ideological, class, and political-economic relationships (indeed, differences) that can only be grasped by taking into consideration spatial and temporal relationships that, in our present moment of globalization, are transnational and often global in their reach.[5]

Lacan's style takes a different double imperative as its motive force: this is the imperative to describe both the subject and the symbolic universe that she inhabits while also indicating that which falls outside of and over-determines this universe. In Lacan, the forces of overdetermination are not only the unconscious but also the various manifestations of the real, from uncoded materiality, to death, to the *objet petit a*, to the drives, to trauma.[6] As these shifting definitions of the real indicate, Lacan keeps his very terminology in motion during the many revisions of his thought over the many years of his seminar. The reason for this constant revision is precisely to disrupt his listening subjects' fantasies of mastery over the contents of his teachings. While Lacan's own ambiguous relationship to the performance of mastery is well documented, at its best (such as in his account of the four discourses), his teaching suggests the implication of the teacher in the same fantasy structure of mastery as the student, particularly within the canonized and thus deadened discourse of the university.[7] When the fantasy of mastery is satisfied, the knowledge is no longer alive for the subject because its object is no longer recognized as heterogeneous. Instead the object is integrated, via language, into the subject's symbolic universe and ceases to trouble or disrupt the systems of conscious knowledge adhered to by the subject. Lacan's style, with its constant puns, its troubled syntax, and its whiplash changes in direction, is designed to keep the listeners' sense of mastery at bay by calling attention to aspects of the object that are exogamous to his conscious understanding.

Thus both Lacan and Adorno work to maintain the object's negativity— it's refusal to be fully integrated into the smooth workings of the former's conception of the symbolic and the latter's version of the dialectic (indeed this is, in part, what defines Adorno's dialectic as negative). This emphasis on negativity leads to my next proposition.

2. *The negative is crucial for any theoretical approach that wants to
attend to the material and articulate a transformative politics around it.*

It is not a coincidence that both Lacan and Adorno foreground the negative in their approaches to the question of the object or, more broadly, to
the question of materiality. For each of them (and for me in this book),
the negative is crucial for marking the heterogeneity, the resistance, and
indeed, the insistence of the material. Without an account of the material's
force, its resilience, contingency, and obduracy—in short its negativity—it is too easy to integrate it into our systems of representation and
linguistic denotation. In arguing for the value of the negative in this context, I am not arguing that subject and object are mutually exclusive or that
language and other forms of materiality are always separate—indeed to do
so would be to reproduce a version of the Cartesian mind/body split that
Elizabeth Grosz rightly critiques as being at heart of too many Western
conceptions of the body.[8] As I have tried to show throughout *Insistence*,
subjectivity, for me (particularly given the embodied history I detailed in
the preface), as for most psychoanalytic and certain phenomenological
accounts of the body such as Grosz's or Merleau-Ponty, is always embodied.[9] Instead what I am suggesting is that there is what Žižek terms a "not
all" at the heart of our engagement with matter and even our cognitive,
egoic, and even unconscious mappings of our bodies; aspects of materiality refuse, exceed, and resist our attempts to fully control or map it.[10] As
object-oriented ontologist Levi Bryant puts it, "The split at the heart of all
being is not simply characteristic of those objects we would seek to know,
but are also characteristics of the particular object we are."[11]

It is crucial to theorize this spit at the heart of the material (or what
Graham Harman describes as the object's withdrawn qualities) for reasons
ecological, economic, and subjective. In ecological terms, a recognition of
the negative relationship between our uses of the material and its composition indicates the way in which our understanding of the material remains
epistemologically limited when we (often in important, valuable, and
necessary ways) appropriate it for human use. This remains true even as
science does the necessary work of attempting to understand the material
world more fully. Constructing our relationship to the material as negative
forces us to recognize it in its particularity and partial autonomy—the ways
in which it refuses to fully adhere to our economic, ecological, or social
scripts. In maintaining this recognition—including a recognition of the

unexpected and unintended consequences that our interaction with the material may produce—we cease to treat it as inert fodder, as merely the input to our political-economic and political-ecological calculi. Such a recognition thus can be part of producing a more ecologically sustainable relationship to the material world—one in which we attend to the forms of materiality (e.g., resources, "waste," infrastructure, and embodied labor) that are too often rendered invisible or disavowed within our political-economic calculations. This attention to the material, then, can become a version of what Latour terms *political ecology*—one based on the recognition of nonhuman actors as well as human actors.[12]

As I argued at greater length in *Hard-Boiled Masculinities*, negativity is also crucial for thinking about subjectivity and intersubjective relations.[13] The unconscious, as articulated by psychoanalytic theory, represents a crucial source of those forms of affect and fantasy that form in a negative relationship to the materials of consciousness (and this is the case in spite of the fact that, for Freud, the actual materials of the unconscious are positive).[14] I think we need to continue to think about the workings of the unconscious even after what Jameson describes as the advent of postmodernism, which he argues is characterized by, among other things, the colonization of the unconscious.[15] The unconscious may be colonized by commodity culture, avatar culture, and the logic of neoliberalism, but what the unconscious contains and enacts is still unruly, oneiric, and in a negative relationship with consciousness. Hence, we see the forms of late-capitalist unconscious explored in Ballard's fiction. This is not an id or presocial unconscious. Rather, it is one largely produced by the social world inhabited by his characters. Yet it is no less disruptive for being so produced.

Similarly, as Silko and Burroughs differently demonstrate, it is crucial to recognize the social and fantasmatic negativity that is produced by exploitative class relationships, imperial violence, and the systematic maintenance of unequal social hierarchies. Without such a recognition, any progressive or radical politics threatens to repeat the erasures of bourgeois liberalism. As Benjamin Noys articulates, such a conception of negativity must inform "a practice" forceful enough for "the necessary destruction of existent positivities."[16] Similarly, Dodie Bellamy's work reminds us that, while transitivity and sociopolitical connection is possible and necessary between subjects, intersubjective negativity is valuable for the ways it refuses and resists the subject's easy appropriation of the other's subjectivity. A positive politics that is worth its name can only occur by tarrying with and working through the negative. The dangers of a purely positive account of the social are particularly marked in the contemporary United States, which as Lauren Berlant has demonstrated, is organized around the cultural logic of what she terms "cruel optimism."[17]

In contrast, the novels addressed in *Insistence of the Material* are notable for their aesthetic negativity and their refusal to affirm the cultures of (neo)liberalism and late capitalism. Thus their aesthetic negativity can be understood as more than a practice of mere artistic transgression, which is always easily reassimilable by the cultures of capitalism; it can also be understood as an insistence on negativity not only of the subjects they write about but of the object of the text itself—its refusal to affirm the subject's appropriation or mastery of the text. This leads to my next proposition.

3. Theories of biopolitics and thanatopolitics need to be supplemented with an account of the material and its insistence.

Biopolitics and thanatopolitics are powerful ways of conceptualizing power and the regulation of subjectivity in relationship to contemporary forms of governmentality and political-economic production. Indeed, they hold the distinct advantage of functioning as a theoretical means to bypass imaginary social relationships such as citizenship (as important as these are) and attend to the way in which social and economic power is increasingly structured in relationship to the direct organization and shaping of life and death. As theoretical categories, biopolitics and thanatopolitics, with their emphasis on the interface of power with biological life, hold great materialist promise. Yet, as I have argued throughout *Insistence of the Material*, this promise has too often gone unrealized. A biopolitics worth its name would need a theory of the body and its materiality that is both shaped by yet not reducible to the discourses and practices by which biopolitics is enacted. An account of the material body as it is shaped by contemporary biopolitical practice, from the workings of biomedicalization to the dictates of human capital, needs to theorize both the psychoanalytic mapping of the body image as well as what I have been terming the real body of uncoded or miscoded materiality. The body needs to be understood as more than a passive site of inscription—a *tabula rasa* upon which biopolitics and thanatopolitics inscribe their insistent and sometimes terrifying scripts. Instead, we need to theorize the

ways in which the body—and the psyche as it intersects with and overdetermines the body—resists and complicates the logic of biopolitics. Such
an account would situate the body as a locus of resistance and counterac-
tion (as an "actor," in Bruno Latour's terms)—one that complicates the
one-way movement that is too often assumed by theories of biopolitics
and thanatopolitics.[18] Psychoanalysis and other materialist theories of the
body seem crucial in this regard for constructing a more adequate account
of biopolitics' and thanatopolitics' intersections with the lived body.

Another dimension of psychoanalysis that seems promising in relationship to biopolitics and thanatopolitics—one that I have only touched
upon in *Insistence of the Material*—is a theorization of libido and the death
drive (or Eros and Thanatos) in relationship to the workings of the two
forms of power. Such a theorization would begin to articulate how biopolitics and thanatopolitics are lived and complicated on the level of the
psyche. It would also suggest how fantasy, desire, and enjoyment are structured by and yet also complicate the workings of the two forms of power.

Similarly, biopolitics and thanatopolitics need to be articulated more
fully in relationship to political economy and the forms of material production that are central to much twenty-first-century life. Hardt and
Negri, to their credit, have made strides in developing a conception of
biopolitics as an economic category and as a category of active making
with their notion of biopolitical production. This conception represents
an important advance over conceptions of biopolitics that figure subjects
as passive vessels shaped by the workings of biopower.[19] Yet this notion
is too bound up with their concept of immaterial production and the
notion that all production is taking on an imminent and communicative
character that obviates the need for larger forms of political organization.
Such a vision, while suggestive, avoids the difficult work of tracing the
complex relationships between different kinds of production and different
kinds of political and economic positioning. As Saskia Sassen has compellingly argued, so-called immaterial production is always undergirded by
material production on another scene.[20] Moreover, these forms of material
production are often the most symbolically and materially marginalized
elements of contemporary production. Those of us who live in the global
North tend to focus on the work on our computer screens rather than
the work done to assemble and produce the materials that make up our
computers—work that often takes place in deregulated spaces under the
worst of working conditions. Similarly, the celebratory discourse around

the digitalization of all forms of cultural life in the present tends to suggest that the "dematerialization" of everyday objects, like our books, music, and films, is a positive ecological good, without attending to the exponential growth in electricity use and in the forms of material production (from laying cables to making our digital devices) that coincides with this digital revolution. This is not to say that digitization does not potentially have positive ecological consequences. It is rather to say that we will not be able to effectively assess these consequences without theorizing and attending to the irreducibly material dimensions of these activities.

For reasons political and ecological, then, our theories of biopolitics and thanatopolitics need to take into consideration the political economic and the forms of materiality bound up with it. If we are going to talk about the production and regulation of life and death by power, then we should think through the ways in which the global political-economic system is absolutely bound up with these determinations. Which lives get protected and valorized and which lives, as Henry Giroux and Zigmunt Bauman have differently theorized, are rendered disposable? What forms of death are made acceptable in the name of economically immunizing and maximizing the potential of certain lives?[21] For biopolitics and thanatopolitics to more effectively describe our present, then, we should theorize their limits in relation to both subjects and objects.

4. Theory, if it is to be true to its most radical impulses, should refuse to validate our fantasies of transcending the material.

Too many theoretical accounts of contemporary existence in the global North work to efface materiality. This has been true of work that has taken place under the cultural and linguistic turns, but it is also surprisingly true of many other accounts of contemporary life, whether these fall under the rubric of postmodernism, postindustrial society, new media studies, the digital humanities, or biopolitics and thanatopolitics. The will to theorize the emergence of new forms of cultural life is both necessary and commendable. There is no question that, within late capitalism and the emergence of digital culture, the very fabric of everyday life has changed in ways both subtle and profound. In order to theorize these transformations, new theoretical instruments and frameworks are necessary. Yet these theoretical frameworks ignore the material dimensions and underpinnings of these transformations only at the peril of reproducing the worst aspects of avatar fetishism.

A retooled conception of biopolitical production can be productively invoked to help us rethink our own moment of the emergence of the digital in a way that doesn't reproduce the logic of avatar fetishism. We should to attend to all the emergent forms of production—electronic, financial, affective, service—that Hardt and Negri term immaterial, but we need to also attend to the way in which these forms of production are dialectically tied to various forms of agricultural and industrial production and to the laboring bodies reshaped and deformed by such forms of production.[22] As Antony Bryant and Griselda Pollock put it, "Behind the surface of virtual worlds lie still very concrete processes of material production, labor, capital, and work by grounded beings in space and time."[23] Such a focus on labor and production, both material and so-called immaterial, enables us to avoid the celebratory and market-happy rhetoric that inflects much writing on new media and the digital humanities.

Fortunately, there are theorists of the virtual and digital who have been more cognizant of the complex political-economic, bodily, and epistemological issues raised by the digitization. Thus, rather than conceptualizing the digital realm as a space of dematerialization and endless possibility, theorists such as Brian Massumi, N. Katherine Hayles, and Pierre Lévy have stressed that the digital realm itself is a domain of materiality—one that intersects in complicated ways with the materialities of the body and of the nondigital world.[24] This emphasis on the virtual realm as also material is a crucial insight for challenging the logic of avatar fetishism. Yet much of this work (with the exception of Hayles) employs a conception of the materiality that blurs the distinction between different registers of the material, treating the linguistic, bodily, natural, and virtual as equally weighted in their material properties. While this understanding of materiality importantly challenges the tendency to see the virtual as a site of dematerialization, it runs the danger of not distinguishing enough between, say, the soft materialities of writing and digital production, on the one hand, and the more intransigent materialities of the fleshly body, earth, and tools and objects of electronic, affective, industrial, and agricultural production, on the other.

Attending to the forms of labor and materiality that are too often obscured by theories of the virtual involves taking a dialectical position outside of either contemporary boosterish rhetoric about the virtues of the digital or its opposite, Luddite condemnations of contemporary technology. To put it bluntly, digital technology will neither save us nor be the cause our downfall. Like all technology, its value is entirely dependent on how it is used. It opens up new possibilities but also puts in motion new problems. Accordingly, we should maintain what Fredric Jameson has termed a "properly ambivalent" relationship to it.[25] However, if we are able to move beyond the fantasy of dematerialization that is bound up with it, we will sidestep some of the most pressing problems currently attached to its uses and perhaps be able to reap more of its genuine benefits.

It is in theorizing these intransigent materialities that our theories still need to take account of a negative version of the subject/object dialectic, as well as related dialectics between the linguistic and the material, virtual and the actual. In the name of deconstructing these distinctions or rethinking materiality (for example, as virtuality), too many theories of contemporary life write everything under the signs of the subjective, linguistic, and virtual.

5. No subjects without objects; no objects without subjects.

The first part of this injunction should be self-evident by now. It is a version of the argument presented throughout *Insistence of the Material*. We can no longer afford to neglect the forms of materiality that shape our everyday existences, whether they comprise our bodies, our ecosystems, the objects that surround us, or the material dimensions of political-economic production. While Jane Bennett has eschewed the term object in her own conception of vibrant matter, I want to retain the term for its polemical force.[26] It is precisely because the word *object* indicates not only materiality shaped by change and processes of becoming but, more forcefully, materiality that has weight, force, and persistence (in short, being) that it remains crucial. While we do not want to think about our bodies or any other form of materiality as an object in the degraded sense with which the term is used in instrumental rationality, object-oriented ontologists such as Graham Harman and Levi Bryant have powerfully rethought the concept of the object as a way of attending not only to the realms of culture and subjectivity theorized so cogently during the linguistic and cultural turns but also to all that exceeds the domains of language and culture. As Bryant persuasively argues, "The domain of nature and the object has been foreclosed" within the logic of the linguistic and cultural turns.[27] He instead proposes to theorize "a *subjectless* object, or an object that is *for itself* rather than an object that is an opposing pole before or in front of a subject."[28] To the degree that Bryant posits the object as for itself, its being outside of any dependence on a subject, his theory represents a major advance over the limits of the cultural and linguistic turns and what Quentin Meillassoux has termed *correlationism*.[29] Such a position enables us to develop a political ecology and a political economy of valuing, respecting, and working with the objects that make up our material world, including the materiality of our own bodies and the possibilities and limits they produce.

Yet there is an ambiguity in Bryant's position. While I entirely agree that we need to theorize objects for themselves, it is important that this does not lead to the further step that we abandon theorizing the subjective, linguistic, or cultural. It may be important to suspend the relationship to the "opposing pole" of the subject in theorizing the object, yet this suspension should only be temporary and theoretical. For Bryant, it is indeed temporary, his book being an impressive example political and social force of the new posthumanism at its best. However, for other object-oriented ontologists, such as Ian Bogost, the turn to the object seems to be a corresponding turn away from the subject. It is here where Adorno's model of negative dialectics becomes an important corrective because it allows us to theorize the insistence and resistance of the object without abandoning a relationship to subjectivity. Hence I offer my second injunction: no objects without subjects.

This latter injunction functions as a mode of autocritique for the work many of us are starting to do as part of the material turn. The material turn has been invigorating and necessary for humanities and the social sciences work in the present, producing a range of work in fields as diverse as object-oriented ontology (OOO), animal studies, food studies, Deleuzian accounts of the body in process, political ecology, political economy, and so on. Yet I think it is crucial that in constructing what Cary Wolfe describes as the "posthumanities," in which we remove the human subject from the center of academic inquiry, that we do not come to ignore the subjective entirely.[30] Thus while we need to engage with and attend to the material, this engagement only takes on its full meaning as it relates to the subjective; however, broadly, we may want to define the latter category (inclusive of animals, for example). Moreover, it is crucial that posthumanism and the materialist turn not participate in a devaluation of human life or a rejection of human concerns, even as we rightly expand our ethical, political, and economic concerns beyond the circle of the human. There are too many pressing issues—of economic justice, social equality, and building a sustainable global life together—for us to turn away from the human, even as we necessarily turn toward that which is outside the human, sets limits on the human, and is obscured by the human. Similarly, there are too many forces in contemporary life that degrade human life, such as neoliberalism, neoimperialism, global warfare, and various discourses of social exclusion and exploitation, for it to be acceptable that theory even unconsciously participates in the denigration of the human. I am not calling for a return to humanism but rather a recognition that we have to think the posthumanities in a dialectical relationship to the older ethical force carried by the term and practice of the humanities at their best.

The subjective and subjectivity, as they are conceptualized in psychoanalytic theory, are still crucial terms for political theorizing—ones that we abandon only at our peril. As a critical vocabulary, psychoanalytic theory initially seems relentlessly centered on the human and so may appear to be outmoded in the moment of the material turn. Yet, as I have demonstrated throughout *Insistence of the Material*, psychoanalysis gives us a powerful account of how embodied subjects interact with the material world. More thoroughly than any other form of critical theory, it traces the complex dynamics of attraction and repulsion, fetishism and disavowal, pleasure and enjoyment, and incorporation and excorporation by which subjects engage with the material world and the materiality of their own bodies. It also provides a theoretical framework for conceptualizing embodiment and the intersections of the symbolic, fantasmatic, and the material that shape both our maps of the body and that which lies outside these maps. Thus, if part of the material turn is to produce a different relationship between human subjects and the materiality, then psychoanalysis is indispensable.

6. In order to deal with the challenges of the material turn and the growth of biopolitics, we need to be politically creative and theoretically impure.

A willful theoretical impurity has been central to the work undertaken in *Insistence of the Material*. This theoretical impurity has been neither accidental nor arbitrary. It is, instead, a product of the very movement outward, from the certainties of subjectivity and culture and from the fantasies of control that language and our theoretical systems provide to the heterogeneity and alterity of the material world itself. Thus I have attempted to let the objects—in terms of both the literary texts examined and the mate-rialities engaged by these texts—dictate the theory I employ. Part of this work can be described as the opening out of thought to the contingencies of the material world and to its insistence. To attend to the material, then, means learning to also be contingent in the theory we employ and in the political solutions we suggest.

The importance of theoretical heterodoxy is also dictated by the growth of biopolitics and thanatopolitics as central forms of political and econom-ic power in the present. If, in an earlier twentieth-century moment, it was somewhat easier to separate the workings of political-economic exploita-tion from the operations of the state and to look for protection from the latter in relationship to the former, in our twenty-first century dominated by neoliberal biopolitics, the forms of governmentality taken up by the state and other sovereign or semisovereign bodies have been thorough-ly saturated with the logic of human capital and the economic calculus underwritten by the capitalist world system. Thus we will need a politics that challenges both economic forms of exploitation and the violence underwritten by various forms of governmentality (whether state based or grounded in transnational bodies such as nongovernmental organiza-tions or the United Nations). This double manifestation of contemporary biopolitics (both economic and governmental) perhaps suggests the rea-sons for the reemergence of anarchism in the last twenty years as both a theoretical and political project. While I have many of the same theoretical problems with anarchistic notions of completely stateless governance that I do with Hardt and Negri's conception of a purely communicative and immanent conception of production, I think we can productively borrow from anarchism its suspicion of both capitalist and governmental power.

We can also borrow from Hardt and Negri's conception of the "com-mons" as distinct from both the private and the public.[31] If the private is the product of accumulation by dispossession and capitalist exploitation and the public is that which is owned and maintained by governments, the commons is that which is owned as common wealth by the people. We need a politics and an economics that will preserve and enhance the global commons, for it is only within such a self-managed sphere that biopolitics does not function as a form of subjugation and exploitation; rather, the creation of a positive or affirmative biopolitics, as we saw in Silko's *Almanac of the Dead*, becomes possible—literally a politics of life. Such an affirma-tive biopolitics is central to the vision of both Hardt and Negri and Silko.

We can only access such a positive biopolitics by first attending to the negative, whether this is the negativity presented by subjects in their resistance to biopolitics and economic exploitation; the negativity presented by subjects in relationship to each other around global histories of exclusion and violence; or the negativity exerted by the material insistence of our bodies, of the material and ecological world in which we exist, and of the material dimensions of production. Thus we need to articulate a conception of global life that allows for the expression and "working-through" of the forms of negativity and conflict that are central to democratic struggle.[32] The commons can only be a common source of wealth and productivity if a process of material struggle and democratic negotiation has allowed it to indeed become a common resource for all actors and as well a space that recognizes all material actors, as Latour has theorized them. We also, however, should never imagine it as a pure space of positivity—for in doing so, we deny the space of the negative to challenge this positivity as exclusionary and negating even (especially) in its claims to be fully inclusive.

7. No common without the commons.

In different elaborations of the idea of the commons by Michael Hardt and Jodi Dean, both theorists make a distinction between the common (as Hardt describes it, "The results of human labor and creativity, such as ideas language, affects, and so forth") and the commons ("the earth and all the resources associated with it: the land, the forests, the water, the air, minerals and so forth").[33] Both theorists go on to focus their accounts entirely on the common as the source of human productivity. Yet, while perhaps theoretically helpful for attending to the distinctive features of human productivity, this distinction runs the danger of again divorcing the linguistic, cultural, and affective from the material, object-oriented, and ecological. If we are to make this distinction, then we also need the injunction no common without the commons. While the common may be characterized by abundance, this abundance is predicated on limits (historically changing limits but limits nonetheless): the finite and material domain of the commons. We may find new ways to nurture and expand the resources of the commons, but this can only be done if we theorize our continuing reliance and dependence on them, as well as the dependence of immaterial production on material production and resource extraction.

The political economic concept of the common also needs to be a political-ecological conception of the commons. We need forms of theory and conceptions of politics that will allow us to attend to the ecological dimensions of our shared world. Part of this is developing a politics of attending to the material, both the material dimensions and possibilities of everyday life and the way in which all our actions have ecological and material effects. In balancing political-economic justice and political-ecological sustainability, we will need to be creative. On one level, given the reach and interconnectedness of the world system, our solutions will have to be global in their outlook. Yet, in working toward global solutions, we can learn from and link together a range of more regional and localized forms of alternative political-economic and political-ecological organizations.

The models of economic solidarity and cooperative production that are being practiced in sectors of the contemporary Brazilian economy present one productive model of a way (as Boaventura de Sousa Santos puts it) "beyond the capitalist canon."[34] Moreover, groups like the EZLN and the global peasant movement, La Via Campesina, represent other ways forward. What is distinctive about each of these forms of organization is that they are neither capitalist nor state oriented but rather represent the fruits of autonomous organizing and production in the present. They are not necessarily opposed to states, but they are movements grounded in the commons rather than the public or the private.

The measure of such forms of praxis should not be their doctrinal purity or their revolutionary or reformist rhetoric but how well they contribute to the on-the-ground work—literally the *material* work—of global economic justice, democracy, and sustainability. Just as the material should be that against which we gauge the explanatory power of our theories, it should also be that against which we measure of our conceptions of justice, democracy, and sustainability.

8. The impure resources of the humanities can be invaluable guides for helping us think through a workable posthumanism and a new relationship to the material world.

The literature I have examined throughout *Insistence of the Material* made the material turn long before contemporary critical theory. This should be an indication that we should look to literature and other forms of cultural production as indices of the way forward. Because of their gloriously impure and sensuous nature—they generally put the material (their own materials) and the affective above the dictates of reason or argument—the texts generated by artistic and cultural production have usually been more oriented toward the material than the sphere of theoretical production. Accordingly, we should take our cue from artistic and cultural production in tarrying with the material.

If we take as axiomatic the two propositions with which I began *Insistence of the Material*—(1) we need to attend to the material and (2) language and other forms of materiality exist in necessary contradiction—then literature and the arts become some of the crucial media through which we can access the material. The artistic work (conceived broadly as including the works of popular culture as well as the traditional arts), wherever it is primarily motivated by its own internal formal challenges or by the attempt to make reference to the larger world, takes the engagement with materiality as its central focus. Moreover, since its attempts at a solution are sensuous and material in and of themselves, we can look to art as a guide for how we should engage the material.

As Cary Wolfe has demonstrated, posthumanism does not mean the death of the humanities but their renewed relevance. While we may finally want to rename them as the posthumanities, the humanities can point us in the direction of attending to all that falls outside the human, cultural, and linguistic. What might such a different conception of the humanities—the posthumanities—look like? The answer to this question is being explored by those who are making the material turn in contemporary humanities scholarship.

It has also been answered, in a myriad of different ways, by contemporary writers. Accordingly, as an indication of the way in which we should let the arts and cultural production guide us in our theoretical endeavors, I want to conclude *Insistence of the Material* not with my own words but with the words of Karen Yamashita in her brilliant novel *Tropic of Orange*. The novel constructs a willfully failed allegory of contemporary Los Angeles and its relationship to the larger transnational spaces of the Americas and the pacific rim.[35] By all rights, Yamashita deserves a chapter of her own in *Insistence of the Material*. Her book traverses some of the same ground as *Almanac of the Dead* but does so in a finally more affirmative and playful manner (while still importantly negative at points).

Her vision is a thoroughly political one, reading Los Angeles and the space of the U.S./Mexico border from the bottom up through the eyes of immigrants, laborers, and cultural workers from a myriad of transnational backgrounds and presenting an image of the commons in the homeless living in a permanently stalled traffic jam on Interstate 405. It is also economic, detailing the violence of NAFTA and charting the five hundred years of imperialism that have shaped the spaces of greater Los Angeles and greater Mexico. Finally, it is brilliantly ecological—attending to the forms of materiality and the ecosystems that shape, constrain, and enable human existence. I end *Insistence of the Material* with a stunning passage that moves between the human-built environment and the larger non-human environment in which it is embedded as well as between human rhythms (represented by the homeless conductor, Manzanar, who conducts the sounds of the city) and much longer ecological rhythms. This passage can perhaps serve as an augur of the theoretical work we still have to do in insisting on the material:

The past spread out like a great starry fan and then folded in upon itself.

Encroaching on this vision was a larger one: the great Pacific stretching along its great rim, brimming over long coastal shores from one hemisphere to the other. And there were the names of places he had never seen, from the southernmost tip of Chile to the Galapagos, skirting the tiny waist of land at Panama, up Baja to Big Sur to Vancouver, around the Aleutians to the Bering Strait. From the North, that peaceful ocean swept from Vladivostok around the Japan Isles and the Korean peninsula to Shanghai, Taipei, Ho Chi Minh City, through a thousand islands of the Philippines, Malaysia, Indonesia, and Micronesia, sweeping about that giant named Australia and her sister New Zealand. Manzanar looked out on this strange end and beginning: the very last point West, and after that it was all East. The inky waves with their moonlit spume stuttering against the shore seemed to speak this very truth—garbage jettisoned back prohibiting further progress.

And there was the great land mass to the south, the southern continent and the central Americas. Everything was for a brief moment fixed. Fixed as they had supposedly always been.

Of course, with continental drift, the changing crust of the Earth's surface had over billions of years come to this, cracked into continents, spread apart by large bodies of water. Now human civilization covered everything in layers, generations of building upon building upon building the residue, the burial sites, and garbage that defined people after people for centuries. Manzanar saw it, but darkly, before it would shift irrevocably.[36]

Acknowledgments

Writing is, of course, a material practice. The material practice of writing this book has been sustained by many different individuals and communities. Without this sustenance, this book would have never congealed into its present form. Thus I want to acknowledge all those who helped me materialize this book, while recognizing that such acknowledgments always remain inadequate. The practice of writing is oddly divided between the solitary and the collective. While I typically face the computer screen in the intentionally isolated spaces of my office (at home and at work), I write with the knowledge that I have thought and rethought my ideas in the context of various communities.

Before turning to the communities that have sustained me, I want to acknowledge specific individuals who have been central in catalyzing the object that is *Insistence of the Material*. First and foremost, I want to thank Elizabeth Hatmaker, who not only is the love of my life and my central intellectual interlocutor but whose poetry gave me intimations of what a materialist poetics and writing practice could look like. Next, I thank Dodie Bellamy, whose writing taught me that language and embodiment, signification and materiality, could be brilliantly and often vulnerably intertwined. Thank you for your unswerving friendship, mentorship, and support throughout this book project. I would also like to thank Earl Jackson Jr., one of my mentors in graduate school and the person who initially introduced me to almost all the novels that I analyze in *Insistence of the Material*. If I do justice to these novels, it is because of his inspiration. I also thank my graduate student Ericka Wills, who taught me how to think about biopolitics in the context of Marxist theory and whose work on *Almanac of the Dead* influenced my own. If her own work has taken on a more activist trajectory, it is a tribute to her commitment to materialist praxis. I hope my own work can measure up. I want to thank José David Saldívar, Sophia McClennen, and Russ Castronovo, all three of whom have been wonderful mentors, intellectual interlocutors, and friends throughout the process of this book's composition. I also thank John Ferrari, a wonderful research assistant during this book's genesis.

I thank the editor I have now worked with on two different books at the University of Minnesota Press, Richard Morrison. Richard is a remarkable editor and a sage and patient guide. He has become an excellent friend. I thank you for making this book as strong as it could possibly be. I also thank Richard's editorial assistant, Erin Warholm-Wohlenhaus, and all of the other tireless folks at Minnesota who enabled the production of this book. I wish to thank five of my colleagues at Illinois State University and elsewhere who read and contributed greatly to different chapters: Rebecca Saunders, Valerie Kaussen, Robert McLaughlin, Tim Hunt, and Gabriel Gudding.

I also recognize the communities that have sustained me. First and foremost is my home institution, Illinois State University (ISU). While as an interdisciplinary English studies program we have our share of productive disagreements, such disagreements are always generative. I regularly find my thought challenged and reshaped by my discussions with colleagues, graduate students, and undergraduate students at ISU. ISU is complexly poised between the research university and the teaching college, and this distinctive positioning forces all of us toward self-accounting, recognizing how the different forms of work undertaken in higher education pull us in creative and sometimes conflicting directions. There is a tradition of sustained engagement with and production of experimental literature at ISU, and this book has benefited from that tradition in ways both subtle and profound. Many of my colleagues have been crucial contributors to my work on this book, including Lee Brasseur, Karen Coats, Ricardo Cortez Cruz, Chris De Santis, Kristin Dykstra, Katherine Ellison, Kass Fleisher, Duriel Harris, Angela Hass, Julie Jung, Hilary K. Justice, Susan Kim, Brooklynn Lehner, Francesco Levato, Josette Lorig, Krishna Manavalli, William McBride, Brian Rejack, Amy E. Robillard, Jerry Savage, K. Aaron Smith, Ron Strickland, Curtis White, Michael Wollitz, Jessica Zhang, and Kirstin Hotelling Zona.

Another community central to the genesis of this book has been my adopted Canadian home, McMaster University, in Hamilton, Ontario, where I was the recipient of a Fulbright Research Grant at the Center on Globalization and the Human Condition. My thanks to Fulbright Canada and the wonderful community of scholars, researchers, and staff at McMaster, including Henry Giroux, Nancy Johnson, Susie O'Brien, Tony

Porter, Petra Rethmann, Peter Walmsley, and Rachel Zhou. Hamilton with its thriving art and music scene was a fantastic home away from home.

Another community is my extended group of academic and personal friends, a number of whom contributed to the final shape taken by *Insistence of the Material*. I thank Sally Bachner, Robin Baldridge, Thomas Banks, Renee Bergland, Cathy Birkenstein-Graff, Ashley Byock, Sam Cohen, Scott Davis, Carla Freccero, Kevin Floyd, Michael Gillespie, Gerald Graff, Sean Grattan, Kirsten Silva Gruesz, Christian Haines, Peter Hitchcock, Andrew Hoberek, Kevin Killian, Sophia McClennen, Christoph Ribbat, Max Rovner, Kirsti Sandy, David Schmid, Carsten Strathausen, and Rob Wilson.

I would like to acknowledge the love and support of my immediate family: my parents, Joseph and Giovanna Breu, and my sister, Eugenia Baron, her husband, Randall Baron, and daughters, Zoe and Alexis Baron. Acknowledgments would not be complete, of course, without recognition of our trio of cats, Irma, Chester, and Freddy, who alternately helped and hindered the writing process. Finally, I acknowledge my extended Facebook community. While this book questions the boosterish rhetoric around virtuality, my Facebook friends have truly been sustaining throughout this process. Despite the site's commercialism and problematic relationship to the production of the commons, it has often been a place in which I floated ideas, marked milestones in my writing, or just blew off steam while I was in the process of composing. It helped keep me intellectually loose and stopped me from pacing so much. Thank you for that (and for putting up with my periodic spelling and grammar errors as well)—you know who you are!

Finally, I thank the community of intersex activists and scholars who have illuminated and challenged the medical procedures that I chronicle in the Preface. You have truly made a difference in my life and the lives of many others. You have also enabled me to be mentally and physically healthy enough to write this book. I dedicate it to you.

Notes

Preface

1. For extended accounts of intersex (i.e., forms of embodiment that do not fully correspond to the binary of sex), see the following texts: Anne Fausto-Sterling, *Sexing the Body: Gender Politics and the Construction of Sexuality* (New York: Basic Books, 2000); Katrina Karkazis, *Fixing Sex: Intersex, Medical Authority, and Lived Experience* (Durham, N.C.: Duke University Press, 2008); Elizabeth Reis, *Bodies in Doubt: An American History of Intersex* (Baltimore: Johns Hopkins University Press, 2009); Saron E. Preves, *Intersex and Identity: The Contested Self* (New Brunswick, N.J.: Rutgers University Press, 2003); Alice Domurat Dreger, *Hermaphrodites and the Medical Invention of Sex* (Cambridge, Mass.: Harvard University Press, 2000); Alice Domurat Dreger and April Herndon, "Progress and Politics in the Intersex Rights Movement," *GLQ: A Journal of Lesbian and Gay Studies* 15, no. 2 (2009): 199–24. There has also been a recent attempt to move away from the language of *intersex* and toward the clinical designation of *disorder of sex development* (DSD), because such a nomenclature enables those who need surgery (rather than those, like myself, who didn't initially need it) to receive it and have it covered by insurance. There are also those in the intersex community who feel stigmatized by the term *intersex*. For myself and many intersex activists, however, there is something lost by this shift, especially as it repathologizes a condition that many of us have been arguing should not be pathologized. It also tends to reinforce a binary gender model. Elizabeth Reis's suggestion of renaming DSD as "divergence of sex development" solves the first issue but not the second (159). Ellen K. Feder has tried to make the argument that DSD is a more progressive designation because it does not constitute an identity in the Foucauldian sense, but I find her argument far from persuasive. Indeed, as I will argue throughout this book, it points to the limits of the linguistic and cultural turns for theorizing about intersex and for embodiment more generally. I am not concerned with preserving intersex as an identity (since it is one I at best only partially identify with, as I basically identify as a man and am embodied and ideologically interpellated largely as such) but as an embodiment and as an account of bodies that does not forcefully inscribe gender/sex dualisms. See Ellen K. Feder, "Imperatives of

Normality: From 'Intersex' to 'Disorders of Sex Development,'" *GLQ: A Journal of Lesbian and Gay Studies* 15, no. 2 (2009): 225–47.

2. This information is drawn from the U.S. government's "PubMed Health" website: http://www.ncbi.nlm.nih.gov/pubmedhealth/PMH0002265. From everything I have read, this is a relatively conservative estimate of the number of occurrences, yet even with these statistics, the frequency is higher than most other "congenital birth defects."

3. Reis, *Bodies in Doubt*, 23–55.

4. See Patricia Cornwell, *Portrait of a Killer: Jack the Ripper—Case Closed* (New York: Putnam, 2003).

5. Karkazis, *Fixing Sex*, 7.

6. Adele Clarke, Janet K. Shim, Laura Mamo, Jennifer Ruth Fosket, and Jennifer R. Fishman, "Biomedicalization: A Theoretical and Substantive Introduction," in *Biomedicalization: Technoscience, Health, and Illness in the U.S.,* ed. Adele Clarke, Janet K. Shim, Laura Mamo, Jennifer Ruth Fosket, and Jennifer R. Fishman (Durham, N.C.: Duke University Press, 2010), 1.

7. For thoughtful accounts of the material dimensions of intersex, in addition to Fausto-Sterling's account cited previously, see Iain Morland, "What Can Queer Theory Do for Intersex?," *GLQ: A Journal of Lesbian and Gay Studies* 15, no. 2 (2009): 285–312; and Vernon Rosario "Quantum Sex: Intersex and the Molecular Destruction of Sex," *GLQ: A Journal of Lesbian and Gay Studies* 15, no. 2 (2009): 267–84.

8. Fausto-Sterling, Preves, and Reis each describe hypospadias as one of the forms of intersex, as do Dreger and Herndon in their jointly authored article, although Dreger argues that it should not be considered a form of hermaphroditism in her book. Karkazis argues that intersex activists tend to categorize it as a form of intersex, while clinicians do not. The latter, though, do categorize it as a DSD. (See Karkazis, *Fixing Sex*, 144–46.)

9. Given this preface and the personal and material context it provides for the work of literary criticism that follows, readers may ask why I have not analyzed Jeffery Eugenides's Pulitzer Prize–winning novel, *Middlesex*. While I admire Eugenides's novel, have taught it, and indeed have recommended it in print as a way of teaching high school students about intersex, the novel itself is more metafictional than materialist in its engagement with intersex. Thus it does not fall into the category of the "late-capitalist literature of materiality" that I am explicating in this book; it instead falls into the tradition of metafiction against which the literature of materiality, in part, emerged. Eugenides's lack of engagement with the material and his turn to metafiction is why I find his book less than fully compelling as an account of intersex, as powerful and thoughtful as it is. See Jeffrey Eugenides, *Middlesex: A Novel* (New York: Picador, 2007); and Christopher Breu, "Middlesex Meditations: Understanding and Teaching Intersex," *English Journal* 98, no. 4 (2009): 102–8.

Introduction

1. Diana Coole and Samantha Frost, "Introducing the New Materialisms," in *New Materialisms: Ontology, Agency, and Politics*, ed. Diana Coole and Samantha Frost (Durham, N.C.: Duke University Press, 2010), 1–43: 6; Richard Terdiman, *Body and Story: The Ethics and Practice of Theoretical Conflict* (Baltimore: Johns Hopkins University Press, 2005), 14.

2. The texts I have in mind in thinking about biopolitics, biopolitical production, and thanatopolitics are Michel Foucault, *The History of Sexuality, Volume 1: An Introduction*, trans. Robert Hurley (New York: Vintage, 1978), 135–59; Foucault, *"Society Must Be Defended": Lectures at the Collège de France 1975–1976*, trans. David Macey (New York: Picador, 2003), 239–64; Foucault, *The Birth of Biopolitics: Lectures at the Collège de France, 1978–1979*, trans. Graham Burchell (New York: Picador, 2010); Giorgio Agamben, *Homo Sacer: Sovereign Power and Bare Life*, trans. Daniel Heller-Roazen (Stanford, Calif.: Stanford University Press, 1998); Michael Hardt and Antonio Negri, *Empire* (Cambridge, Mass.: Harvard University Press, 2000); Hardt and Negri, *Multitude: War and Democracy in the Age of Empire* (New York: Penguin, 2004); Hardt and Negri, *Commonwealth* (Cambridge, Mass.: Harvard University Press, 2009); Achille Mbembe, "Necropolitics," trans. Libby Meintjes, *Public Culture* 15, no. 1 (2003): 11–40; Roberto Esposito, *Bíos: Biopolitics and Philosophy*, trans. Timothy Campbell (Minneapolis: University of Minnesota Press, 2008); Adele Clarke, Laura Mamo, Jennifer Ruth Fosket, Jennifer R. Fishman, and Janet K. Shim, eds., *Biomedicalization: Technoscience, Health, and Illness in the U.S.* (Durham, N.C.: Duke University Press, 2010).

3. Fredric Jameson treats the cultural turn and postmodernism as fully coincident (and it is he who first coined the former phrase). See Fredric Jameson, *The Cultural Turn: Selected Writings on the Postmodern, 1983–1998* (London: Verso, 1998).

4. Quentin Meillassoux, *After Finitude: An Essay on the Necessity of Contingency*, trans. Ray Brassier (London: Continuum, 2008), 5.

5. Stacy Alaimo, "Trans-corporeal Feminisms and the Ethical Space of Nature," in *Material Feminisms*, ed. Stacy Alaimo and Susan Hekman (Bloomington: Indiana University Press, 2008), 237–64: 242.

6. Stacy Alaimo and Susan Hekman, "Introduction: Emerging Models of Materiality in Feminist Theory," in *Material Feminisms*, ed. Stacy Alaimo and Susan Hekman (Bloomington: Indiana University Press, 2008), 1–19: 6.

7. Coole and Frost, "Introducing the New Materialisms," 6.

8. See Sarah Ahmed, "Orientations Matter," in *New Materialisms: Ontology, Agency, and Politics*, ed. Diana Coole and Samantha Frost (Durham, N.C.: Duke University Press, 2010), 234–57; Sonia Kruks, "Simone de Beauvoir: Engaging Discrepant Materialisms," in *New Materialisms: Ontology, Agency, and Politics*,

ed. Diana Coole and Samantha Frost (Durham, N.C.: Duke University Press, 2010), 258–80.

9. For some of the more compelling critiques of the linguistic, cultural, and rhetorical turns, see Susan Hekman, "Constructing the Ballast: An Ontology for Feminism," in *Material Feminisms*, ed. Stacy Alaimo and Susan Hekman (Bloomington: Indiana University Press, 2008), 85–119; Ian Hacking, *The Social Construction of What?* (Cambridge, Mass.: Harvard University Press, 1999); Bruno Latour, "Why Has Critique Run Out of Steam? From Matters of Fact to Matters of Concern," *Critical Inquiry* 30, no. 2 (2004): 225–48.

10. For Butler's classic theorization of performativity, see Judith Butler, *Gender Trouble: Feminism and the Subversion of Identity*, 2nd ed. (New York: Routledge, 1999), 175–204.

11. See Teresa de Lauretis, *Freud's Drive: Psychoanalysis, Literature, and Film* (New York: Palgrave Macmillan, 2010); Elizabeth Grosz, *Jacques Lacan: A Feminist Introduction* (New York: Routledge, 1991); Grosz, *Volatile Bodies: Toward a Corporeal Feminism* (Bloomington: Indiana University Press, 1994), 27–61; Lee Edelman, *No Future: Queer Theory and the Death Drive* (Durham, N.C.: Duke University Press, 2004); Bruce Fink, *The Lacanian Subject: Between Language and Jouissance* (Princeton, N.J.: Princeton University Press, 1996).

12. De Lauretis, *Freud's Drive*, 10.

13. Frantz Fanon, *Black Skin, White Masks*, trans. Charles Lam Markmann (New York: Grove Press, 1967), 112.

14. Louis Althusser, *For Marx*, trans. Ben Brewster (London: Verso, 2010), 111.

15. See Grosz, *Volatile Bodies*; Rosi Braidotti, *Metamorphoses: Towards a Materialist Theory of Becoming* (Cambridge: Polity, 2002); Anne Fausto-Sterling, *Sexing the Body: Gender Politics and the Construction of Sexuality* (New York: Basic Books, 2000); Stacy Alaimo and Susan Hekman, eds., *Material Feminisms* (Bloomington: University of Indiana Press, 2008).

16. Grosz, *Volatile Bodies*, 23.

17. Alice Dreger, *Hermaphrodites and the Medical Invention of Sex* (Cambridge, Mass.: Harvard University Press, 2000); C. Jacob Hale, "Sex Change, Social Change: Reflections on Identity, Institutions, and Imperialism," *Hypatia* 23, no. 1 (Winter 2008): 204–7; Hale, "Tracing a Ghostly Memory in My Throat: Reflections on FTM Feminist Voice and Agency," in *Men Doing Feminism*, ed. Tom Digby (New York: Routledge, 1998), 99–130.

18. Grosz, *Volatile Bodies*, 23.

19. Alain Badiou, "Lacan and the Pre-Socratics," in *Lacan: The Silent Partners*, ed. Slavoj Žižek (London: Verso, 2006), 7–17; Slavoj Žižek, *The Parallax View* (Cambridge, Mass.: MIT Press, 2006), 26.

20. For Lacan's account of the real as uncoded or only partly coded materiality, see his discussion of the real in seminar III and his discussion of "Das Ding" in seminar VII: Jacques Lacan, *The Psychoses, 1955–1956: The Seminar of Jacques Lacan*

Book III, trans. Russell Grigg (New York: Norton, 1993), 9; Jacques Lacan, *The Ethics of Psychoanalysis, 1959–1960: The Seminar of Jacques Lacan Book VII*, trans. Dennis Porter (New York: Norton, 1992), 43–70.

21. Lacan, "The Mirror Stage as Formative of the I Function as Revealed in Psychoanalytic Experience," in *Écrits: The First Complete Edition in English*, trans. Bruce Fink (New York: Norton, 2006), 75–81: 78.

22. Fink, *Lacanian Subject*, 26–28. For Lacan's most provocative discussion of the *objet petit a*, see Jacques Lacan, *The Four Fundamental Concepts of Psychoanalysis: The Seminar of Jacques Lacan Book XI*, trans. Alan Sheridan (New York: Norton, 1977), 263–76.

23. Fausto-Sterling, *Sexing the Body*, 60–63.

24. See Graham Harman, *The Quadruple Object* (Winchester, U.K.: Zero Books, 2011); Levi Bryant, *The Democracy of Objects* (Ann Arbor, Mich.: Open Humanities Press, 2011); Ian Bogost, *Alien Phenomenology, or What It's Like to Be a Thing* (Minneapolis: University of Minnesota Press, 2012); Jane Bennett, *Vibrant Matter: A Political Ecology of Things* (Durham, N.C.: Duke University Press, 2010); Bill Brown, *A Sense of Things: The Object Matter of American Literature* (Chicago: University of Chicago Press, 2004); Bruno Latour, *The Politics of Nature: How to Bring the Sciences into Social Democracy* (Cambridge, Mass.: Harvard University Press, 2004); Bruno Latour, *Reassembling the Social: An Introduction to Actor-Network-Theory* (Oxford: Oxford University Press, 2005), 63–86.

25. Brown, *Sense*, 18.

26. Brown, *Material*, 12–18.

27. Ahmed, "Orientations Matter," 172.

28. Bryant, *Democracy of Objects*, 18–19.

29. Ibid., 203.

30. Bennett, *Vibrant Matter*, 21, 94; Latour, *Politics of Nature*, 246–47.

31. Bennett, *Vibrant Matter*, 103; Latour, *Politics of Nature*, 238.

32. Latour, *Politics of Nature*, 67; Bennett, *Vibrant Matter*, 21.

33. Theodor Adorno, *Negative Dialectics*, trans. E. B. Ashton (New York: Continuum, 1973).

34. Adorno, *Negative Dialectics*, 183.

35. Max Horkheimer and Theodor Adorno, *Dialectic of Enlightenment*, trans. John Cumming (New York: Continuum, 1999).

36. Horkheimer and Adorno, *Dialectic of Enlightenment*, 17.

37. Adorno, *Negative Dialectics*, 176.

38. Ahmed, "Orientations Matter," 34.

39. Foucault, *"Society Must Be Defended,"* 240.

40. Ibid., 242.

41. My understanding of neoliberalism comes primarily from David Harvey, Henry Giroux, and Foucault. See David Harvey, *A Brief History of Neoliberalism* (Oxford: Oxford University Press, 2005); Henry Giroux, *Against the Terror of*

Neoliberalism: Politics beyond the Age of Greed (New York: Paradigm Publishers, 2008); Foucault, *Birth of Biopolitics*.

42. Foucault, *Birth of Biopolitics*, 226–29.

43. Clarke et al., *Biomedicalization*, 1–87.

44. Agamben, *Homo Sacer*, 1–2.

45. Mbembe, "Necropolitics," 11.

46. Ibid., 11.

47. Esposito, *Bios*, 44–77. My thinking about death in relationship to politics and embodiment has, of course, also been shaped by Russ Castronovo's *Necrocitizenship: Death, Eroticism, and the Public Sphere in the United States* (Durham, N.C.: Duke University Press, 2001).

48. Hardt and Negri, *Empire*, 30.

49. Hardt and Negri, *Multitude*, 114–15.

50. Guy Debord, *The Society of the Spectacle*, trans. Donald Nicolson-Smith (Detroit: Black and Red, 2010).

51. See N. Katherine Hayles, *How We Became Post Human: Virtual Bodies in Cybernetics, Literature, and Informatics* (Chicago: University of Chicago Press, 1999), esp. 1–25; and Hayles, "Traumas of Code," in *Digital and Other Virtualities: Renegotiating the Image*, ed. Antony Bryant and Griselda Pollock (London: I. B. Taurus, 2010), 23–41.

52. Arjun Appadurai, *Modernity at Large: Cultural Dimensions of Globalization* (Minneapolis: University of Minnesota Press, 1997), 27–47.

53. Arif Dirlik, *Global Modernity: Modernity in the Age of Capitalism* (London: Paradigm, 2001); David Harvey, *The Enigma of Capital and the Crises of Capitalism* (Oxford: Oxford University Press, 2010); Harvey, *Brief History of Neoliberalism*; Immanuel Wallerstein, *The Essential Wallerstein* (New York: New Press, 2000), esp. 71–106; Giovanni Arrighi, *The Long Twentieth Century: Money, Power, and the Origins of Our Times* (London: Verso, 1994); Aníbal Quijano, "Coloniality of Power, Eurocentrism, and Latin America," in *Coloniality at Large: Latin America and the Postcolonial Debate*, ed. Mabel Moraña, Enrique Dussel, and Carlos A. Jáuregui (Durham, N.C.: Duke University Press, 2008), 181–224; Wallerstein and Quijano, "Americanity as a Concept, or the Americas in the Modern World System," *International Social Science Journal*, no. 44 (1992): 549–57.

54. Saskia Sassen, *The Global City: New York, London, Tokyo* (Princeton, N.J.: Princeton University Press, 2001); Sassen, *Globalization and Its Discontents: Essays on the New Mobility of People and Money* (New York: New Press, 1998).

55. My thinking on the world system in relationship to literature has also been shaped by José David Saldívar, *Trans-Americanity: Subaltern Modernities, Global Coloniality, and the Cultures of Greater Mexico* (Durham, N.C.: Duke University Press, 2011).

56. Wallerstein, *The Essential Wallerstein*, 93.

57. David Harvey, *Neoliberalism*, 159–60.

58. See Žižek, *The Parallax View*, 370.

59. See, for example, Kevin Floyd, *The Reification of Desire: Toward a Queer Marxism* (Minneapolis: University of Minnesota Press, 2009); and Robert Babe, *Cultural Studies and Political Economy: Toward a New Integration* (Lanham, Md.: Lexington Books, 2008).

60. Immanuel Wallerstein, *Decline of American Power* (New York: New Press, 2003), 49–52.

61. David Harvey, *The Limits to Capital*, new and updated ed. (London: Verso, 2007), 123.

62. Karl Marx, *Capital*, vol. 1, trans. Ben Fowkes (New York: Vintage, 1976), 163–64.

63. On the dynamic of racial borrowing in the early twentieth century, see Christopher Breu, *Hard-Boiled Masculinities* (Minneapolis: University of Minnesota Press, 2005), esp. 11–13.

64. For the canonical accounts of these different versions of postmodernism, see Jean-François Lyotard, *The Postmodern Condition: A Report on Knowledge*, trans. Geoff Bennington and Brian Massumi (Minneapolis: University of Minnesota Press, 1984); McHale, *Postmodernist Fiction* (New York: Routledge, 1987), 3–36; Linda Hutcheon, *A Poetics of Postmodernism*, 2nd ed. (New York: Routledge, 2002), 3–21; Fredric Jameson, *Postmodernism, or, the Cultural Logic of Late Capitalism* (Durham, NC: Duke University Press, 1991), esp. 1–54; David Harvey, *The Condition of Postmodernity: An Enquiry into the Origins of Cultural Change* (Oxford: Blackwell, 1990), 39–65.

65. Majorie Perloff, *21st-Century Modernism: The "New" Poetics* (Oxford: Blackwell, 2002), iii; Andreas Huyssen "High/Low in an Expanded Field," *Modernism/Modernity* 9, no. 3 (2002): 366. See also Huyssen's more recent elaboration of the multiple modernities model: "Introduction: World Cultures, World Cities," in *Other Cities, Other Worlds* (Durham, N.C.: Duke University Press, 2008), 1–21; see also Appadurai's now classic formulation of "modernity at large" in *Modernity at Large*, 27–47.

66. See the following for articles that make use of the "post-postmodern" signifier in a range of different contexts: Alan Kirby, "The Death of Postmodernism and Beyond," *Philosophy Today: A Magazine of Ideas* (May/June 2009); Jeffrey T. Nealon, "Periodizing the 80s," in *A Leftist Ontology: Beyond Relativism and Identity Politics*, ed. Carsten Strathausen (Minneapolis: University of Minnesota Press, 2009), 54–79; Robert McLaughlin, "Post-Postmodern Discontent: Contemporary Fiction and the Social World," *Symplokē* 12, nos. 1–2 (2004): 53–68; See also Andrew Hoberek's thoughtful comments on the issue in Hoberek, "Introduction: After Postmodernism," *Twentieth Century Literature* 53, no. 3 (Fall 2007): 233–47.

67. Marianne DeKoven, *Utopia Limited: The Sixties and the Emergence of the Postmodern* (Durham, N.C.: Duke University Press, 2004).

68. Rachel Adams, "The Ends of America, the Ends of Postmodernism," in *Twentieth Century Literature* 53, no. 3 (Fall 2007): 250.

69. Phillip Wegner, *Life between Two Deaths, 1989–2001: U.S. Culture in the Long Nineties* (Durham, N.C.: Duke University Press, 2009).

70. Hardt and Negri, *Multitude*, xvi.

71. William Whyte Jr., *The Organization Man* (Philadelphia: University of Pennsylvania Press, 2002); C. Wright Mills, *White Collar: The American Middle Classes* (Oxford: Oxford University Press, 2002).

72. As Debord nicely puts it, "The spectacle is not a collection of images, but a social relationship among people, mediated by images" (2). See Guy Debord, *The Society of the Spectacle*, trans. Donald Nicolson-Smith (Detroit: Black and Red, 2010).

73. Enrique Dussel, "World-System and 'Trans'-Modernity," *Nepantla: Views from the South* 3, no. 2 (2002): 221–44.

74. Ibid., 223.

75. Victor Burgin, *In/Different Spaces: Place and Memory in Visual Culture* (Berkeley: University of California Press, 1996), 179.

76. David Harvey, *The Condition of Postmodernity*, 3.

77. For a thoughtful questioning of the privileging of violence in postwar American fiction, see Sally Bachner, *The Prestige of Violence: American Fiction, 1962–2007* (Athens: University of Georgia Press, 2011). While my analysis of violence in twentieth-century fiction runs counter to Bachner's in a number of ways, her book is a bracing reminder of the dangers of turning violence into an artistic sublime.

1. The Novel Enfleshed

1. The epigraph to this chapter is from David Cronenberg, *Cronenberg on Cronenberg*, ed. Chris Rodley (London: Faber, 1992), 80.

2. On post-postmodernism, see Robert McLaughlin, "Post-Postmodern Discontent: Contemporary Fiction and the Social World," *Symplokē* 12, nos. 1–2 (2004): 53–68: 53.

3. Davis Schneiderman and Philip Walsh, eds., *Retaking the Universe: William S. Burroughs in the Age of Globalization* (London: Pluto Press, 2004).

4. Ann Douglas, "Punching a Hole in the Big Lie: The Achievement of William S. Burroughs," in *Word Virus: The William S. Burroughs Reader*, ed. James Grauerholz and Ira Silverberg (New York: Grove Press, 2000), xv–xxx.

5. See Jameson's account of literary forms and modes of production in Fredric Jameson, *Postmodernism, or, the Cultural Logic of Late Capitalism* (Durham, N.C.: Duke University Press, 1991), 297–418.

6. See Raymond Williams, *Marxism and Literature* (Oxford: University of Oxford Press, 1977), 121–27.

7. Jameson, *Postmodernism*, 302.

8. My account of the prescient dimensions of Burroughs's narrative draws upon Fredric Jameson's discussion of literature as anticipatory in relationship to overlapping modes of production. See Jameson, *Marxism and Form: Twentieth Century Dialectical Theories of Literature* (Princeton, N.J.: Princeton University Press, 1971), 389–90; Jameson, *The Political Unconscious: Narrative as a Socially Symbolic Act* (Ithaca, N.Y.: Cornell University Press, 1981), 95. In the latter, Jameson draws upon Nicos Poulantzas's theory of overlapping modes of production to theorize the anticipatory potential of the literary text. For a recent account of *Naked Lunch* that also draws upon Poulantzas, this time his theory of the state, see Andrew Pepper, "State Power Matters: Power, the State, and Political Struggle in the Post-War American Novel," *Textual Practice* 19, no. 4 (2005): 467–91. Pepper's reading, while making an important argument for the consideration of state power in the era of globalization, runs largely counter to mine. What he sees as the novel's limitation, its figuring of power as largely outside the structure of the state, I see as its prescience.

9. On brecciated time, see Victor Burgin, *In/Different Spaces: Place and Memory in Visual Culture* (Berkeley: University of California Press, 1996), 179–276. On transmodernity, see Enrique Dussel, "World-System and 'Trans'-Modernity," *Nepantla: Views from the South* 3, no. 2 (2002): 221–44.

10. Brian Edwards, *Morocco Bound: Disorienting America's Maghreb from Casablanca to the Marrakech Express* (Durham, N.C.: Duke University Press, 2005), 158–97.

11. In reading Burroughs against conventional ideas of postmodernism, I am of course indebted to Timothy S. Murphy's excellent *Wising Up the Marks: The Amodern William Burroughs* (Berkeley: University of California Press, 1997), esp. 16–45.

12. Oliver Harris puts it this way: "Nothing Burroughsian is abstract," and while I do think there are moments of abstraction in Burroughs (see my discussion of dematerialization later), I agree wholeheartedly with Harris's claim as a general description of Burroughs's writing practice. See Harris, "Can You See a Virus? The Queer Cold War of William Burroughs," *Journal of American Studies* 33, no. 2 (1999): 243–66: 246.

13. For an account of the real as trauma, see Jacques Lacan, *The Four Fundamental Concepts of Psychoanalysis: The Seminar of Jacques Lacan Book XI*, trans. Alan Sheridan (New York: Norton, 1981), 43–64; for an account of the real as materiality, see Jacques Lacan, *The Ethics of Psychoanalysis, 1959–1960: The Seminar of Jacques Lacan Book VII*, trans. Dennis Porter (New York: Norton, 1986), 43–70.

14. My understanding of abjection comes, of course, from Julia Kristeva. See Julia Kristeva, *The Powers of Horror: An Essay on Abjection*, trans. Leon S. Roudiez (New York: Columbia, 1982), 1–31.

15. For the classic discussions of the function of language in Burroughs's texts, see Robin Lyndenberg, *Word Cultures: Radical Theory and Practice in William S. Burroughs's Fiction* (Urbana: University of Illinois Press, 1987), 120–26; and Ihab Hassan, "The New Gnosticism: Speculations on an Aspect of the Postmodern Mind," in *Early Postmodernism: Foundational Essays*, ed. Paul A. Bové (Durham, N.C.: Duke University Press, 1995), 77–99.

16. William Burroughs, *Nova Express* (New York: Grove Press, 1994), 48.

17. William Burroughs and Brion Gysin, *The Third Mind* (New York: Viking, 1978), 27.

18. Timothy S. Murphy, "Exposing the Reality Film: William S. Burroughs among the Situationists," in *Retaking the Universe: William S. Burroughs in the Age of Globalization*, ed. Davis Schneiderman and Philip Walsh (London: Pluto Press, 2004), 29–57: 39. For an account of the logic of Burroughs's cut ups that finally runs counter to my own reading, see Michael Clune, *American Literature and the Free Market, 1945–2000* (Cambridge: Cambridge University Press, 2010), 77–102.

19. Giorgio Agamben, *Homo Sacer: Sovereign Power and Bare Life*, trans. Daniel Heller-Roazen (Stanford, Calif.: Stanford University Press, 1998), 8.

20. Roberto Esposito, *Bíos: Biopolitics and Philosophy*, trans. Timothy Campbell (Minneapolis: University of Minnesota Press, 2008), 110–45.

21. William Burroughs, *Naked Lunch: The Restored Text*, ed. James Grauerholz and Barry Miles (New York: Grove Press, 2001), 199. Note that all direct quotes taken from this title are cited parenthetically in the running text from this point forward.

22. Levi R. Bryant, *The Democracy of Objects* (Ann Arbor, Mich.: Open Humanities Press, 2011), 19.

23. Theodor Adorno, *Negative Dialectics*, trans. E. B. Ashton (London: Continuum, 1973), 187; Bryant, *Democracy of Objects*, 23.

24. See the discussion of Burroughs's routines in Barry Miles, *William Burroughs, El Hombre Invisible: A Portrait* (New York: Hyperion, 1992), 77.

25. Jameson, *Postmodernism*, 38.

26. See John Vernon, "The Map and the Machine," in *Retaking the Universe: William S. Burroughs in the Age of Globalization*, ed. Davis Schneiderman and Philip Walsh (London: Pluto Press, 2004), 203–24, esp. 218–19.

27. Kristeva, *Powers of Horror*, 2.

28. The concept of base materialism comes from Georges Bataille. See Georges Bataille, "Base Materialism and Gnosticism," in Bataille, *Visions of Excess: Selected Writings, 1927–1939*, trans. Alan Stoekl, with Carl R. Lovitt and Donald M. Leslie Jr. (Minneapolis: University of Minnesota Press, 1985), 45–52.

29. For Freud's discussion of the body-ego, see Sigmund Freud, *The Standard Edition of the Complete Psychological Works of Sigmund Freud*, vol. 19, trans. James Strachey (London: Hogarth Press, 1955), 25–26. Lacan's definition of the mirror

stage can, of course, be found in Jacques Lacan, "The Mirror Stage as Formative of the I Function as Revealed in Psychoanalytic Experience," in *Écrits: The First Complete Edition in English*, trans. Bruce Fink (New York: Norton, 2006), 75–81.

30. Jacques Lacan, *Écrits: The First Complete Edition in English*, trans. Bruce Fink (New York: Norton, 2006), 78. See also Jacques Lacan, *Freud's Papers on Technique 1953–1954: The Seminar of Jacques Lacan Book I*, trans. John Forrester (New York: Norton, 1988), 82–83.

31. Michael Hardt and Antonio Negri, *Multitude: War and Democracy in the Age of Empire* (New York: Penguin, 2004), xiii.

32. Hardt and Negri, *Multitude*, 192.

33. For an account of Burroughs's writings in relationship to the theories of Hardt and Negri, including the concept of the biopolitical, see the following essays: Murphy, "Exposing the Reality Film," 29–57; Jason Morelyle, "Speculating Freedom: Control and Rescriptive Subjectivity in the Work of William S. Burroughs," in *Retaking the Universe*, 74–86; Jamie Russell, "Guerilla Conditions: Burroughs, Gysin, and Balch Go to the Movies," in *Retaking the Universe*, 161–74; and Oliver Harris, "Cutting up Politics," in *Retaking the Universe*, 175–97.

34. My discussion of the fleshly "excluded remainder" is, of course, influenced by Slavoj Žižek's account of the indivisible remainder in his book of the same name. See Slavoj Žižek, *The Indivisible Remainder: On Schelling and Related Matters* (London: Verso, 1996), 1–9.

35. The prescient dimensions of Burroughs's representation of Interzone as an orientalized figuration of late capitalist space is compellingly delineated in Timothy Yu, "Oriental Cities, Postmodern Futures: *Naked Lunch, Blade Runner, Neuromancer*," *MELUS* 33, no. 4 (Winter 2008): 45–71. While Yu rightly critiques Burroughs for refiguring modernist orientalisms for the postmodern era, he also attends to the way in which this space destabilizes sexual and racial hierarchies and functions as part of a more generalized economic critique (49–53). On Interzone and the dynamics of racialization and consumption in Burroughs's text, see also Jonathan Eburne, "Trafficking in the Void: Burroughs, Kerouac, and the Consumption of Otherness," *Modern Fiction Studies* 43, no. 1 (1997): 53–92.

36. Edwards, *Morocco Bound*, 158–83.

37. Allen Hibbard, "Shift Coordinate Points: William S. Burroughs and Contemporary Theory," in *Retaking the Universe*, 13–28, 16.

38. David Harvey, *The Condition of Postmodernity: An Enquiry into the Origins of Cultural Change* (Oxford: Blackwell, 1990), 285–307.

39. See Saskia Sassen, *Globalization and Its Discontents: Essays on the New Mobility of People and Money* (New York: New Press, 1998), xxvii–xxx.

40. On the distinctive conception of space in Burroughs's oeuvre, see Alex Houen, "William Burroughs's Cities of the Red Night Trilogy: Writing Outer Space," *Journal of American Studies* 40, no. 3 (2006): 523–49.

41. On sexuality in *Naked Lunch*, see Jamie Russell, *Queer Burroughs* (New York: Palgrave Macmillan, 2001), 1–56; and Oliver Harris, *William Burroughs and the Secret of Fascination* (Carbondale: University of Southern Illinois Press, 2006), 215–48. In attending to the predatory dimensions of sexuality in Burroughs, I don't want to slight the more utopian figurations of queer sexuality that are also present in *Naked Lunch* and that are developed more fully in a novel like *The Wild Boys*, but I do want to suggest that part of the challenge represented by Burroughs to queer theory is the way in which he insists on us thinking about the intersections of queer sexualities with the predatory dimensions of global capitalism. In Burroughs, questions of sexual and economic liberation are necessarily intertwined. See William Burroughs, *The Wild Boys* (New York: Grove Press, 1969).

42. Karl Marx, *Capital*, vol. 1, trans. Ben Fowkes (New York: Vintage, 1977), 164–65.

43. See Adele Clarke, Laura Mamo, Jennifer Ruth Fosket, Jennifer R. Fishman, and Janet K. Shim, eds., *Biomedicalization: Technoscience, Health, and Illness in the U.S.* (Durham, N.C.: Duke University Press, 2010), 1–87.

44. The *Oxford English Dictionary* presents the earliest use of the term in 1828. It also takes on a secondary derogatory meaning of remaining "aloof or independent, especially politically" in 1889.

45. On the apathy of de Sade's sadists, see Gilles Deleuze, "Coldness and Cruelty," trans. Jean McNeil, in *Masochism* (New York: Zone Books, 1989), 9–141: 29.

46. Lacan, *Écrits*, 645–68.

47. Ibid., 667.

48. See Guy Debord, *Society of the Spectacle*, trans. Donald Nicolson-Smith (Detroit: Black and Red, 2010), 11–35.

49. For the most developed reading of the talking asshole passage, one upon which my own reading draws, see Lyndenberg, *Word Cultures*, 19–43.

50. Graham Harman, *The Quadruple Object* (Winchester, U.K.: Zero Books, 2011), 125.

51. Bryant, *Democracy of Objects*, 23–24.

2. Vital Objects

1. Theodor Adorno, *Negative Dialectics*, trans. E. B. Ashton (New York: Continuum, 1973), 183. Theodor Adorno, "Subject and Object," in *The Essential Frankfurt School Reader*, ed. Andrew Arato and Eike Gebhardt (New York: Continuum, 1993), 497–511. The epigraph provided appears on p. 499.

2. Thomas Pynchon, *V.* (New York: Harper and Row, 1961), 62. Note that all direct quotes taken from this title are cited parenthetically in the running text from this point forward.

3. On late modernism, see Tyrus Miller, *Late Modernism: Politics, Fiction, and the Arts between the World Wars* (Berkeley: University of California Press, 1999).

4. See Robert McLaughlin, "Unreadable Stares: Imperial Narratives and the Colonial Gaze in Gravity's Rainbow," *Pynchon Notes* 50, no. 1 (2002): 76–96; Michael Harris, "Pynchon's Postcoloniality," in *Thomas Pynchon: Reading from the Margins*, ed. Nyan Abbas (Cranbury, N.J.: Associate University Presses, 2003), 199–214.

5. Giorgio Agamben, *Homo Sacer: Sovereign Power and Bare Life*, trans. Daniel Heller Roazan (Stanford, Calif.: Stanford University Press, 1998), 8.

6. On the posthuman and posthumanism, see Cary Wolfe, *What Is Posthumanism?* (Minneapolis: University of Minnesota Press, 2010), xi–31. While I do not share Wolfe's theoretical inclinations, which are made up of a mix of systems theory and deconstruction, his call to move beyond the frame of the human (or what I have been calling the *subjective*) seems a necessary corrective to the epistemological blindness produced by both humanism and the forms of antihumanism that were grounded in a version of social or cultural constructivism.

7. Jacques Lacan, *The Four Fundamental Concepts of Psychoanalysis: The Seminar of Jacques Lacan Book XI*, trans. Alan Sheridan (New York: Norton, 1977), 267.

8. Slavoj Žižek, *The Sublime Object of Ideology* (London: Verso, 1989), 183. See also Melanie Klein, "The Importance of Symbol Formation in the Development of the Ego," in *The Selected Melanie Klein*, ed. Juliet Mitchell (New York: Free Press, 1986), 95–111.

9. Lacan, *Four Fundamental Concepts of Psychoanalysis*, 263.

10. See Sigmund Freud, "Fetishism," in *The Standard Edition of the Complete Psychological Works of Sigmund Freud*, vol. 21, trans. James Strachey (London: Hogarth Press, 1961), 149–57.

11. See Stefan Mattessich, *Lines of Flight: Discursive Time and Countercultural Desire in the Work of Thomas Pynchon* (Durham, N.C.: Duke University Press, 2002), 23–42.

12. See Andreas Huyssen, *After the Great Divide: Modernism, Mass Culture, Postmodernism* (Bloomington: University of Indiana Press, 1986), 44–62.

13. See Michael Hardt and Antonio Negri, *Multitude: War and Democracy in the Age of Empire* (New York: Penguin, 2004), 64–69.

14. Karl Marx, *Capital*, vol. 1, trans. Ben Fowkes (New York: Vintage, 1977), 163.

15. Brian McHale, *Postmodern Fiction* (New York: Routledge, 1987), 21–25.

16. Cary Wolfe, *What Is Posthumanism?*, ix.

17. Michel Foucault, *"Society Must Be Defended": Lectures at the College de France, 1975–1976*, trans. David Macey (New York: Picador, 1997), 252–53.

18. See Adele E. Clarke, Laura Mamo, Jennifer Ruth Fosket, Jennifer R. Fishman, and Janet K. Shim, eds., *Biomedicalization: Technoscience, Health, and Illness in the U.S.* (Durham, N.C.: Duke University Press, 2010), esp. 1–87.

19. Giorgio Agamben, *State of Exception*, trans. Kevin Attell (Chicago: University of Chicago Press, 2005), 1.

20. Donna Haraway, "A Cyborg Manifesto," in *The Cultural Studies Reader*, 3rd ed., ed. Simon During (New York: Routledge, 2007), 314–34: 317.

21. Slavoj Žižek, *Looking Awry: An Introduction to Jacques Lacan through Popular Culture* (Cambridge, Mass.: MIT Press, 1992), 29–31.

22. See Theodor Adorno and Max Horkheimer, *Dialectic of Enlightenment*, trans. John Cumming (London: Continuum, 1999), 3–42.

23. Žižek, *Sublime Object of Ideology*, 11–21.

24. I am, of course, paraphrasing Lacan's famous account of fetishism at the end of seminar XI as "in you more than you." See Lacan, *Four Fundamental Concepts of Psychoanalysis*, 263.

25. Achille Mbembe, "Necropolitics," trans. Libby Meintjes, *Public Culture* 15, no. 1 (2003).

26. Ibid., 17.

27. Frantz Fanon, *Black Skin, White Masks*, trans. Charles Lam Markmann (New York: Grove Press, 1967), 89.

28. See Homi Bhabha, *The Location of Culture* (New York: Routledge, 1994), 85–92.

29. See Edward Said, *Culture and Imperialism* (New York: Knopf, 1993), 62–80.

30. See Joseph Conrad, *Heart of Darkness* (New York: Penguin, 2007).

31. See Fredric Jameson, *The Political Unconscious: Narrative as a Socially Symbolic Act* (Ithaca, N.Y.: Cornell University Press, 1981), 151–84; Georg Lukács, *Studies in European Realism* (New York: Dunlap, 1964).

32. See Jacques Lacan, *The Psychoses, 1955–1956: The Seminar of Jacques Lacan Book III*, trans. Russell Grigg (New York: Norton, 1993), 130–42.

33. David Olusoga and Casper W. Erichsen, *The Kaiser's Holocaust: Germany's Forgotten Holocaust and the Colonial Roots of Nazism* (New York: Faber and Faber, 2010).

34. See Jacques Lacan, *The Ethics of Psychoanalysis, 1959–1960: The Seminar of Jacques Lacan Book VII*, trans. Dennis Porter (New York: Norton, 1992), 43–70.

35. McLaughlin, "Unreadable Stares," 94.

36. See Eva Cherniavsky, *Incorporations: Race, Nation, and the Body Politics of Capital* (Minneapolis: University of Minnesota Press, 2006), 8–11; Aníbal Quijano, "Coloniality of Power, Eurocentrism, and Latin America," in *Coloniality at Large: Latin America and the Postcolonial Debate*, ed. Mabel Moraña, Enrique Dussel, and Carlos A. Jáuregui (Durham, N.C.: Duke University Press, 2008), 181–224.

37. See Slavoj Žižek, *Tarrying with the Negative: Kant, Hegel, and the Critique of Ideology* (Durham, N.C.: Duke University Press, 1993), 200–237.

38. Lacan, *Four Fundamental Concepts of Psychoanalysis*, 263.

39. Agamben, *Homo Sacer*, 8.

40. On Pynchon's ethics, see Aso Takashi, "Pynchon's Alternative Ethics of Writing in *V*.: The Problem of Authorship in the Confessions of Fausto Majistral," *Pynchon Notes* 52–53 (2003): 7–22.

41. See Bruno Latour, *Reassembling the Social: An Introduction to Actor-Network-Theory* (Oxford: Oxford University Press, 2005), 63–86; Edward Said, *Culture and Imperialism*, xi–xxviii.

42. See Sara Ahmed, *Queer Phenomenology: Orientations, Objects, Others* (Durham, N.C.: Duke University Press, 2006), 169–70.

43. Immanuel Wallerstein, *The Capitalist World-Economy: Essays by Immanuel Wallerstein* (Cambridge, U.K.: Cambridge University Press, 1979), 32.

44. Giovanni Arrighi, *The Long Twentieth Century: Money, Power, and the Origins of Our Times*, new and updated ed. (London: Verso, 2010), 49–75.

3. The Late-Modern Unconscious

1. The epigraph to the chapter comes from Timothy Morton, *Ecology without Nature: Rethinking Environmental Aesthetics* (Cambridge, Mass.: Harvard University Press, 2007), 1.

2. Thus accounts of postmodernism can be loosely divided between those that privilege the linguistic without recourse to the material and those that read this privileging itself as a symptom of a specific political-economic condition. Jean Baudrillard's and Jean-François Lyotard's accounts of postmodernism tend to be a version of the former; those of Fredric Jameson, David Harvey, and Michael Hardt and Antonio Negri tend toward the latter. Baudrillard has, of course, written specifically about *Crash*, which he appropriates to his own vision of a thoroughly postmodern and hyperreal world in which the "real" (not in the Lacanian sense) is entirely eclipsed. As has been noted by Aidan Day, Ballard's text (and Ballard himself) resists this reading; Day instead rightly reads the novel "for its protest against the hyperreality that it invokes." See Aidan Day, "Ballard and Baudrillard: Close Reading *Crash*," *English Association* 49 (2000), 277–93: 288. Jean Baudrillard, *Simulations*, trans. Paul Foss, Paul Patton, and Philip Beitchman (New York: Semiotext[e], 1983); Baudrillard, "Ballard's 'Crash,'" trans. Arthur B. Evans, *Science Fiction Studies* 18, no. 1 (1991): 313–20; Jean-Francois Lyotard, *The Postmodern Condition: A Report on Knowledge*, trans. Geoff Bennington and Brian Massumi (Minneapolis: University of Minnesota Press, 1984); Fredric Jameson, *Postmodernism, or, the Cultural Logic of Late Capitalism* (Durham, N.C.: Duke University Press, 1991), 1–54; David Harvey, *The Condition of Postmodernity: An Enquiry into the Origins of Cultural Change* (Oxford: Blackwell, 1990), 39–98; Michael Hardt and Antonio Negri, *Empire* (Cambridge, Mass.: Harvard University Press, 2000), 280–303.

3. Martin Amis, "Introduction," in *The Complete Short Stories*, by J. G. Ballard (New York: Norton, 2010), xi–xiv: xiii.

4. Michael Hardt and Antonio Negri, *Multitude: War and Democracy in the Age of Empire* (New York: Penguin, 2004), 65.

5. Slavoj Žižek, *The Plague of Fantasies* (London: Verso, 1997), 11.

6. Theodor Adorno, *Negative Dialectics*, trans. E. B. Ashton (London: Continuum, 1973), 183; Levi Bryant, *The Democracy of Objects* (Ann Arbor, Mich.: Open Humanities Press, 2011), 18.

7. For Marx's classic formulation of this distinction see Karl Marx, "Preface to *A Contribution to the Critique of Political Economy*," in *Karl Marx: Selected Writings*, ed. David McLelland (Oxford: Oxford University Press, 1977), 388–92. For two particularly influential critiques of this distinction, see Raymond Williams, *Marxism and Literature* (Oxford: Oxford University Press, 1978), 75–83; and Ernesto Laclau and Chantal Mouffe, "Post-Marxism without Apologies," *New Left Review* 1, no. 166 (1987): 79–106.

8. Jameson, *Postmodernism*, xxi.

9. Hardt and Negri, *Empire*, 22.

10. For a brilliant discussion of materiality and architecture in *Concrete Island*—one that has influenced my reading of *Crash*—see Laura Colombino, "Negotiations with the System: J.G. Ballard and Geoff Ryman Writing London's Architecture," *Textual Practice* 20, no. 4 (2006): 615–35.

11. Jameson, *Postmodernism*, 49.

12. Harvey, *Condition of Postmodernity*, 3.

13. Hardt and Negri, *Empire*, 22; Hardt and Negri, *Multitude*, 109.

14. See Bill Brown, *The Material Unconscious: American Amusement, Stephen Crane, and the Economics of Play* (Cambridge, Mass.: Harvard University Press, 1997), 1–26; Bill Brown, *A Sense of Things: The Object Matter of American Literature* (Chicago: University of Chicago Press, 2004), 1–20.

15. J. G. Ballard, *Crash: A Novel* (New York: Picador, 1973), 35. Note that all direct quotes taken from this title are cited parenthetically in the running text from this point forward.

16. On the supplanting of Great Britain by the United States as hegemon of the capitalist world system in the twentieth century, see Giovanni Arrighi, *The Long Twentieth Century: Money, Power, and the Origins of Our Times*, new and updated ed. (London: Verso, 2010), 235–38, 320–31.

17. See Immanuel Wallerstein, *The Decline of American Power* (New York: New Press, 2003), 49–52.

18. Enrique Dussel, "World-System and 'Trans'-Modernity," *Nepantla: Views from the South* 3, no. 2 (2002): 221–44.

19. For Lacan on the relationship between subject and objects, see Jacques Lacan, *The Ethics of Psychoanalysis, 1959–1960: The Seminar of Jacques Lacan Book*

VII, trans. Dennis Porter (New York: Norton, 1992), 43–70; and Jacques Lacan, *The Four Fundamental Concepts of Psychoanalysis: The Seminar of Jacques Lacan Book XI*, trans. Alan Sheridan (New York: Norton, 1998), 174–87, 263–77.

20. As Sam Francis nicely points out, this obsessive fragmentation of the body in *Crash* is informed by the way Ballard is interested in charting intersecting logics of pornography and contemporary science. See Sam Francis, "'Moral Pornography' and the 'Total Imagination': The Pornographic in J.G. Ballard's *Crash*," *English Association* 57, no. 218 (2008): 146–68.

21. On the photographic dimensions of Ballard's narrative and its relationship to its political critique, see Jeannette Baxter, "Radical Surrealism: Rereading Photography and History in J.G. Ballard's *Crash*," *Textual Practice* 22, no. 3 (2008): 507–28.

22. Francis, "'Moral Pornography,'" 157.

23. Graham Harman, *The Quadruple Object* (Winchester, U.K.: Zero Books, 2011), 20–34.

24. Ibid., 35, 36.

25. Slavoj Žižek, *Looking Awry: An Introduction to Jacques Lacan through Popular Culture* (Cambridge, Mass.: MIT Press, 1992), 21. For the full discussion of the notion, see pages 21–39. For a thoughtful reading of Ballard's complex (and changing) political positions over the years that nicely employs Žižek, see Benjamin Noys, "*La Libido Reactionnaire?* The Recent Fiction of J.G. Ballard," *Journal of European Studies* 37, no. 4: 391–406. Noys nicely attends to the reactionary elements that inflect the otherwise left-wing positions of both Ballard and Žižek, locating the emergence of these elements as a product of the contradictory libidinal politics of both figures.

26. See Sigmund Freud, "The 'Uncanny,'" in *The Standard Edition of the Complete Psychological Works of Sigmund Freud*, vol. 17, trans. James Strachey (London: Hogarth Press), 217–56.

27. Adorno, *Negative Dialectics*, 356. For a provocative discussion of second nature and its specifically psychoanalytic resonances, see Slavoj Žižek, *The Metastases of Enjoyment: On Women and Causality* (London: Verso, 1994), 9–15.

28. McHale, *Postmodernist Fiction* (New York: Routledge, 1987), 10. Italics in original.

29. Harman, *Quadruple Object*, 123.

30. See Judith Butler, *Precarious Life: The Powers of Mourning and Violence* (London: Verso, 2006), 27.

31. Adele Clarke, Laura Mamo, Jennifer Ruth Fosket, Jennifer R. Fishman, and Janet K. Shim, eds., *Biomedicalization: Technoscience, Health, and Illness in the U.S.* (Durham, N.C.: Duke University Press, 2010), 1–86.

32. See Lauren Berlant, *The Female Complaint: The Unfinished Business of Sentimentality in American Culture* (Durham, N.C.: Duke University Press, 2008), 107–44.

33. Hardt and Negri, *Multitude*, 192; Donna Haraway, "A Cyborg Manifesto," in *The Cultural Studies Reader*, 3rd ed., ed. Simon During (New York: Routledge, 2007), 314–34.

34. Mark Seltzer, *True Crime: Observations on Violence and Modernity* (New York: Routledge, 2006).

35. Bruno Latour, *Reassembling the Social: An Introduction to Actor-Network-Theory* (Oxford: Oxford University Press, 2005), 71.

36. Ibid., 72.

37. Bryant, *Democracy of Objects*, 25.

38. See Sigmund Freud, "Fetishism," in *The Standard Edition of the Complete Psychological Works of Sigmund Freud*, vol. 21, trans. James Strachey (London: Hogarth Press, 1961), 149–57.

39. See Slavoj Žižek, *The Sublime Object of Ideology* (London: Verso, 1989), 11–54.

40. Kevin Floyd, *The Reification of Desire: Toward a Queer Marxism* (Minneapolis: University of Minnesota Press, 2009), 38–79.

41. Sara Ahmed, *Queer Phenomenology: Orientations, Objects, Others* (Durham, N.C.: Duke University Press, 2006), 171.

42. Ibid., 171.

43. Andrzej Gasiorek, *J. G. Ballard* (Manchester: Manchester University Press, 2005), 62–63.

4. Disinterring the Real

1. The epigraph for this chapter comes from Dodie Bellamy, "Body Language," in *Academonia* (San Francisco: Krupskaya, 2006), 69–82: 82.

2. For an analysis of these different accounts of postmodernism, see my discussion of postmodernism and transmodernity in the introduction. For an account of post-postmodernism in aesthetic practices, see Robert McLaughlin, "Post-Postmodern Discontent: Contemporary Fiction and the Social World," *Symplokē* 12, nos. 1–2 (2004): 53–68. For an account of post-postmodernity as an era, see Jeffrey Nealon, "Periodizing the 80s," in *A Leftist Ontology: Beyond Relativism and Identity Politics*, ed. Carsten Strathausen (Minneapolis: University of Minnesota Press, 2009), 54–79; and Alan Kirby, "The Death of Postmodernism and Beyond," *Philosophy Today: A Magazine of Ideas*, 58 (May/June 2009), http://www.philosophynow.org.

3. Lee Edelman, *No Future: Queer Theory and the Death Drive* (Durham, N.C.: Duke University Press, 2004), 11.

4. Slavoj Žižek, *Looking Awry: An Introduction to Jacques Lacan through Popular Culture* (Cambridge: MIT Press, 1992), 3.

5. My discussion of Bellamy's engagement with the abject, of course, draws upon Julia Kristeva's famous formulation of the concept in Julia Kristeva, *Powers

of Horror: An Essay on Abjection, trans. Leon S. Roudiez (New York: Columbia, 1982), 1–31.

6. Sarah Brophy, *Witnessing AIDS: Writing, Testimony, and the Work of Mourning* (Toronto: University of Toronto Press, 2004), 3–4. In addition to the texts cited further on, my thinking about the signification of the AIDS crisis has also been influenced by Priscilla Wald, *Contagious: Cultures, Carriers, and the Outbreak Narrative* (Durham, N.C.: Duke University Press, 2008).

7. Roberto Esposito, *Bíos: Biopolitics and Philosophy*, trans. Timothy Campbell (Minneapolis: University of Minnesota Press, 2008), 10.

8. For Bellamy, the horror genre is particularly laden with meanings for feminist issues of embodiment: "Horror films are obsessed with the division between inside and outside, with the very integrity of our bodies, a sense of physical invasion. I think these are core concerns for many women. I find it enlightening to study how women are so often associated with the monstrous." Quoted in Julia Bloch, "Steamy Pages: Dodie Bellamy," in *Curve*, http://www.highbeam.com/doc/1G1-127079073.html.

9. See Linda Hutcheon, *The Politics of Postmodernism*, 2nd ed. (New York: Routledge, 2002), 1–28; Brian McHale, *Postmodernist Fiction* (New York: Routledge, 1987), 26–30; Jean François Lyotard, *The Postmodern Condition: A Report on Knowledge*, trans. Geoff Bennington and Brian Massumi (Minneapolis: University of Minnesota Press, 1984), 9–11, 53–60; Fredric Jameson, *Postmodernism, or, the Cultural Logic of Late Capitalism* (Durham, N.C.: Duke University Press, 1991), 1–54; and David Harvey, *The Condition of Postmodernity: An Enquiry into the Origin of Cultural Change* (Oxford: Blackwell, 1989), 39–65.

10. My understanding of new narrative fiction has been shaped by Earl Jackson Jr., *Strategies of Deviance: Studies in Gay Male Representation* (Bloomington: University of Indiana Press, 1995), 179–254.

11. Ian Bogost, *Alien Phenomenology, or What It's Like to Be a Thing* (Minneapolis: University of Minnesota Press, 2012), 36. Bogost here is quoting technology scholar Michael Lynch.

12. Giorgio Agamben, *Homo Sacer: Sovereign Power and Bare Life*, trans. Daniel Heller-Roazen (Stanford, Calif.: Stanford University Press, 1998), 8.

13. See Adele Clarke, Laura Mamo, Jennifer Ruth Fosket, Jennifer R. Fishman, and Janet K. Shim, "Biomedicalization: Technoscientific Transformations of Health, Illness and U.S. Biomedicine," in *Biomedicalization: Technoscience, Health, and Illness in the U.S.*, ed. Adele Clarke, Laura Mamo, Jennifer Ruth Fosket, Jennifer R. Fishman, and Janet K. Shim (Durham, N.C.: Duke University Press, 2010), 47–87.

14. Ibid., 48.

15. Jacques Lacan, *The Psychoses, 1955–1956: The Seminar of Jacques Lacan Book III*, trans. Russell Grigg (New York: Norton, 1993), 9.

16. Jacques Lacan, *The Four Fundamental Concepts of Psychoanalysis: The Seminar of Jacques Lacan Book XI*, trans. Alan Sheridan (New York: Norton, 1977),

53–64; Jacques Lacan, *The Ethics of Psychoanalysis, 1959–60: The Seminar of Jacques Lacan Book VII*, trans. Dennis Porter (New York: Norton, 1992), 43–70.

17. Nina Auerbach, *Our Vampires, Ourselves* (Chicago: Chicago University Press, 1995), 1–9; Laurence Rickels, *The Vampire Lectures* (Minneapolis: University of Minnesota Press, 1999), xii–xiv.

18. See Judith Butler, *Gender Trouble: Feminism and the Subversion of Identity* (New York: Routledge, 1990); Donna Haraway, "A Cyborg Manifesto," in *The Cultural Studies Reader*, 3rd ed., edited by Simon During (New York: Routledge, 2007), 314–34; and Rosi Braidotti, *Metamorphoses: Towards a Materialist Theory of Becoming* (Cambridge, U.K.: Polity, 2002), 11–64. There are, of course, significant differences between the paradigms proposed by each of these thinkers, with Braidotti's woman being closest to what Bellamy is articulating with her vampires. Yet, with each of these paradigms, there is a turn toward the discursivization of the material. It is precisely such a turn that Bellamy's vampires resist. For Butler's take on Braidotti's criticisms of her performative subject, see Judith Butler, *Undoing Gender* (New York: Routledge, 2004), 192–98. I find Haraway's recent work in animal studies a much more amenable paradigm for thinking about bodily materiality as Bellamy represents it. See Donna Haraway, *When Species Meet* (Minneapolis: University of Minnesota Press, 2008), 3–42.

19. Jacques Derrida, *Specters of Marx: The State of the Debt, the Work of Mourning, and the New International* (New York: Routledge, 1994), 96.

20. On Stoker's Mina as a figuration of modernity, see Jennifer Fleissner, "Dictation Anxiety: The Stenographer's Stake in Dracula," in *Nineteenth-Century Contexts* 22, no. 3 (Fall 2000): 417–56; and Jennifer Wicke, "Vampiric Typewriting: Dracula and Its Media," in *English Language History* 59, no. 2 (Summer 1992): 467–93.

21. David Buuck, "The Powers of Horror," *EBR* 7 (Summer 1998).

22. Dodie Bellamy, interview with the author, August 2007. I conducted this interview with Bellamy on August 3, 2007, in the Chicago queer and queer-friendly neighborhood of Andersonville.

23. Ibid.

24. Dodie Bellamy, *The Letters of Mina Harker* (Madison: University of Wisconsin Press, 1998), 90. Note that all direct quotes taken from this title are cited parenthetically in the running text from this point forward.

25. For Bellamy's discussion of her battle with bulimia, see Dodie Bellamy, *Academonia* (San Francisco: Krupskaya, 2006), 103–9.

26. See Judith Halberstam, *Skin Shows: Gothic Horror and the Technology of Monsters* (Durham, N.C.: Duke University Press, 2005), 1–27; and Eve Kosofsky Sedgwick, *Between Men: English Literature and Male Homosocial Desire* (New York: Columbia University Press, 1985), 83–96.

27. The distinction between the Fordist and the post-Fordist city comes, of course, from David Harvey. See Harvey, *The Condition of Postmodernity*, 66–98. For his discussion of neoliberalism, see David Harvey, *A Brief History of Neoliberalism* (Oxford: Oxford University Press, 2005), 1–38.

28. Saskia Sassen, *Globalization and Its Discontents: Essays on the New Mobility of People and Money* (New York: New Press, 1998), xxv–xxvi.

29. David Harvey, *Spaces of Global Capitalism: Toward a Theory of Uneven Geographical Development* (London: Verso, 2006), 9.

30. For a discussion of habitus, see Pierre Bourdieu, *Distinction: A Social Critique of Taste*, trans. Richard Nice (Cambridge, Mass.: Harvard University Press, 1984), 169–225.

31. Esposito, *Bíos*, 46.

32. These meanings are part of what Paula Treichler has described as the "epidemic of signification" that accompanied the AIDS epidemic. See Treichler, *How to Have Theory in an Epidemic: Cultural Chronicles of AIDS* (Durham, N.C.: Duke University Press, 1999), 11.

33. Douglas Crimp, *Melancholia and Moralism: Essays on AIDS and Queer Politics* (Cambridge, Mass.: MIT Press, 2002), 1–26.

34. See Lauren Berlant, *The Queen of America Goes to Washington City: Essays on Sex and Citizenship* (Durham, N.C.: Duke University Press, 1997), 1–24; and Edelman, *No Future*, 1–31.

35. Here I am drawing on Freud's classic account of the primal scene in the "Wolf Man" case history. See Sigmund Freud, "From the History of an Infantile Neurosis," in *The Standard Edition of the Complete Psychological Works of Sigmund Freud*, vol. 17, trans. and ed. James Strachey (London: Hogarth, 1955), 29–47.

36. On the real as traumatic kernel, see Žižek, *The Sublime Object of Ideology* (London: Verso, 1989), 161–64.

37. Lauren Berlant and Michael Warner, "Sex in Public," in *The Cultural Studies Reader*, 2nd ed., ed. Simon During (New York: Routledge, 2000), 354–67: 355.

38. David Harvey, *A Brief History of Neoliberalism* (Oxford: Oxford University Press, 2005), 5–38.

39. Bourdieu, *Distinction*, 190–96.

40. Ross Chambers, *Untimely Interventions: AIDS Writing, Testimonial, and the Rhetoric of Haunting* (Ann Arbor, Mich.: Michigan University Press, 2004), xxviii.

41. Jacques Lacan, *Écrits: The First Complete Edition in English*, trans. Bruce Fink (New York: Norton, 2006), 80.

42. Lacan, *Four Fundamental Concepts of Psychoanalysis*, 85–90.

43. Žižek, *Looking Awry*, 1.

44. Lacan, *Four Fundamental Concepts of Psychoanalysis*, 88.

45. Bellamy, interview with the author, August 2007.

46. Alenka Zupančič, *Ethics of the Real: Kant, Lacan* (London: Verso, 2000), 35.

47. Lacan, *Ethics of Psychoanalysis*, 55.

48. Sigmund Freud, "Beyond the Pleasure Principle," in *The Standard Edition of the Complete Psychological Works of Sigmund Freud, Volume XVIII (1920–1922): Beyond the Pleasure Principle, Group Psychology and Other Works*, trans. James Strachey (London: Hogarth, 1955), 1–64.

49. For a brilliant, extended discussion on the ethical dimension opened up by the real, one that has had a strong influence on my own related but slightly different account of the ethics of the real, see Zupančič, *Ethics of the Real*, 211–45.

50. Bellamy, interview with the author, August 2007.

51. Sara Ahmed, *Queer Phenomenology: Orientations, Objects, Others* (Durham, N.C.: Duke University Press, 2006), 162.

52. Bellamy, *Academonia*, 82.

5. Almanac of the Living

1. This chapter was conceptualized in dialogue with Ericka Wills. I directed Wills's brilliant MA thesis on *Almanac of the Dead*, and my thinking on the novel, especially as it relates to biopolitics, has emerged in dialogue with her work. Her work on *Almanac* is currently slated to become a chapter in her dissertation, which is also under my direction, so I am happy to report that she will have the last word in this dialogue. See Ericka Wills, "Orbiting Biospheres, Blackmarket Biomaterials, and the New Geography of Revolution: Manipulations of Techno-Scientific Innovations in Silko's *Almanac of the Dead*" (master's thesis, Illinois State University, 2008). The epigraph for this chapter is taken from Theodor Adorno, *Negative Dialectics*, trans. E. B. Ashton (New York: Continuum, 1973), 191.

2. Silko herself talks about the connection of the novel to the revolutionary activities of the Zapatistas (or EZLN). See Ellen Arnold's interview with Silko. Ellen Arnold, "Listening to the Spirits: An Interview with Leslie Marmon Silko," *Studies in American Indian Literatures* 10, no. 3 (1998): 8–9. Also on this issue, see Kimberly Roppolo, "Vision, Voice, and Intertribal Metanarrative: The American Indian Visual-Rhetorical Tradition and Leslie Marmon Silko's *Almanac of the Dead*," *American Indian Quarterly* 31, no. 4 (Fall 2007): 534–58, esp. 543–44.

3. Silko uses both the terms *almanac* and *novel* to characterize her text and its genre. As I discuss later, the text is modeled on ancient Mayan codex and almanacs, as well as the farmer's almanacs of more recent vintage. I will follow Silko's usage and alternate between these terms to emphasize the structural uniqueness of this text and its distance from a conventional understanding of the novel form. See Ellen L. Arnold, *Conversations with Leslie Marmon Silko* (Jackson: University of Mississippi Press, 2000), 119–20.

4. Enrique Dussel, "World-System and Trans-modernity," *Nepantla: Views from the South* 3, no. 2 (2002): 221–43.

5. On geographical space in *Almanac*, see Ann Brigham, "Productions of Geographic Scale and Capitalist-Colonialist Enterprise in Leslie Marmon Silko's *Almanac of the Dead*," *MFS: Modern Fiction Studies* 50, no. 2 (2004): 303–31.

6. For a superb account of time and temporality in relationship to Silko's political vision, see Caren Irr, "The Timeliness of *Almanac of the Dead*, or a Postmodern Rewriting of Radical Fiction," in *Leslie Marmon Silko: A Collection of Essays*, ed. Louise K. Barnett and James L. Thorson (Albuquerque: University of New Mexico Press, 1999), 223–44.

7. On thanatopolitics, see Roberto Esposito, *Bíos: Biopolitics and Philosophy*, trans. Timothy Campbell (Minneapolis: University of Minnesota Press, 2008), 110–45; on neoliberalism, see David Harvey, *A Brief History of Neoliberalism* (Oxford: Oxford University Press, 2005).

8. Adele E. Clarke, Laura Mamo, Jennifer Ruth Fosket, Jennifer R. Fishman, and Janet K. Shim, "Biomedicalization: Technoscientific Transformations of Health, Illness and U.S. Biomedicine," in *Biomedicalization: Technoscience, Health, and Illness in the U.S.*, ed. Adele E. Clarke, Laura Mamo, Jennifer Ruth Fosket, Jennifer R. Fishman, and Janet K. Shim (Durham, N.C.: Duke University Press, 2010), 47–87.

9. Arnold, *Conversations*, 110.

10. Esposito, *Bíos*, 46.

11. See Aníbal Quijano, "Coloniality of Power, Eurocentrism, and Latin America," trans. Michael Ennis, *Coloniality at Large: Latin America and the Postcolonial Debate*, ed. Mabel Moraña, Enrique Dussel, and Carlos A. Jáuregui (Durham, N.C.: Duke University Press, 2008). For a brilliant use of Dussel's notion of "coloniality" to read subaltern texts, one that has influenced my own reading of Silko, see José David Saldívar, "Unsettling Race, Coloniality, and Caste: Anzaldúa's *Borderlands/La Frontera*, Martinez's *Parrot in the Oven*, and Roy's *The God of Small Things*," *Cultural Studies* 21, nos. 2–3 (2007): 339–67. Silko's understanding of race as, in part, an economic category is one of the things that Walter Benn Michaels misses in his ungenerous and rather cursory reading of *Almanac of the Dead* in *The Shape of the Signifier* (Princeton, N.J.: Princeton University Press, 2004), 23–24.

12. Quijano, "Coloniality of Power," 184.

13. Harvey, *Brief History of Neoliberalism*, 178.

14. Eva Cherniavsky, *Incorporations: Race, Nation, and the Body Politics of Capital* (Minneapolis: University of Minnesota Press, 2006), 8–11.

15. Chela Sandoval, *Methodology of the Oppressed* (Minneapolis: University of Minnesota Press, 2000), 15–39.

16. The novel's representation of political struggle and revolutionary alliance has, understandably, been its most written about feature. See Laura Shackleford,

"Counter-networks in a Network Society: Leslie Marmon Silko's *Almanac of the Dead*," *Postmodern Culture* 16, no. 3 (2006): 1–24; Channette Romero, "Envisioning a 'Network of Tribal Coalitions': Leslie Marmon Silko's *Almanac of the Dead*," *American Indian Quarterly* 26, no. 4 (2002): 623–40; T. V. Reed, "Toxic Colonialism, Environmental Justice and Native Resistance in Silko's *Almanac of the Dead*," *MELUS: Multi-Ethnic Literature of the U.S.* 34, no. 2 (Summer 2009): 24–42; Miriam Schact, "'Movement Must Be Emulated by the People': Rootedness, Migration, and Indigenous Internationalism in Leslie Marmon Silko's *Almanac of the Dead*," *Studies in American Indian Literatures* 21, no. 4 (Winter 2009), 53–70; Shari M. Huhndorf, *Mapping the Americas: The Transnational Politics of Contemporary Native Culture* (Ithaca, N.Y.: Cornell University Press, 2009), 140–71.

17. Gerald Vizenor, *Native Liberty: Natural Reason and Cultural Survivance* (Lincoln: University of Nebraska Press, 2009), 57–83.

18. Leslie Marmon Silko, *Almanac of the Dead* (New York: Penguin, 1992), 14. Note that all direct quotes taken from this title are cited parenthetically in the running text from this point forward.

19. Michael Hardt and Antonio Negri, *Empire* (Cambridge, Mass.: Harvard University Press, 2000); Hardt and Negri, *Multitude: War and Democracy in the Age of Empire* (New York: Penguin, 2004); Hardt and Negri, *Commonwealth* (Cambridge, Mass.: Harvard University Press, 2009).

20. Hardt and Negri, *Multitude*, 97–137.

21. Hardt and Negri, *Commonwealth*, 115–18.

22. Levi Bryant, *The Democracy of Objects* (Ann Arbor, Mich.: Open Humanities Press, 2011), 23.

23. See Jane Bennett, *Vibrant Matter: A Political Ecology of Things* (Durham, N.C.: Duke University Press, 2010), 1–38; Bruno Latour, *Politics of Nature: How to Bring the Sciences into Democracy*, trans. Catherine Porter (Cambridge, Mass.: Harvard University Press, 2004), 1–52; and Bruno Latour, *Reassembling the Social: An Introduction to Actor-Network-Theory* (Oxford: Oxford University Press, 2005), 63–86.

24. See Louise Barnett and James Thorton's introduction to their collection of critical essays on Silko for a text that does comment on Silko as an experimental writer. Louise K. Barnett and James Thorton, "Introduction," in *Leslie Marmon Silko: A Collection of Critical Essays*, ed. Louise K. Barnett and James Thorton (Albuquerque: University of New Mexico Press, 1999), 1–13.

25. Silko puts it this way in an interview with Rolando Hinojosa, in which they are discussing the dangers of ghettoization: "Well, let's talk about something that just occurs to me. Let's talk about how America might be one of the few countries where some of the best writers have to have international recognition before our own nation recognizes us. . . . In Norway, there's only 4 million of those Norwegians and what do they know? What they know is what interests them about

America. And they think that the Latino writers, the Afro-American, the Native American, that's American to them" (Arnold, *Conversations*, 88).

26. For discussions of the text as almanac, see Roppolo, "Vision, Voice, and Intertribal Metanarrative," 538–45; Shackelford, "Counter-networks in a Network Society," 16–18; Irr, "Timeliness of *Almanac of the Dead*," 186; and Silko herself, in Arnold, *Conversations*, 121–22.

27. For accounts of the novel's ecological vision, see Bridget O'Meara, "The Ecological Politics of Leslie Silko's Almanac of the Dead," *Wicazo Sa Review* 15, no. 2 (Fall 2000): 63–73.

28. Bryant, *Democracy of Objects*, 45; Alain Badiou, *Being and Event*, trans. Oliver Feltham (London: Continuum, 2005), 189–91.

29. Wills, "Orbiting Biospheres, Blackmarket Biomaterials, and the New Geography of Revolution," 92–97.

30. Achille Mbembe, "Necropolitics," trans. Libby Meintjes, *Public Culture* 15, no. 1 (2003): 11–40.

31. Giorgio Agamben, *Homo Sacer: Sovereign Power and Bare Life*, trans. Daniel Heller-Roazen (Stanford, Calif.: Stanford University Press, 1998), 8.

32. Giorgio Agamben, *State of Exception*, trans. Kevin Attell (Chicago: University of Chicago Press, 2005), 1.

33. Achille Mbembe, "Necropolitics," 11.

34. Reed, "Toxic Colonialism, Environmental Justice, and Native Resistance," 32.

35. Esposito, *Bíos*, 32.

36. Brigham, "Productions of Geographic Scale," 313. On Silko's representation of the trade in biomaterials, see also Anne Folwell Stanford, "'Human Debris': Border Politics, Body Parts, and the Reclamation of the Americas in Leslie Marmon Silko's *Almanac of the Dead*," *Literature and Medicine* 16, no. 1 (1997): 23–42, and Wills, "Orbiting Biospheres, Blackmarket Biomaterials, and the New Geography of Revolution," 74–102.

37. Adele Clarke, Janet K. Shim, Laura Mamo, Jennifer Ruth Fosket, and Jennifer R. Fishman, "Biomedicalization: Technoscientific Transformations of Health, Illness, and U.S. Biomedicine," in *Biomedicalization: Technoscience, Health, and Illness in the U.S.*, ed. Adele E. Clarke, Laura Mamo, Jennifer Ruth Fosket, Jennifer R. Fishman, and Janet K. Shim (Durham, N.C.: Duke University Press, 2010), 47–87: 57.

38. Adele E. Clarke, Janet K. Shim, Laura Mamo, Jennifer Ruth Fosket, and Jennifer R. Fishman, "Biomedicalization: A Theoretical and Substantive Introduction," in *Biomedicalization: Technoscience, Health, Illness in the U.S.*, ed. Adele E. Clarke, Janet K. Shim, Laura Mamo, Jennifer Ruth Fosket, and Jennifer R. Fishman (Durham, N.C.: Duke University Press, 2010), 1–44: 1.

39. Gilles Deleuze, "Coldness and Cruelty," trans. Jean McNeil, in *Masochism* (New York: Zone Books, 1989), 9–141: 73.

40. Christopher Breu, *Hard-Boiled Masculinities* (Minneapolis: University of Minnesota Press, 2005), 12–15; Eric Lott, *Love and Theft: Blackface Minstrelsy and the American Working Class* (Oxford: Oxford University Press, 1995), 1–63.

41. See Cherniavsky, *Incorporations*, 49–70; Huhndorf, *Mapping the Americas*, 140–70; Roppolo, "Vision, Voice, and Intertribal Metanarratives"; Romero, "Envisioning a 'Network of Tribal Coalitions.'"

42. Huhndorf, *Mapping the Americas*, 141.

43. Karl Marx and Friedrich Engels, *The Communist Manifesto* (Oxford: Oxford University Press, 2008), 65.

44. Hardt and Negri, *Multitude*, 129–38.

45. Quijano, "Coloniality of Power, Eurocentrism, and Latin America," 186.

46. Theodor Adorno and Max Horkheimer, *Dialectic of Enlightenment*, trans. John Cumming (London: Continuum, 1999), 1–35.

47. Graham Harman, *The Quadruple Object* (Winchester, U.K.: Zero Books, 2011), 7.

48. Ibid., 28; Bryant, *Democracy of Objects*, 21.

49. Walter Mignolo, "The Geopolitics of Knowledge and the Colonial Difference," in *Coloniality at Large: Latin America and the Postcolonial Debate*, ed. Mabel Moraña, Enrique Dussel, and Carlos A. Jáuregui (Durham, N.C.: Duke University Press, 2008), 225–58: 242.

50. Timothy Morton, *Ecology without Nature: Rethinking Environmental Aesthetics* (Cambridge, Mass.: Harvard University Press, 2004), 21.

51. Harman, *Quadruple Object*, 125.

Conclusion

1. Georg Wilhelm Friedrich Hegel, *The Phenomenology of Spirit*, trans. A. V. Miller (Oxford: Oxford University Press, 1979), 1–44.

2. Ferdinand de Saussure, *Course in General Linguistics*, trans. Wade Baskin (New York: Open Court, 1983), 65–70.

3. Theodor Adorno, *Minima Moralia: Reflections from Damaged Life*, trans. E. F. N. Jephcott (London: Verso, 2010).

4. See Slavoj Žižek, *Interrogating the Real* (London: Continuum, 2005), 26–55; Žižek, *Tarrying with the Negative: Kant, Hegel, and the Critique of Ideology* (Durham, N.C.: Duke University Press, 1993), 125–64; Fredric Jameson, *The Hegel Variations: On the Phenomenology of Spirit* (London: Verso, 2010); Jameson, *Valences of the Dialectic* (London: Verso, 2010), 3–73.

5. For Jameson's spirited and persuasive defense of the concept of totality, see Fredric Jameson, *Valences of the Dialectic*, 201–22. In unpacking the notion of "totality" in Lukács, Jameson offers the following defense of the term: "The 'aspiration to totality,' famously invoked by Lukács in *History and Class Consciousness* . . .

would then in the narrative realm involve a refusal of these habitual limits and boundaries [produced by reification] and even a defamiliarization of our habitual sense of the recognition and the understanding of human acts and passions" (*Valences*, 206). For two of the most cogent critiques of the imperializing dangers of totalizing when it is used to efface difference, see Gayatri Chakravorty Spivak, *In Other Worlds* (New York: Routledge, 1988), 197–21; and Walter D. Mignolo, "The Geopolitics of Knowledge and the Colonial Difference," in *Coloniality at Large*, ed. Mable Moraña, Enrique Dussel, and Carlos A. Jáuregui (Durham, N.C.: Duke University Press, 2008), 225–58.

6. Bruce Fink, *The Lacanian Subject: Between Language and Jouissance* (Princeton, N.J.: Princeton University Press, 1996), 7–11.

7. Jacques Lacan, *The Other Side of Psychoanalysis: The Seminar of Jacques Lacan Book XVII*, trans. Russell Grigg (New York: Norton, 2007), 11–27.

8. Elizabeth Grosz, *Volatile Bodies: Toward a Corporeal Feminism* (Bloomington: Indiana University Press, 1994), 3–26.

9. See Maurice Merleau-Ponty, *The Phenomenology of Perception* (New York: Routledge, 2002), 77–202.

10. Žižek, *Interrogating the Real*, 31.

11. Levi Bryant, *The Democracy of Objects* (Ann Arbor, Mich.: Open Humanities Press, 2011), 61.

12. Bruno Latour, *The Politics of Nature: How to Bring the Sciences into Democracy*, trans. Catherine Porter (Cambridge, Mass.: Harvard University Press, 2004), 264.

13. See Christopher Breu, *Hard-Boiled Masculinities* (Minneapolis: University of Minnesota Press, 2005), 23–57.

14. See Sigmund Freud, "Negation," in *The Standard Edition of the Complete Works of Sigmund Freud Volume XIX (1923–1925): The Ego and the Id and Other Works*, trans. James Strachey (London: Hogart, 1955), 19: 223–40; Jacques Lacan, *Freud's Papers on Technique, 1953–1954: The Seminar of Jacques Lacan Book I*, trans. John Forrester (New York: Norton, 1988), 66–67.

15. Fredric Jameson, *Postmodernism, or, the Cultural Logic of Late Capitalism* (Durham, N.C.: Duke University Press, 1991), 49.

16. Benjamin Noys, *The Persistence of the Negative: A Critique of Contemporary Continental Theory* (Edinburgh: Edinburgh University Press, 2010), 14.

17. Lauren Berlant, *Cruel Optimism* (Durham, N.C.: Duke University Press, 2011).

18. Latour, *Politics of Nature*, 238.

19. For Hardt and Negri's precise articulation of their positive and active version of biopolitics and their criticism of Agamben's more negative and passive formulation, see Michael Hardt and Antonio Negri, *Empire* (Boston: Harvard University Press, 2000), 366.

20. Saskia Sassen, *Globalization and Its Discontents: Essays on the New Mobility of People and Money* (New York: New Press, 1998), xi–xxxv.

21. See Henry A. Giroux, *Youth in a Suspect Society: Democracy or Disposability?* (New York: Palgrave Macmillan, 2010), 145–88; Zigmunt Bauman, *Wasted Lives: Modernity and Its Outcasts* (Cambridge, U.K.: Polity, 2004).

22. For a powerful account of the importance of thinking about the materiality and material effects of agricultural production in the present, see Philip McMichael, "Food System Sustainability: Questions of Environmental Governance in the New World (Dis)Order," *Global Environmental Change* 21 (2011): 804–12.

23. Antony Bryant and Griselda Pollock, "Introduction," in *Digital and Other Virtualities: Renegotiating the Image*, ed. Antony Bryant and Griselda Pollock (London: I. B. Tauris, 2010), 1–22: 14.

24. See Pierre Lévy, *Becoming Virtual: Reality in the Digital Age*, trans. Robert Bonnono (New York: Plenum, 1998); Brian Massumi, *Parables for the Virtual: Movement, Affect, Sensation* (Durham, N.C.: Duke University Press, 2002); N. Katherine Hayles, *How We Became Post Human: Virtual Bodies in Cybernetics, Literature, and Informatics* (Chicago: University of Chicago Press, 1999); Hayles, "Traumas of Code," in *Digital and Other Virtualities: Renegotiating the Image*, ed. Antony Bryant and Griselda Pollock (London: I. B. Taurus, 2010), 23–41.

25. Fredric Jameson, "Reification and Utopia in Mass Culture," in *The Jameson Reader*, ed. Michael Hardt and Kathi Weeks (Oxford: Blackwell, 2000), 123–48.

26. Jane Bennett, *Vibrant Matter: A Political Ecology of Things* (Durham, N.C.: Duke University Press, 2010), vii.

27. Bryant, *Democracy of Objects*, 15.

28. Ibid., 19.

29. Quentin Meillassoux, *After Finitude: An Essay on the Necessity of Contingency*, trans. Ray Brassier (London: Continuum, 2008), 5.

30. Cary Wolfe, *What Is Posthumanism?* (Minneapolis: University of Minnesota Press, 2010), xii–xxxi.

31. See Michael Hardt and Antonio Negri, *Commonwealth* (Cambridge, Mass.: Harvard University Press, 2009), 39–56, 165–79.

32. On my understanding of "working-through," which I borrow, of course, from Freud, see Breu, *Hard-Boiled Masculinities*, 175–88.

33. Jodi Dean, *The Communist Horizon* (London: Verso, 2012), 119–56. See also Michael Hardt, "The Common in Communism," in *The Idea of Communism*, ed. Costas Douzinas and Slavoj Žižek (London: Verso, 2010), 131–44: 136.

34. See Boaventura de Souza Santos, ed., *Another Production Is Possible: Beyond the Capitalist Canon* (London: Verso, 2007), xvii–lxii.

35. Karen Tei Yamashita, *Tropic of Orange* (Minneapolis: Coffee House Books, 1997).

36. Yamashita, *Tropic of Orange*, 170.

Index

Abbas, Niran, 63

abjection, 39, 213n14, 222n5; abject forms of materiality, in Burroughs's *Naked Lunch*, 40, 41, 43, 44, 49, 50, 53, 58; Bellamy's engagement with, 32, 122, 123–24, 126, 127, 145, 146; Lacan on, 39, 53, 127; Pynchon's ethical stance of attending to the abjected, 90; within the symbolic of late capitalism, in Ballard's *Crash*, 101, 110. *See also* AIDS epidemic; bare life (*zoē*); thanatopolitics

accumulation by dispossession, 20; brecciated conception of time and space and, 30–31; founding moments of, in the Americas, 155; "return" of, as central dynamic of neoliberalism, 155–56, 157; in Silko's *Almanac*, 162–63, 164, 166; violence in initial instances of, in intersections of body with macrotechnology, 108–9

Adams, Henry, 62

Adams, Rachel, 24, 212n68

administered society, 27

Adorno, Theodor, 61, 151, 183, 209nn33–37, 214n23, 216n1, 218n22, 220n6, 226n1, 230n3, 230n46; on administered society, 27; aphoristic style of, 184; critique of identity, 176, 177; on disjunction between subject and object in advanced capitalist life, 61–62, 70, 81; on negative relationship between subject and object (negative dialectics), 13–14, 185, 186, 193; on postwar adoption of technologies of fascist Germany, 69; on preponderance of object, 94, 158; on productive irrationalities produced by rationalities, 75; on second nature, 104

Agamben, Giorgio, 14, 15, 40, 207n2, 214n19, 217n5, 218n19, 223n12, 229nn31–32; bare life (*zoē*) concept, 16, 17, 56, 63, 78, 82, 86–87, 125, 163, 164; bare life (*zoē*) concept, distinction between life of citizen (*bios*) and, 16, 40, 56, 59; on biopolitics, 16, 17; on concentration camp as *locus classicus* of the biopolitical, 82; Hardt and Negri's criticism of, 231n19; *homo sacer*, 56, 87; on state of exception, 69, 163, 164

agency: of citizen, shift to potential for agency embodied in bare life, 56, 59; of matter, importance of attending to, 178–79, 180

agricultural capitalism: lynching as disciplinary tactic within plantation economies, 166; slave labor as central feature of, 165

CHRISTOPHER BREU is associate professor of English at Illinois State University, where he teaches American literature and culture, global literature and culture, and cultural and critical theory. He is the author of *Hard-Boiled Masculinities* (Minnesota, 2005). His writing on subjects ranging from globalization to noir fiction has been published in *ELN, Textual Practice, Callaloo, MFS: Modern Fiction Studies, Twentieth-Century Literature, Men and Masculinities, Prospects,* and *English Journal.*